OTHER BOOKS BY MICHAEL STEWART:

Keynes and After
The Jekyll and Hyde Years: Politics and Economic Policy since 1964
Controlling the Economic Future: Policy Dilemmas in a Shrinking World

OTHER BOOKS BY PETER JAY:

The Crisis for Western Political Economy and Other Essays

APOCALYPSE 2000

Economic Breakdown and the
Suicide of Democracy

1989–2000

PETER JAY and MICHAEL STEWART

SIDGWICK & JACKSON
LONDON

First published in Great Britain in 1987
by Sidgwick & Jackson Limited
1 Tavistock Chambers, Bloomsbury Way
London WC1A 2SG

ISBN 0-283-99440-1

Typeset by Hewer Text Composition Services, Edinburgh
Printed and bound in Great Britain by Adlard & Son Ltd
The Garden City Press, Letchworth, Hertfordshire SG6 1JS
for Sidgwick & Jackson Limited

To Kitty

CONTENTS

PREFACE

We are not saying that this is what will happen: we cannot forecast the future. Dates will be different; locations will be different; events themselves will, of course, be different.

What we are saying is that something of the kind is likely to happen unless the Western democracies learn to cope with their fundamental economic problems much more successfully than they have been doing until now.

Peter Jay
Michael Stewart

January 1987

PROLOGUE

As 1989 began, the inhabitants of the great industrial democracies of Western Europe, North America and Japan were, by and
large, taking a sanguine view of their economic prospects. There
were, to be sure, some intractable problems: high unemployment in Europe, budget and balance of payments deficits in the
United States, and, in Japan, some unease over the rest of the
world's resentment of its economic successes. On the other
hand, the great inflationary surges of the 1970s were a thing of
the past, and for the majority of the citizens of these countries
living standards were higher than they had ever been. Income
taxes were lower than for many years, and for individuals willing
to work hard and seize their chances the good things in life all
appeared within reach. Very few people, it seems safe to say,
had any understanding of the momentous forces that were
moving beneath this tranquil surface, or any inkling of the
débâcle that the next decade was to bring.

Optimism was, appropriately enough, particularly high in the
United States, a country which had long prided itself on its
ability to surmount any obstacle that might lie in its path. Even
the weather in Washington DC, on 20 January 1989, seemed to
symbolize the spirit of the ceremony which took place that day
on the steps of the Capitol. It was crisp and sunny and brilliantly
clear, bracing and exhilarating, but with just a hint in the
intermittent breeze that blew from the south that, though
winter was not yet done, spring was not far away. As the new
Democratic President took the oath of office, there was an
excitement and expectancy in the air that had not been felt at
this occasion since the swearing-in of John Fitzgerald Kennedy a
generation earlier. The drift and confusion of the last few years
were over. The nation now had at its helm a dynamic, highly
intelligent, relatively youthful man, already experienced in the

1

ways of government, but open-minded and full of new ideas; a man conscious of the magnitude of the problems facing the United States both at home and abroad, but bolstered in his confidence that he could solve them by the unexpectedly large margin of his Presidential victory, and the significant Democratic majority which continued to exist in both houses of Congress.

The President was, however, going to need all the self-confidence he could muster. He was taking over at a strange moment in American history. Eight years earlier, on this same spot, Ronald Reagan had been inaugurated as 40th President of the United States. Reagan had been an extraordinary political phenomenon. He was the oldest man ever to occupy the Presidency, and, by all accounts, one of the least hard-working and least well-informed. Yet he had been elected, and then re-elected, by an overwhelming majority. He undoubtedly benefited from his association, in his younger days, with two of the most potent forces shaping the American way of life and the American dream, first as a sports commentator and later as a Hollywood film star. These activities not only vested him with a certain glamour but, more practically, had given him an unrivalled mastery of the medium of radio and television. He had touched another chord, too, in the American psyche – the notion that things had been better in the old days, that since Lyndon Johnson's Great Society programmes of the 1960s – perhaps since Franklin Roosevelt's New Deal of the 1930s – government had got too big, taxes had got too high. And – what had come across clearly, particularly at times of national tragedy – he was a warm-hearted and decent man.

But there was a reverse side to the coin. Reagan's immense popularity, at any rate during the first six years of his term of office, combined with his lack of grasp of economic issues, had resulted in a deterioration in the underlying strength of the American economy that not many other Presidents could have got away with. But although the country's economic difficulties had contributed to the defeat of the Republican candidate in the 1988 Presidential election, few Americans yet realized how deep-seated they were, and thus it was that optimism was the predominant mood in the US in January 1989.

On the other side of the Atlantic, too, optimism generally prevailed at the beginning of 1989, though it varied in degree

2

from country to country. It was least pronounced, perhaps, in Britain.

The surprise departure from office of Mrs Thatcher, after the longest continuous occupation of 10 Downing Street of any Prime Minister for more than seventy years, had been greeted with widespread relief in Britain. Her early successes in bringing down the inflation rate, breaking up state bureaucracies, curbing the power of the trade unions, and liberating the Falklands after the Argentine invasion, had gradually faded from the public memory. Increasingly, what the nation saw was a domineering and obstinate person, who seemed unconcerned about the trebling of the unemployment rate and the declining standards of provision in the health and education services.

Towards the end of her period in office she had in fact, under mounting pressure from within her own party, reversed some of her earlier policies, allocating more resources to health and education and permitting a rise in the budget deficit, and a growth in the money supply, on a scale of which she would have been highly critical a few years earlier. But these expansionary policies had done little to put right nearly a decade's neglect of the country's social infrastructure, or to reduce unemployment. Their main effect had been to give a boost to inflation, already beginning to rise again, after the low figures achieved in the mid-1980s, in response to the slide in the sterling exchange rate and a level of pay settlements much higher than the growth in productivity. Moreover, the country's balance of payments, which had been in healthy surplus during the first half of the 1980s thanks to North Sea oil, had plunged into heavy deficit, partly because of the fall in world oil prices in 1986, but also because of the weak performance of Britain's manufacturing exports, combined with its apparently insatiable appetite for imports.

Although, therefore, the real purchasing power of the 88 per cent of the labour force which had a job was at the highest level ever, although unemployment was slowly falling, and although inflation was still running at a much lower rate than in the 1970s, the real state of affairs was considerably less favourable than it looked. The country as a whole might be feeling reasonably cheerful; but the new Prime Minister had now been in office long enough to know that storms lay ahead.

3

Across the Channel, in France, optimism was more pronounced than in Britain, and perhaps with some reason. The shift towards more market-oriented policies had come later in France than in Britain and the US – tentatively at first, in 1982, when President Mitterrand's socialist government had been forced by pressure on the franc to do a U-turn in its conduct of economic policy; and more vigorously only after March 1986, when a conservative coalition government had taken power. Moreover, the long-standing tradition of *dirigisme* by the central government, together with resistance by the organized working class, had meant that policies of providing greater tax incentives, of public expenditure cuts, of privatization and the relaxation of price and exchange controls, had been implemented more slowly than the government would have liked. Nevertheless, in spite of intermittent labour unrest, the country had moved towards a greater degree of flexibility and efficiency in its economic arrangements and the economy had grown, albeit rather slowly. Inflation had remained low, at any rate by the standards of the 1960s and 1970s, and in some parts of the advanced technology sector French industry had performed well, particularly in certain key export markets.

Politically, too, the barometer seemed set reasonably fair. At one time it had been thought that the institutions of the Fifth Republic – a system designed by de Gaulle for de Gaulle – might founder if a President of one political persuasion had to coexist with a Prime Minister of another. But when this situation had arisen, in March 1986, *cohabitation* between a socialist President and a conservative Prime Minister had on the whole worked quite smoothly. It soon became apparent that on economic and social matters, as long as he commanded a majority in the National Assembly, it was the Prime Minister who ultimately wielded power. At the same time, this power had to be exercised with skill and discretion, because of the President's prerogative – skilfully played on by Mitterrand – to call a snap Presidential election at a time of his own choosing. Thus although the incumbent President at the beginning of 1989 did not see eye to eye with the Prime Minister, this did not really matter: it was the Prime Minister who effectively ran the show.

In spite of this evidence of economic success and political stability, there were one or two clouds on the horizon at the beginning of 1989. The shift towards market-oriented policies had led to a considerable shakeout of labour, particularly in some of the older industries and occupations, and unemployment had risen quite sharply. This had aggravated racial tensions, already being exploited and promoted by the anti-North African immigrant propaganda of Jean-Marie Le Pen's National Front. It had also widened the gap between the rich, who had done well out of economic liberalization and cuts in high marginal tax rates, and the poor in low-paid jobs or no jobs at all, who were the principal victims of the rightward shift in economic policy.

If optimism was widespread in France, something closer to downright complacency was the order of the day in West Germany. German citizens – though not the foreign guest-workers who did the menial jobs – now enjoyed the highest living standards in the world. Even more important, perhaps, in view of the indelible folk-memory of the hyper-inflation which had destroyed the German middle class in the early 1920s, inflation had been almost eliminated: the price level was hardly any higher than it had been three years earlier. The Deutsche-mark was a rock-hard currency, the balance of payments was in surplus, and the country's net external assets, second in size only to Japan's, continued to grow. Germans, with some reason, attributed this happy state of affairs to hard work and self-discipline – virtues they saw no great evidence of in some of their neighbours and allies. Politically, although there were certainly marked differences of opinion, there was also a wide degree of consensus on most issues across the four main parties. Within the past decade, after all, the small Free Democratic Party had been in alliance first with the Social Democrats (the SPD) and later with the Christian Democrats (the CDU); and even Bavaria's conservative and xenophobic Christian Social Union (the CSU) had edged somewhat closer to the consensus centre after the disappearance from the scene of its charismatic leader, Franz-Josef Strauss.

There were some, however, who did not subscribe to this consensus, and its tolerance of high unemployment and the environmental degradation which seemed to be the inseparable by-product of industrial processes. Many of them – mainly young – rejected what they saw as the materialist ethos and

5

selfish, uncaring value system of late 20th-century German society: the costs of conventional economic success, in their opinion, often outweighed the benefits. Many of them expressed their point of view through the medium of the Greens, a party which should have been able to play an important political role under an electoral system which guaranteed parliamentary representation to any group that succeeded in obtaining more than 5 per cent of the total vote. But the Greens also attracted a motley collection of extreme leftists, anarchists and cranks, and had always found it very difficult to agree on any coherent programme. The party's political credibility was accordingly low, and those of its members who wished to argue their case within the context of the parliamentary system found it difficult to do so.

This strengthened the hand of extremists, both within and outside the Greens. Over the last two or three years, there had been increasing resort to 'direct action' – demonstrations, which sometimes turned violent, aimed at physically preventing construction work on nuclear facilities of all kinds, and at disrupting the smooth operation of existing nuclear power plants and factories identified as generating high levels of pollution. And from time to time the heirs of the Baader-Meinhof gang and the original Red Army Faction indicated that they were alive and well by engaging in isolated acts of urban terrorism, and the occasional assassination of prominent 'representatives of the corrupt bourgeois state'.

Thus as the airports filled up, in January 1989, with affluent Germans on their way to Caribbean beaches and East African game parks, life in Germany was very comfortable for the great majority of its citizens, but not without a certain shadowy menace.

Urban terrorism was not the problem in Italy, even though it had been in that country that the most spectacular political assassination in Europe during the last fifteen years had taken place, with the kidnapping and murder in 1978 of the President of the Christian Democratic Party, and former Prime Minister, Aldo Moro. Italy's problem lay in a combination of fundamental economic imbalances and an unstable political system that made radical reform, particularly of the bloated and inefficient state bureaucracy, exceedingly difficult. Tax evasion by employers and self-employed was widespread, which meant that employees from whom taxes were deducted at source bore a wholly disproportionate share of the burden, and were increasingly intolerant of a system which required them to pay as much as 50 per cent of their income in taxes. The budget deficit was colossal – over 15 per cent of gross domestic product (GDP), compared with an average for Western European countries of less than 3 per cent. Unemployment was higher than in any other major industrial country; and inflation – despite some success in recent years in breaking the *scala mobile*, the hitherto sacrosanct link between price increases and wage increases – was only just under double figures. And the country was now observing the political manoeuvrings of its 50th post-war government.

Yet, somehow, miraculously, the whole contraption flew. Italy, as a country which needed to import 80 per cent of its energy, had benefited enormously from the fall in oil prices in the mid-1980s; and Italian clothes, shoes and accessories still dominated the world of high fashion – no mean advantage in a decade in which the wealth of the better-off inhabitants of the major industrial countries had grown so handsomely. These factors did not seem to provide a full explanation of the generally happy and prosperous face which Italy presented to the world at the beginning of 1989. Nevertheless, somehow or other, the country had succeeded in defying the forces of political and economic gravity for many years in the past, and with luck might manage to go on doing so in the future.

In the smaller countries of Europe, both within and outside the European Economic Community, there was a fair degree of contentment as 1989 dawned, though this was tinged with growing impatience at the slowness with which unemployment was being reduced, and apprehension at the fact that inflation had apparently begun to rise again. There was some connection between the movement of these two key indicators. The expansionary measures which a number of other governments, as well as the British, had been forced by mounting hostility to high unemployment to take over the past couple of years had not done much to create new jobs for the unskilled and long-term unemployed, but had soon led to shortages of many kinds of skilled labour, and this in turn had led to substantial wage and price increases in some sectors of the economy. At the same time, other factors were at work raising inflation above the very low levels achieved in the middle of the decade. One was the disappearance (indeed to some extent the reversal) of a major favourable factor – the big fall in oil prices in 1986. Another was the very sharp rise which had occurred over the last two years in the prices of certain key minerals, as South Africa, the major supplier, retaliated against the tightening noose of the world's economic sanctions against it, and as the armed struggle in and around that country continued to escalate.

Within the EEC itself, there were grumblings of discontent about the way that some countries continued to benefit at the expense of others, and at the fact that millions of inefficient farmers continued to be heavily subsidized by taxpayers and consumers. But it was not obvious that these complaints were any more meaningful or dangerous than they had been for the past twenty years. And there was one thing in which, compared with twenty years ago, the European Community could take some pride. In 1969 three of the present members of the Community – including Greece, birthplace of democracy – had been fascist dictatorships (and only a year before that France itself had appeared to teeter on the edge of a revolution which could have ended in a totalitarian regime of either left or right). All that now seemed far away. In Spain and Portugal, as well as in Greece, the democratic systems set up in the mid-1970s looked well-established and robust. From the Atlantic to the Iron Curtain, from the Arctic Ocean to the Mediterranean, Europe was as prosperous and as free as at any time in its history. Sanguine spirits gave thanks; only the churlish, it seemed, were filled with a sense of foreboding.

Meanwhile, in the Far East (as Europeans still thought of it) or the western rim of the Pacific basin (as Americans tended to view it), what looked increasingly like the coming economic powerhouses of the 21st century continued to grow and flex their muscles. Principal among these, of course, was Japan, now the world's second largest economy. Unemployment in Japan, though a little higher than it had been a few years earlier, was still very low by North American and Western European standards; and inflation was negligible. The main problem was that over the past two or three years the growth rate had been slow, because the sharp appreciation of the yen in 1985–6 had checked the expansion of Japanese exports, and measures to raise the growth of domestic demand to compensate for this, though continually promised by the government, and occasionally actually adopted, had not proved vigorous enough to take up the slack.

In spite of the brake that the rising yen had imposed on its export growth, Japan was still running a large balance of payments surplus on current account. This reflected, in part, the relentless aggressiveness with which it continued to seek out new overseas markets and cultivate existing ones. But the explanation went deeper than that – deeper even than the 'export or die' philosophy which had been part of Japan's response to the trauma of its defeat in the Second World War, and the basic ingredient in its remarkable post-war economic growth.

The key lay, perhaps, in the Japanese genius for production engineering. This had first been demonstrated over a century before, in the startling speed with which Japan assimilated Western technology in the decades after Commodore Perry had forced the country to open its doors to the rest of the world in 1854; and the point had been forcibly driven home by its defeat of the Russian Empire in the Russo-Japanese War of 1904–5. Behind the country's spectacular economic success in the period since the Second World War lay its unrivalled capacity to take over a technology, improve it, and translate it quickly, efficiently, and cheaply into advanced, high-quality products that plenty of people wanted to buy. There might be some truth in the conventional European and American view that Japan was a nation that was very good at copying other people's inventions, but no good at coming up with inventions of its own – though this view was much more difficult to sustain in 1989 than it had been a couple of decades earlier. But few close observers of global economic developments over the past quarter century could doubt that Japan's ability to trade continuously up-market, first in consumer goods and later in capital goods, creating and then satisfying an ever-growing demand for its products, was unequalled by any other nation in the world, with the possible exception of Germany. As the last decade of the 20th century began to heave into view, Japan was more than ever the nation to beat.

Such was Japan's self-confidence – or, as hostile critics sometimes put it, its arrogance and contempt for other races, only thinly masked by an elaborate veil of humility – that few of its citizens doubted their ability to stay ahead in the economic race, increasing their share of world markets and their command over the mineral and energy resources of which Japan itself had so little. But by the beginning of 1989 some of the more internationally minded Japanese politicians and economists were feeling a certain apprehension about the future. The huge balance of payments surpluses that Japan had been running throughout most of the 1980s had created resentment abroad, particularly in the United States. Americans, unable to believe that their vast trade deficit with Japan was mainly a reflection of the excellence and value for money of Japanese goods, were convinced that Japan was not playing fair in the international trading game, and was resorting to illegitimate tactics to exclude American goods from its market. Anecdotal evidence of this abounded: American baseball bats that did not quite meet Japanese technical specifications; American skis that were not quite suitable for Japanese snow. This kind of thing had proved invaluable ammunition to the already very powerful protectionist lobby in the US Congress, and might at any time provoke the imposition of even more real and massive trade barriers against Japanese exports than those already in existence.

Nor was the prospect of American or West European protectionism the only threat to Japanese exports. For other economic powers had been emerging in the western Pacific. Of the newly-industrializing countries (or NICs), the so-called Asian Gang of Four, or super-NICs, were among the most formidable. Two of these – Hong Kong and Singapore – remarkable though their achievements had been, were relatively small and somewhat preoccupied with their own problems, Hong Kong with its forthcoming partial absorption into the People's Republic of China in 1997, and Singapore with a fluctuating level of internal dissension. But the other two – Taiwan and, to an even greater extent, South Korea – were now major industrial nations, with a manufacturing capacity whose size and sophistication in some sectors rivalled that of Japan itself, yet which benefited from a significantly lower wage level. Moreover, by little more than an accident of history, the currencies of these two countries had for a long time been tied to the American dollar, so that their sales to the United States had not suffered, as Japan's had, from the depreciation of the dollar after March 1985, and their sales to many other markets had benefited from it. Korea's Hyundai car, for example, had swept America, selling over a million units in 1988 and displacing Japanese cars to a much greater extent than American or European ones.

Overall, of course, neither Taiwan nor South Korea, at the beginning of 1989, was in anything like the same economic league as Japan or Germany; but Japan was beginning to look over its shoulder at them, and if the less powerful middle-ranking countries like Britain and France were not also doing so, it was arguable that they should have been. Ferocious competition from the super-NICs – in Latin America as well as South-east Asia – was to play an important, if subsidiary, role in precipitating the traumatic events of the 1990s in both Europe and the United States.

CHAPTER I

The United States: A New Beginning

The new American Administration looked good. Not only the President himself, but his Cabinet officers and the team of aides he had assembled in the White House, inspired widespread confidence both in the United States and abroad. Much in evidence were those in their thirties and forties – the generation, as the new President had remarked, that remembered nothing of the Second World War, but a great deal about the war in Vietnam. In their views on economic and social matters, these people reflected the shift in the terms of the debate which had occurred in the 1970s and 1980s. They had less faith than their predecessors in the Kennedy Administration in the superior wisdom of government, or its power to bring about widespread and desirable change; and they endorsed the need for incentives, and the importance of market forces generally, in securing the efficient allocation of resources.

Nevertheless, the views of the majority of these men and women were in marked contrast to those which had character-ized the Reagan Administration, according to which market forces should normally be the sole determinant of the level and pattern of economic activity, regulation by government agen-cies should be reduced or eliminated, and the role of the government in the economy should be minimized. The new President's aides believed that government had a crucial role to play in influencing the level of output and employment, in alleviating poverty, in preventing the free play of market forces from leading to the emergence of ruthless monopolies, the exploitation of those with little bargaining power, and unaccept-able damage to the environment; and, more generally, in

12

promoting the kind of fairness and justice which had been foreshadowed in the mid-1960s in President Lyndon Johnson's vision of the 'Great Society'. There was a feeling among many of these people that during the 1980s the worship of market forces had gone too far, and that despite its undoubted economic progress in some directions, America had reverted to the pattern of an earlier and harsher era, in which the strong and the lucky had amassed huge fortunes and the weak and disadvantaged had gone to the wall. The more idealistic among them, indeed, argued that redressing the balance between rich and poor should be one of the main priorities of the new Administration; though they readily accepted that this could only be done within the context of a strong and expanding economy.

However, the President was too astute a politician to give youthful idealism too loose a rein. His Administration also contained a goodly quota of older and wiser heads, accustomed to distinguish ideals from illusions. These men were determined that there would be no equivalent of the Bay of Pigs fiasco which has so marred the early months of Kennedy's Presidency, and that there would be no repetition of the economic mistakes made by the incoming Reagan Administration eight years earlier, when decisions to slash taxes and boost military expenditure had been taken without any clear understanding of the effect on the federal budget or the economy as a whole. No harm in lifting our eyes to the horizon now and again, their attitude was; but let's make sure while doing so that we don't shoot ourselves in the foot.

The mixture of idealism and realism which he envisaged as the hallmark of his Administration was articulated in the President's inaugural speech. He dwelt both on what could be, and what was; on the limitations on improving the lot of the people that were inevitably imposed by the accidents of climate and geology, and the frailties of human nature, and those that were unnecessary, imposed simply by a lack of will, of courage and of compassion. In a celebrated passage – one that consciously echoed a section of President Kennedy's great inaugural speech – he said, 'The time has come to dedicate ourselves anew to the fulfilment of the promise held out by our Founding Fathers. There is no limit to what America can achieve, no end to the progress we can make, no barriers to the development of each

13

and every one of us to our fullest potential as human beings, provided only that we have the vision to hope, the courage to strive, the compassion to care. In a country still marred by unemployment and poverty, and a world still torn by strife and disfigured by deprivation, we must think not of what others can do for us, but of what we can do for others. We have no choice but to start from where we are; but we must move into a better future, our confidence never to be diminished, our resolve never to be eroded.'

In another, less quoted, part of the speech, but one equally important to an understanding of his aims and intentions, the new President spoke of 'huge distortions and imbalances which currently afflict our economy, powerful forces which will fight to the last ditch to preserve the status quo . . . there will be decisions which will be hard to make and unpopular to carry out; but made and carried out they nevertheless will be.'

The rhetoric may have soared like a rocket, but it had been launched from a solid foundation, and it carried a significant payload. In the six months that had elapsed since the new President had won the Democratic nomination, his team had done its homework. The new Administration had a reasoned diagnosis of what had gone wrong, and a coherent strategy for putting things right.

The economic problems facing the nation were clear enough, and had been highlighted again and again by the Democrats in the course of the election campaign. The most immediate issue was that for some time the economy had been moving into recession, and unemployment had risen from less than 7 per cent (itself a figure that would have been regarded as unacceptably high in earlier decades) to over 10 per cent. In spite of this increase in unemployment, and the weakened bargaining power of labour which it signified, inflation was rising again, from the low point of less than 2 per cent achieved in 1986–7, chiefly because of the effects of the big fall in the dollar on American import prices. Economic and social inequality had deepened, as rising unemployment and the onslaughts of the Reagan Administration on social programmes had driven larger numbers into poverty: nearly 50 million Americans now had incomes that fell below the official poverty line. The farm sector was still in

14

deep crisis. Environmental conditions had worsened, both in the big cities, as federal funding of urban housing and mass-transit systems had been cut back, and more generally, as deregulation had allowed a freer hand to private interests, and as expenditures on everything from aircraft maintenance to toxic waste disposal were reduced in response to fiercer competition and cuts in federal spending. Yet in spite of these and other efforts to reduce government expenditure, the budget deficit was still far too high. Moreover, in spite of the fall in the value of the dollar compared with a few years earlier, the balance of payments on current account was now in deficit for the seventh year running. So big had these deficits become that the US, which had started the decade as the world's largest creditor nation, was now far and away the world's largest debtor. Finally, underlying these more immediate concerns there was the worry – at least in the minds of some close observers of the way the international economic system was evolving – that the American economy, for all the famous dynamism and flexibility so envied in Western Europe, might be beginning to lag behind in the race with competitors on the other side of the Pacific.

What had caused things to go wrong? In the view of the new President and his advisers, the philosophy and policies of the Reagan Administration had been deeply flawed in three crucial respects.

First, it had assumed that the economy was essentially self-regulating: that if left to itself it would achieve satisfactory levels of growth, employment and price stability, and that what had gone wrong in the past was that the government had interfered too much. This classical 19th-century view of how the economy works was thought by many to have been destroyed in 1936, when John Maynard Keynes published *The General Theory of Employment, Interest and Money*; but in fact it had merely gone underground, and reappeared in the later 1960s in the guise of monetarism. Though monetarism had yielded some useful insights about inflation and the nature of inflationary expectations, it was, in the view of most of the economists who were advising the new President, fundamentally misconceived. When tried, it had simply not worked. And the basic reason for this was that the economy was no longer self-regulating in the

15

way it perhaps had been in the early 19th century when conditions were totally different, and when the classical economic theory had been developed.

Secondly, President Reagan, in common with right-wing politicians everywhere, had been convinced that a large part of existing government expenditure was wasteful and unnecessary, and could be cut with relatively little difficulty. As was later documented in detail by David Stockman, Reagan's Budget Director for more than four years, this proved not to be the case. Waste and inefficiency in expenditure by the federal government there certainly had been, and continued to be: it became clear during the later part of Reagan's Presidency, for example, that under his Administration there had been a scandalous degree of waste and inefficiency in military procurement (toilet seats that cost several hundred dollars being one much-quoted example) and in the activities of the National Aeronautics and Space Administration (NASA). Nevertheless, it had soon become apparent to independent observers, if not to the Reagan Administration itself, that the big cuts in civil expenditures which Reagan had promised his supporters in 1980 were simply not going to happen: in the last resort (some would say in the first resort) the American people and their elected representatives were not going to stand for the wholesale dismantling of the social reforms that were the legacy of Franklin Roosevelt in the mid-1930s and Lyndon Johnson in the mid-1960s. President Reagan might believe that he could cut back the scale of government to where it had been fifty or a hundred years earlier; to his critics, the complexity of late 20th-century life made this an absurd idea, and a sign that the President had acted in too many Westerns.

The third, and perhaps most serious, mistake of the Reagan Administration had been its brief but fatal flirtation with supply-side economics. The notion that slashing the *rate* of income tax can actually increase the total *yield* of income tax because it leads to such a big rise in output and income is as beguiling as belief in Father Christmas and the Tooth Fairy, and needs to be treated with equal scepticism until incontrovertible proof is provided. Unfortunately Reagan himself (described by Stockman as a man who thought in terms of anecdotes rather than concepts) found the basic message of

16

supply-side economics to be entirely consistent with his own experience in Hollywood. During the 1940s marginal tax rates had been as high as 90 per cent, so that there came a point during the financial year when it no longer paid an actor to go on working: you made four movies and then went off on holiday. Therefore supply-side economics was correct; therefore income tax could be slashed in 1981 and total revenue would rise enough to pay for the huge increase in military expenditure that Reagan believed to be essential.

Alas, government by anecdote proved to be a colossal blunder, as the vast budget deficits of the mid- to late-1980s demonstrated. The country could not have guns *and* butter *and* tax reductions without going ever more heavily into debt with other countries, and that is exactly what happened. By the beginning of 1989 the country's net external debt was approaching $500 billion. One per cent of the national income was now needed each year simply to pay interest on this debt; and the situation was still deteriorating.

On the basis of this diagnosis of what had gone wrong with the economy under Reagan, the new President and his advisers had formulated what, in his State of the Union Address, the President described as a 'two-tier strategy'. The first part of this strategy called for the government to use the various instruments of economic policy to influence the level and pattern of demand so as to promote a return to full employment and rapid growth, without permitting any reignition of high rates of inflation. This approach would be more than a simple return to the kind of demand management practised in the 1960s and 1970s, since it would have to take account of the much more open nature of the US economy and the greater relevance of events and decisions overseas to developments within the US itself; but it would involve a return to the basic idea that the government has a central responsibility for monitoring and influencing the behaviour of the economy.

The second part of the two-tier strategy would be more specific: it would consist of measures – including structural and supply-side measures – to deal with the immediate issues confronting the country: the high level of unemployment, the budget and balance of payments deficits, and the worsening problem of poverty. But the question was, how to do it?

17

Outlining the strategy in a speech was one thing; putting it into effect was quite another.

The main difficulty lay, as it so often does in economic policy-making, in the fact that action to achieve one objective was likely to militate against the achievement of other objectives. The conventional Keynesian answer to unemployment was to cut taxes or increase public expenditure, so as to raise the level of effective demand in the economy, even though this would lead to a temporary budget deficit. This, of course, was exactly what – without realizing it – the Reagan Administration had done immediately upon taking office. In 1981 it had cut rates of income tax by approximately 25 per cent across the board, and had simultaneously embarked on a defence build-up which raised the level of military expenditure, in real, inflation-adjusted terms, by more than 50 per cent over the next five years. But although the resulting budget deficits had made sense in the early 1980s, when the US economy was in deep recession, they should have been phased out in 1983 or 1984, as the economic recovery gathered strength. But they had not been. The consequence was that in 1989 the budget deficit was still much too large, and action that would increase it even further would almost certainly be counter-productive, leading to a loss of confidence and a rise in interest rates that would make the recession worse.

Moreover, even if demand could be expanded and unemployment reduced by measures – such as a stimulus to private consumption or investment – which did not increase the budget deficit, past experience suggested that a rise in domestic demand would be accompanied by a rise in imports and a worsening of the balance of payments; and the balance of payments, like the budget, was still in unacceptably large deficit. An attractive alternative possibility, at least in theory, was a further decline in the value of the dollar, and thus an increase in American competitiveness, which would lead, via a rise in exports and a fall in imports, to both an improvement in the balance of payments and a rise in American output and employment – which would in turn raise tax revenues and thus help to close the budget gap. But in a world in which – despite some degree of co-ordinated official intervention – exchange rates were mainly determined by market forces, it was not clear how a controlled

18

fall in the dollar could actually be achieved; and in any case such a fall would add further to the already rising inflation rate. And some people argued that the fall in the dollar since 1985 had already been too big.

'Okay,' the President-elect is reputed to have said to the group of advisers who had explained all these difficulties to him during a meeting shortly after the election, 'it's impossible. Now that we've got that settled, I want to be told how we're going to do it. In a paper on my desk by 8.00 a.m. tomorrow.' The answer the paper provided – to judge by the relevant passage in the State of the Union Address delivered to a joint session of the 101st Congress a couple of months later – fell into three parts.

First, very high priority would be assigned to cutting the budget deficit. A significant contribution to this would come from an increase in the income tax paid by those in roughly the top third of the income distribution: these people, said the President, had benefited mightily from the Reagan tax cuts of 1981, and the further cuts embodied in the Packwood-Rostenkowski tax reform legislation of 1986, and could afford to contribute a little more towards meeting the nation's needs. Some contribution to a reduction in the budget deficit would also come on the expenditure side, but this would be more limited. The President judged that the military build-up under the Reagan Administration had been out of all proportion to what was needed to ensure the nation's security, and had worsened rather than improved the prospects of successful arms control agreements. Accordingly, he proposed to cut back hard on military procurement and on the development of new weapons systems (including the controversial Strategic Defence Initiative or 'Star Wars' anti-missile defence system), reducing military expenditure by 3 per cent a year, in real terms, over each of the next four years. A second cut in government expenditure would come from reducing the cost-of-living adjustments (the so-called COLAs) to Social Security and federal and military pensions by 50 per cent during each of the next three years, so that over this period these entitlements would be increased at only half the inflation rate. With the inflation rate still relatively low, this would impose no great degree of hardship on retired people, and would permit

19

significant savings to be made on items which together now accounted for well over a quarter of the entire federal budget.

However, not all of the money saved by cutting military expenditure and COLAs would go to reducing the deficit; approximately a third of it would go to improving the kind of welfare provision which had been so ruthlessly attacked by the Reagan Administration. Such programmes as food stamps, housing allowances, supplementary social security, aid to families with dependent children, etc., which benefited people in roughly the bottom 15–20 per cent of the nation's income distribution, would receive substantially increased funding. This would be the spearhead of the new Administration's attack on poverty, though it would be supplemented in other ways, notably by making increased provision for the education and training of disadvantaged groups, and of course by the effects of economic expansion in reducing unemployment.

Encouraging this economic expansion formed the second priority in the President's programme. A rapid reduction in the budget deficit should lead to improved confidence, a fall in interest rates and a reduction in inflationary expectations. In this climate, the Federal Reserve Board should be able to pursue a somewhat more relaxed monetary policy, easing credit conditions and facilitating the strong rise in investment which improved confidence and lower interest rates would promote. In the short to medium term, lower interest rates would lead to some decline in the value of the dollar and hence an improvement in American competitiveness and the eventual restoration of a balance of payments surplus; in the longer term the rise in investment would strengthen the economy and improve the prospects for sustainable non-inflationary growth.

Nevertheless – and it was at this point, as he delivered his Address to the two Houses of Congress, that the President came to the crucial third part of his answer to the nation's immediate problems – the first two parts of the programme would not, by themselves, be enough. The problem of unemployment, which was wasting the lives of millions, and the problem of the balance of payments deficit, which was daily plunging the United States deeper and deeper into debt, were too urgent to wait for their solution on the other measures he had outlined to take hold, effective though those measures would prove to be in the medium and longer term. What was needed was drastic though temporary action to stop the bleeding – action to prevent more jobs from being destroyed and more external debts from piling up. Such action could only take the form of temporary import controls.

The President recognized, he said, that such action would be unpopular with America's trading partners. But most of these countries had done very well out of the US over the past five or six years: they had exported freely to the relatively open American market, while themselves often restricting in various ways the access of American exporters to their own markets. One consequence of this was that American jobs had suffered. Another was that while the US had been running balance of payments deficits, and piling up external debt, these other countries had been running surpluses, and accumulating assets overseas – the majority of them in the form of US Treasury bonds, US corporations, American real estate and other forms of American financial and physical capital. It was time for this to stop, the President said: the party was over. The import controls he would ask Congress to approve would be designed to bring the US balance of payments back into healthy surplus within two years. When that had been achieved, the controls would be removed. By that time the other measures he had announced to strengthen the American economy and increase its competitiveness would make continued protection unnecessary. In the meantime, he concluded, he was confident that America's trading partners would accept the temporary setback to their exports that his measures would involve as a small price to pay for the structural adjustment to the American economy which not only had to be made in the interests of the US itself, but which was essential to the continued healthy functioning of the world economy as a whole.

It had been Franklin Roosevelt, in 1933, who established the principle, followed to varying degrees by all subsequent Presidents, that the main agenda of each new Congress would be a programme of legislation submitted to it by the President. There had been another feature of the start of Roosevelt's first term, not copied by his successors, but which some of his advisers now urged on the new President at the beginning of 1989. This was

Roosevelt's famous Hundred Days, a period during which Congress came under such intensive pressure to accept the President's proposals for action that – as one observer remarked – it did not so much debate the bills it passed as salute them as they went sailing by. The new President considered this suggestion, but rejected it. At the beginning of 1933 the nation had been in the grip of an acute economic crisis, manifest to all. The dramatic nature of the Hundred Days had been appropriate to the situation, and widely understood and welcomed. The situation now was different. The economic prospects were indeed disturbing – sufficiently disturbing to have impelled him to break temporarily with the free trade policies that the US had been pursuing, and urging on others, for half a century. But the country at large entertained little sense of crisis, and might react in a profoundly negative way to any attempt to bounce Congress into passing wholesale emergency legislation within a three-month period. It was better to proceed, certainly with urgency, but in a systematic and orderly way, aiming to do no more than get most of the necessary measures through Congress by the start of the summer recess in six months' time.

For one item on the agenda, however, time was of the essence: the proposal to impose temporary controls on imports. Although the President had not committed himself to such controls during the election campaign, he had made it clear that in principle he favoured them. Even before his election, therefore, some canny importers had started to accelerate shipments; after it, the trickle became a flood. The November and December 1988 statistics revealed a marked worsening of the trade gap, and this contributed to a weakening of the dollar. It was clear that the stockpiling of imports would continue until the anticipated controls came into effect; the sooner they came into effect, therefore, the better. The President moved swiftly, and by the end of January a bill was under consideration in the relevant committees of both Houses of Congress. Essentially, the bill provided for a temporary tariff of 50 per cent on all imports of manufactured goods from countries whose exports to the US exceeded their imports from the US by more than 20 per cent. In the case of a few sectors particularly hard hit by foreign competition protection was provided not by tariffs, but by quotas, which limited in absolute

22

terms the quantity of goods admitted into the country from all foreign sources.

In the House of Representatives, the trade sub-committee of the Ways and Means Committee rapidly wrote a bill that was in some ways even tougher than that proposed by the President; and in debate on the floor of the House the strength of support for the legislation was repeatedly underlined. Speaker after speaker rose to tell of jobs lost in their Congressional districts; of unfair competition from suppliers in Japan, and the newly-industrializing countries of Latin America and South-east Asia; of the hidden barriers imposed by these countries on imports from the United States; and of the need for the US to take strong and decisive action to force these countries to abandon their concealed export subsidies and genuinely open up their markets so that US manufacturers could compete on fair and equal terms.

In the Senate, debate was more reasoned and more balanced, as befitted a body whose members each represented a wider range of interests than did their colleagues in the House, and a third of whose members now had six years ahead of them before having to face their next election, and another third of whom were safe for four. The opponents of protectionist legislation made a powerful case. It would fly in the face of the American tradition of free trade and unfettered competition. It would cushion the inefficient sectors of the American economy, instead of forcing them either to become more efficient by innovating and cutting costs, or to release resources to the more dynamic sectors of the economy where America was fully competitive with foreigners. It would be inflationary, and would raise the costs of a wide range of goods to American consumers. One senator quoted figures indicating that the protection of the textile industry that had been exercised under the Reagan Administration had cost consumers as much as $8–10 billion a year in higher prices, and that it was costing American taxpayers as much as $50,000 a year to preserve each worker in inefficient, protected industries in a job. Another senator reminded his colleagues of the disastrous consequences for world trade and output of the Smoot-Hawley Tariff Act which Congress had passed in 1930. Over a thousand economists – virtually every reputable economist in the country – had at

that time petitioned President Hoover not to sign the legislation, he added, but had been ignored. (One irreverent senator
was heard to murmur at this point that surely any proposition
that a thousand economists agreed on *must* be wrong.)

Other speakers stressed the danger that protection would
lead to retaliation by America's trading partners, which would
cut into the export markets of the American industries which
were efficient and competitive, with the perverse result that the
loss of output and jobs, instead of being felt in inefficient and
obsolete industries, would afflict the dynamic and expanding
ones. And a number of senators linked the proposed protectionist legislation to the still precarious international debt problem.
American import controls would hit the exports not only of
Japan, but also of some of the most highly indebted of the
developing countries, making it more difficult for them to earn
the foreign exchange needed to service their external debt, and
increasing the risk of their defaulting, with all the dangers this
would pose to the American banking system.

However, a majority in the Senate came down in support of
the President. They took the view that the urgency of the need
to eliminate the trade deficit and restore confidence in the
dollar, and the fact that the controls would only be temporary,
and would thus give American industry a strong incentive to put
its house in order before the cold winds of foreign competition
started to blow again, together justified the proposed legislation. Several senators pointed out that the revenue from the
temporary tariffs would help, in the short run, to reduce the
budget deficit, and one or two added that the controls would
also be a useful negotiating weapon in inducing a change of
heart in a number of the more advanced developing countries,
which had for many years been resisting the extension of the
provisions of the General Agreement on Tariffs and Trade
(GATT) to cover trade in services: freer trade in services such as
banking, insurance and telecommunications, it was widely
believed, would yield considerable benefits to the US balance of
payments.

Although the Senate and House passed slightly different bills,
reconciliation in a joint conference committee presented few
difficulties, and before the end of February the Temporary
Trade Protection Bill was signed into law by the President.

24

The Trade Bill was needed, as the President had put it, to stop the bleeding; but it was no more than a palliative. The real cure for the nation's economic ills could only come from significant changes within the American economy itself. And the instrument at the heart of the new Administration's strategy for bringing these changes about was the federal budget. Within a few weeks of assuming office the President had submitted to Congress his budget for fiscal 1990 (the twelve months ending on 30 September 1990). This incorporated a carefully costed package of measures designed to reduce the budget deficit along the lines indicated in his State of the Union Address. The net effect of the increases in income tax, cuts in military expenditure and cost of living adjustments to pensions on the one hand, and the increased funding of programmes aimed at helping the poorest and most disadvantaged sections of society on the other, would be a cut of about a half in the budget deficit, from $200 billion to $100 billion, or from 4 per cent to 2 per cent of the GNP. In fact, the President hoped that the reduction in the budget deficit would be bigger than this, as lower interest rates and the fillip to American industry resulting from the temporary import controls led to an expansion of the economy, a fall in unemployment, and a rise in federal tax revenue.

The early stages of the Congressional debate on these proposals were punctuated by a series of incidents in the country at large which, for the President at least, underlined the urgency of some of the measures he was calling for, and in particular of the need to bring down unemployment; though not everyone saw the situation in that light.

Although the 1980s had seen sporadic instances of urban rioting and looting (most notably in Miami in 1980), there had been nothing resembling the near-insurrectionary civil disorder the nation had witnessed in the late 1960s. In the summer of 1967 there had been serious racial riots in twenty-three cities, the worst occurring in Newark and Detroit during a two-week period in July. The following year, after the assassination of Martin Luther King in April, parts of Washington DC itself had been burned to the ground. By the late 1980s all that seemed very far away. The racial discrimination which underlay the rioting appeared to have been largely eliminated by legislation, by executive action, and by court decisions. Even the language

25

of the brilliant Report of the National Advisory Commission on Civil disorders (the Kerner Report), which had been set up by President Johnson in July 1967, with its talk of 'Negroes' and 'Puerto Ricans', now seemed to belong to another era. The events of March 1989 – covered by television much more extensively than those a couple of decades earlier – thus came as a considerable shock to the nation.

The spark for the explosion was provided by a tiny incident in one of the run-down areas of New Jersey which had been involved in the 1967 rioting. A car, driven by a 55-year-old white man whose blood was subsequently shown to contain more than twice the maximum permitted level of alcohol, was in collision with a black child on a bicycle. This collision – in which the child was only slightly injured – occurred at an intersection in a predominantly black neighbourhood where a dozen or so unemployed black teenagers happened to be gathered, several of them, it was later established, high on drugs, and all of them very bored. The collision provided a welcome distraction. The white driver was hauled out of his car and roughed up. A crowd quickly gathered, and within a few minutes a police car appeared. Although most of the patrol cars in this area were manned by black policemen, by an unfortunate coincidence both officers in this one happened to be white. Apparently misunderstanding the situation, they arrested two of the teenagers, ignoring the fact that the white driver had stumbled back into his vehicle and was attempting to drive away. The situation suddenly turned very ugly. One police officer was knocked unconscious by a brick; the other, threatened by a knife, drew his revolver and fired a number of shots into the crowd. One man was killed, several were injured. Other police cars, arriving on the scene, came under attack, first from a hail of bricks and bottles, and later from petrol bombs and sniper fire from adjoining buildings. Within quite a short time, arson and looting were occurring over an area of several square miles, and within hours similar rioting had broken out in half a dozen other cities across the country.

For whatever reason, these riots subsided as quickly as they had begun. Forty-eight hours later order had been restored, and – in contrast to what had happened in 1967 – without recourse to use of the National Guard. But a total of twenty-three people had been killed – five of them police officers – and several hundred injured. The nation, which had grown accustomed in recent years to thinking of violence on this scale as something which happened in Central America or the Middle East, found the experience surprising and disquieting.

The President, too, was disquieted, but not very surprised. To him, the riots and the violence merely confirmed a thesis he had been arguing for a number of years: that while many people had prospered mightily under the 1981–9 Republican Administration, a great many more had done badly. The living standards of more than 50 million Americans had fallen markedly during this period, and not all of them could be expected to suffer this in submissive silence for ever. To him, it did not seem unduly fanciful to see the New Jersey riots as the first puff of smoke from a volcano long, but wrongly, believed to be extinct.

The details of what needed to be done about the underlying conditions which had led to the violence, which might erupt at any time on a much larger scale, were a matter of some dispute among his advisers; but the outline was clear. The conventional wisdom which had developed by the beginning of the 1980s – with which the President was inclined to concur – was that the problems of poverty and deprivation, particularly in the urban ghettos, could not be solved simply by throwing money at them. But – as he had told his Secretary of Health and Human Services when he appointed her — these problems 'sure as hell aren't going to go away *without* our spending a lot of money'. The money would have to be specifically targeted and its disbursement carefully monitored; but money in large quantities there would assuredly have to be. This priority had been reflected in the budget proposals he had sent to Congress early in February, which had called for a major new programme to provide jobs and training for the hard-core unemployed in the 16–25 age group, and for stepped-up federal assistance for housing, education and welfare provision, particularly in derelict industrial areas.

To many Democrats in Congress, the New Jersey riots underlined the urgency of getting these programmes under way, and perhaps increasing their funding above the levels originally contemplated; but to others, mainly Republicans, they were an indication of inadequate policing and a judicial system whose

27

procedures and delays only too often favoured the criminal. Republicans in the Senate, particularly, begrudged extra expenditure on welfare or welfare-related programmes. They endorsed the President's basic aim of eliminating the budget deficit over a two- or three-year period, but resisted the idea that taxes should be increased or military expenditure cut back in order to do it. Given other calls on the public purse (senators from farm states, for example, wished to increase the already high level of agricultural subsidies in the face of low world commodity prices), they were extremely reluctant to countenance more federal tax revenue being allocated to what they regarded as inefficient and often corrupt federal agencies and big-city administrations. Nevertheless, the Democratic majority in the Senate was sufficiently large, and held sufficiently firm, to enable the President to get a bill providing substantial new facilities and resources for the attack on urban deprivation through the Congress, and he signed it in the middle of May.

Although the President had now been in office for nearly four months, he had been too preoccupied with the task of providing the necessary impetus for the key items of his domestic programme to devote much attention to America's relations with other countries. These had been handled, to his complete satisfaction, by the experienced and politically astute former professor and senator whom he had appointed Secretary of State. But this situation was now about to change, with the holding of the annual economic summit in Paris at the end of May.

These economic summits had been held every year since 1975, and were attended by the heads of government of the seven major democratic countries – the United States and Canada, Britain, France, Germany and Italy, and Japan. They were the only regular occasion on which the main economic problems facing the world were discussed, in an informal and even intimate setting, at the very highest level. They were thus, in theory, extremely important. In practice, unfortunately, they had rarely lived up to expectations, at any rate since the late 1970s. One reason for this, in the President's view, was that many of the original participants – Britain's Prime Minister James Callaghan, France's President Giscard d'Estaing,

Germany's Chancellor Helmut Schmidt (though not, admittedly, President Ford) – were former finance ministers, interested in and knowledgeable about economic matters. Most of their successors were less at ease in economic discussions, and preferred to talk about foreign affairs, defence, international terrorism, etc.

Another reason was that with the passage of time the process had evolved into a vast media circus, with the inevitable result that the heads of government – who would not have got where they were if they had not been adroit politicians – became at least as concerned about the figure they were cutting on television back home as about the substance of their discussions. If the summit process were to regain any real value, the President thought, it would have to get back to being a genuine horse-trading operation. The major deadlocks which emerged throughout the year at the innumerable international negotiations of ministers and officials must be broken by heads of government undertaking at summit meetings to pursue policies which might on a narrow short-term view run counter to the interests of their own people, but which were necessary to gain concessions from others that would soon lead to better results for the world as a whole. The summit process ought, therefore, to be a positive sum game, with the whole being greater than the sum of the parts, and everybody benefiting more than they would by simply doing their own thing.

Unfortunately it had not worked out like that in recent years: there had been too much politics, and too little statesmanship. Germany and Japan, in particular, despite frequent assurances (particularly on the part of the Japanese) of impending appropriate action, had in fact done little, either by engineering faster domestic expansion, or through deliberate encouragement of higher imports, to curb their huge balance of payments surpluses on current account. Much of the counterpart of these surpluses was the US current account deficit; and it was the size and persistence of this deficit which had forced the President to adopt the protectionist measures he had announced a few months earlier.

Mainly because of these protectionist measures, and the President's clearly expressed determination to keep them in place until the American balance of payments was back in surplus, the summit was, predictably, a contentious affair. It was the Europeans who seemed to be most unhappy, even though they were much less directly affected by the American import controls than the Japanese. They believed that Japan, seeing its access to the American market being cut back, was girding itself for a massive onslaught on the European market; indeed the first signs of this onslaught were beginning to appear. 'Too bad,' the Secretary of the Treasury apparently said to the President. 'That's their problem.' The President clearly concurred, though some misgivings were expressed by the Secretary of State.

What none of them seem to have realized at the time was that Japan was doing much more than simply switching its export effort from the US to Europe. Japan had seen the American legislation coming, and had reasoned that if America could go protectionist, so could Europe. Its response had been a decision, taken in its usual consensus fashion, to move ahead on three fronts simultaneously. First, it would attack markets in the rest of the world more vigorously than ever. Secondly, it would step up even further the effort it was putting into research and development, design engineering, cost and quality control, and all the other activities which had lain behind its spectacular post-war economic success: Japan was determined that in the 1990s, as in the 1970s and 1980s, its products would be so good and so much in demand that American and European import barriers would be hard put to keep them out. And thirdly, as a kind of backup, it would intensify the strategy it had been pursuing for a number of years now, of direct investment overseas, buying and building factories in the US, Europe and its other major markets, so as to make quite sure that in many cases even the most stringent import controls would be powerless to stop Japanese companies from taking an ever-increasing share of world markets.

Although the Summit only kept the President in Paris for four or five days, his advisers had thought it right that, on this his first visit to Western Europe since his election, he should take the opportunity of having brief talks with the heads of government of some of the countries not directly represented at the Summit. Accordingly, he had spent a day or two in Copenhagen, The Hague, Madrid, Lisbon and Dublin, though the undertone of anti-Americanism he detected in some of these capitals meant that he enjoyed these visits less than he had expected. One consequence of this extended tour was that it was almost a fortnight before he got back to Washington, and a fortnight is a long time in politics. While he had been away the budget process had stalled on Capitol Hill.

The President was too well versed in the ways of Washington to have imagined that he was going to get everything he wanted in his budget, despite the advantage he enjoyed of a Democratic majority in both Houses of Congress, and the favourable wind of a decisive electoral victory barely six months before. But he was shocked to discover now, as he discussed the matter at a meeting with his Chief of Staff and main cabinet officers in the middle of June, how little progress had so far been made. It was almost as if, with the passage of the Trade Protection Bill and the legislation to channel more assistance to the poor and to the derelict inner cities, Congress had for the time being exhausted its willingness to co-operate with the White House.

The news was not all bad. The House Budget Committee had agreed on a sharp rise in the top rate of income tax, and on a proposal that would raise the minimum tax to be paid by wealthy individuals and by corporations, whatever the ingenuity in tax-avoidance of their lawyers and accountants. It had also proposed a big cut in defence expenditure – bigger, in fact, than the President thought altogether prudent. All these proposals seemed likely to be adopted in due course by the whole House. As against this, however, the Committee had adamantly refused to reduce in any way the annual cost-of-living adjustment (or COLA) to be made to social security beneficiaries and other pensioners; and this decision, too, seemed bound to be endorsed by the House as a whole.

In the Senate, things were worse, and the President – normally a moderately spoken man – is said to have used some colourful language at the meeting on a theme he had addressed before: the difficulty of implementing just and equitable policies in a country whose senior legislative body was largely composed of millionaires. The Senate had agreed to the 50 per cent three-year cut in COLAs that the President had asked for, but it had proposed only the most marginal of increases in taxation; it had done no more than slow down the growth of expenditure on the Star Wars programme, and had limited the cut in defence expenditure as a whole to less than 1 per cent a year in real terms; and finally, and to the President's considerable exasperation, it had called for a further major increase in farm subsidies. Worst of all, perhaps, was the marked difference that now existed between the version of the budget passed by the Senate, and the version likely to be passed by the House. If reconciliation of these two versions in the conference committee of the two chambers was going to be possible at all, it would probably be on a basis even further removed from the President's original proposals. In short, things did not look good.

But now a strange thing happened at a meeting in the Oval Office between the President and his closest advisers. Subsequent commentators have disagreed on whether what occurred reflected a strength in the President's character, or a weakness; though it seems unlikely that in the longer run the decision reached made much difference one way or the other.

The President said that it looked to him as though the budget which would eventually be sent down from Capitol Hill might show an unchanged deficit for fiscal 1990 of about $200 billion, compared with the $100 billion deficit he had called for (the Budget Director and the Chairman of the Council of Economic Advisers agreed that this seemed probable). Thinking aloud, the President wondered whether this was necessarily a bad thing. He was not, he reminded his audience, a Keynesian – though he was certainly not a monetarist or supply-sider either. But the fact was that the economy was still in recession; indeed unemployment was continuing to rise. The import controls he had imposed would in due course lead to more jobs, as would the fall in interest rates which he expected to follow the improvement in the balance of payments position. But all that would take time. Meanwhile, did it really make sense to effect a big reduction in the budget deficit, which would lower the level of demand in the economy by about 2 per cent of GNP? The time to do that was surely next year, when the economy was reviving, and when it would be right for the federal government to reduce its call on the nation's savings, so that they could flow into the productive investment which businesses would then be making. In other words, perhaps the arm-twisting of key figures on the Hill that he and some of his staff and cabinet would be engaged on during the next few weeks should be directed not so much at reducing the size of the budget deficit, as at improving the budget's composition – for example by ensuring that the extra money raised by taxation went into urban renewal and education and training programmes rather than into Star Wars and bigger agricultural subsidies.

The discussion which followed this Presidential soliloquy was a lively one. The Secretary of the Treasury, for one, was dead against any amendment to the original timetable for eliminating the budget deficit over the next three years. The Chairman of the Council of Economic Advisers, on the other hand, said that all the indicators suggested that the recession was proving more severe than had been expected at the time of the Presidential election, and that it made sense to adjust the timetable for reducing the budget deficit accordingly. He was backed in this view by the President's Chief of Staff and the Labor Secretary, both of whom feared further urban unrest unless the economy showed rapid signs of recovery.

The President listened to the discussion for some time, and then delivered himself of a judgment of Solomon. For fiscal 1990, he said – the fiscal year beginning in about three months' time – the budget deficit would be left at $200 billion. But by the beginning of fiscal 1991, in fifteen months' time, the economy should be growing strongly, and in that year it would be right to cut the budget deficit back very sharply – by $100 billion or more. Looking one year beyond that – although it was too early to come to any firm conclusions yet – it should prove possible to bring the budget deficit down to zero or thereabouts, thus sticking to the original plan of eliminating the deficit by fiscal 1992.

And so it was left. Over the ensuing few weeks the President and some of his cabinet officers and aides succeeded, by dint of innumerable meetings and phone calls, in effecting some improvement in the structure of the budget – notably by moderating Senate demands for more spending on farm sub-sidies, and by increasing the provision for federal grants for state and local youth training programmes. But overall, the projected budget deficit for fiscal 1990 would be little changed from the expected outcome for fiscal 1989. However, the budget for fiscal 1991 – the one he would be sending Congress next July – would, the President promised his advisers, incorporate a very substan-tial reduction in the size of the deficit.

33

The nation survived a long, hot summer without major disturbances, though rumblings of discontent in the inner cities and demonstrations by groups of farmers over the low level of agricultural prices emphasized the urgency of getting economic recovery under way. Hopeful signs of this were beginning to appear. Unemployment had almost ceased to rise, and although it was still too early for the extra money being poured into the improvement of job prospects and vocational training in the inner cities to be showing significant results, the fact that the programmes were in place was, for the first time in many years, giving new hope and confidence to both professional and volunteer workers in these areas that something effective could really be done.

With the budget issue on the back-burner for the time being, the President, his aides and chief Cabinet officers, reassembling in Washington after Labor Day, in early September 1989, found plenty of other matters to occupy their attention.

The protectionist measures the President had introduced had now been in operation for six months, and some favourable effects were clearly in evidence. New jobs had been created, mainly in manufacturing industry, and in some of the areas benefiting from this process there had been a sharp drop in unemployment. The trade balance had shown a big improvement – though the ever-rising cost of servicing the country's external debt meant that the improvement in the current account as a whole was less impressive.

But there was an unfavourable side to the record as well, and although this had been predictable, some of the effects were worse than had been expected. The inflation rate had jumped from 4 to 7 per cent, not only because many imports now cost more, but also because domestic manufacturers were taking advantage of this to increase their own prices and profit margins. Although the President's Council of Economic Advisers expected this to be a once-for-all effect, with the inflation rate dropping back below 5 per cent within the next six or nine months, the size and speed of price increases to date had taken them by surprise.

Of direct retaliation against America's exports there had, so far, been little. One of the President's younger economic

34

advisers had indeed predicted this, rashly arguing the text book case that even if a country suffers from discrimination against its exports it is irrational for it to retaliate, since that would involve forgoing the benefits of being able to buy in the cheapest market – cutting off its nose to spite its face, in fact. The actual reasons for the relative absence of direct retaliation were less unworldly than this. Japan, whose exports to the US had been hardest hit by the President's import controls, imported so little from America anyway that it did not have much scope for direct retaliation on the manufacturing front; though the Japanese government took the opportunity of further tightening up its controls on imports of such agricultural products as beef and citrus fruits, pleasing its own powerful small farmers' lobby, though further increasing the difficulties facing American farmers. In Europe, protectionist sentiments were growing, but most European countries were not hard hit by the American import controls, and were reluctant to do anything to add a manufacturing dimension to the already bitter transatlantic trade war in agricultural products.

But if direct retaliation had not proved a major problem, the indirect effects of the American import controls were a much more serious matter. It was now beginning to dawn on protectionists in Washington that the Japanese, and indeed some of the other South-east Asian manufacturing countries, were going to respond to their reduced access to the American market by launching a new onslaught on other markets, particularly in Europe, the Middle East, and richer Pacific countries such as Australia and New Zealand. This onslaught would intensify the competitive pressures in all these countries, and American exporters, as well as local producers, would unquestionably lose out. It was by no means certain that, at the end of the day, American manufacturers would gain more from increased protection in their home market than they would lose from more ferocious competition in other markets. Thus the prospects on the trade front were not particularly reassuring.

Even less reassuring was something else. Monitoring the detailed trade and production statistics in the months following the imposition of import controls, one of the young economists on the staff of the President's Council of Economic Advisers found that there had been no fall in the volume of imports of a wide range of goods, particularly sophisticated capital goods; and that in some sectors of US industry production had actually fallen. The explanation of this phenomenon which she offered was not well received by her superiors; but it was difficult to refute.

For a number of reasons, she suggested, including decades of too little civilian research and development and too little investment, and a long period during the 1980s of an overvalued dollar, the US had suffered a form of deindustrialization – similar to, though not yet as bad as, that suffered by Britain. The consequence was that in a number of fields, including not only traditional sectors but some areas of advanced technology as well, American industry could no longer compete; indeed in some cases it had no capacity to produce at all. In such cases, putting a tariff on Japanese goods raised their price to the American customer, but did not significantly reduce the demand for them – or for similar imports from other countries – because there were no domestically-produced substitutes. In other cases, where imports of machinery or equipment were subject not to tariffs but to quotas, the consequences were even worse. If industry could not get hold of necessary parts or components at any price, a situation was created that was normally associated more with the Soviet than with the American economy, with bottlenecks developing at critical points in the productive process, and the output of intermediate and finished goods actually falling.

The case made out by the CEA economist proved sufficiently persuasive to induce the Administration to increase, and in some instances eliminate altogether, the quotas on selected categories of imports. But this action did little to address the underlying problem of America's apparent competitive weakness. Moreover, at about the same time, a number of other developments occurred which raised questions about the country's longer-term ability to hold its own in an increasingly aggressive international economic climate.

One of these was the publication of a new survey of literacy and numeracy in America. Similar surveys had been conducted before, but had often got bogged down in the issue of whether literacy involved the ability to read and write, or the ability to read and write in *English*, which, although still the nation's official language, was hardly even spoken by a sizeable and rapidly increasing proportion of the population. The new survey demonstrated that the ability to read and write with reasonable facility in *any* language was startlingly low for an advanced industrial country at the end of the 20th century – much lower, for example, than in all but the poorest Western European countries. 'Seems like we're almost back to the oral tradition of Homeric Greece,' the President murmured on seeing the figures. 'Only of course, with TV, it's a visual tradition now.' On numeracy, the position was even worse. Of a random cross-section of those in the 16–25 age group, fewer than 50 per cent passed a test routinely set to 10-year-olds in primary schools in England – itself a country with no great reason to pride itself on the standards of its mathematical education. Blame for this state of affairs was bandied about in Congress and the serious press, being variously attributed, according to taste, to the cuts in federal funding under the Reagan Administration, the breakdown of traditional American values, the disintegration of the close-knit American family, and much else besides. But none of this did much to alter the picture of a nation ill-equipped in at least one crucial respect to meet the challenges of the 21st century.

Nor was this by any means the only educational horror story with which his aides presented the President at this time. Another study, comparing various aspects of the American and Japanese educational systems, demonstrated that whereas over 30 per cent of Japanese high school students studied calculus and statistics, in the US less than 4 per cent studied calculus and less than 3 per cent studied statistics. Even more disturbing was a report published by the National Science Foundation. Early in 1986 this federal agency's policy-making board had stated that 'the deterioration of collegiate science, mathematics and engineering education is a grave long-term threat to the nation's scientific and technical capacity, its industrial and economic competitiveness, and the strength of its national defence.' Now, less than four years later, the agency reported that the situation had got even worse, with further cuts in federal funding and a reduction in assistance from private sources since the onset of the recession contributing to the emergence of 'nothing less than a major crisis'.

Although this report was decried as absurdly alarmist by those with an unshakeable conviction in the superiority of American technical prowess, other information available to the President, some of it from highly secret intelligence sources, confirmed that a sense of anxiety was fully justified. In two fields of advanced technology in which American predominance had been taken for granted for decades – aircraft and computers – there was reason to believe that Japan was on the verge of major breakthroughs. Since 1986 a number of Japanese companies had been working on a joint venture with Boeing to develop a new range of civil aircraft designed to dominate the market from the early 1990s until well into the 21st century; but there were signs that the Japanese had now learned all they wanted to from this collaboration, and were ready to forge rapidly ahead on their own. There was also evidence that Japan was poised to leap straight into the production of a fifth generation (artificial intelligence) computer, leaving even the giant IBM well behind.

All of this suggested to the President, as he brooded on the matter in the late fall of 1989, that even he – despite sometimes being labelled a Cassandra – had underestimated the erosion of America's technical base during the past ten or fifteen years. There had, of course, been spectacular progress in the military field, including the invention of a technique to enable submarines to pass messages to each other without surfacing, and the mastery of the problem of how to ensure satisfactory military and civilian communications in the immediate aftermath of a nuclear war; but none of this contributed much to the humdrum task of enabling America to earn its living in the world. Much more useful had been medical discoveries that had come out of the experiments conducted in spacecraft under conditions of weightlessness; but the shuttle disaster early in 1986, when seven astronauts were killed, had cruelly exposed not merely a set of technical weaknesses in the construction of the vehicle, but deficiencies of management and administration in a top federal agency, and some of the country's most prestigious corporations, that had reminded the President of nothing so much as the fate of the British redcoats at the time of his nation's birth two hundred years before. What had long been assumed to be invulnerable had suddenly been shown to be deeply flawed.

38

Much of the blame for this emerging technical weakness in the American economy, the President considered, must be laid at the door of the Reagan Administration, and its utterly irresponsible fiscal policies. The large income tax cuts of 1981, combined with the great defence buildup of the first half of the 1980s, had not merely created the huge budget deficits and external debt burden with which the nation was still struggling; they had also prompted endless determined attempts to cut government spending. But what had actually got cut were not the gigantic programmes such as Social Security, federal pensions and Medicare, which by and large benefited the well-organized middle classes, but welfare programmes for the poor on the one hand, and federal funding of education, training and research on the other. And it was the effect of these latter foolish and short-sighted expenditure cuts that were now beginning to make themselves felt.

But there were other adverse consequences of some of the policies of the Reagan Administration, and of the traditional American preoccupation with money-making which these policies had both reflected and encouraged. One of these was the wave of corporate mergers, acquisitions and so-called 'leveraged buy-outs', or LBOs, which had so dominated the mid-1980s. Although these activities occasionally led to the emergence of more efficient and competitive organizations, this was not the normal outcome; which was hardly surprising, since the motivation of most of the moving spirits in these upheavals was not a more efficient America but a larger personal bank balance.

One particular consequence of all this activity had long been of concern to the President. This was the detrimental effect of takeovers on the research and development expenditures of private corporations. This operated in two ways. First, in order to avoid becoming the target of a hostile takeover bid, companies had a strong incentive to maximize quarterly sales and profits, and thus their stock market valuations. In this emphasis on performance in the very short-term, expenditure on research and development, which could yield a return only in the long run, often got squeezed – in marked contrast, as the President observed sourly to one of his assistants, to the ten- or fifteen-year time horizon frequently operative in Japanese companies.

39

But that was not the end of the matter. For in those many cases where a group of managers had succeeded in effecting a leveraged buy-out of their own company by issuing high-risk, high-yielding 'junk bonds', they had needed to maximize their cash flow in order to service this high-yield capital. In these circumstances, research and development divisions were often regarded as something of a luxury, to be starved of funds or even disbanded. As against this, it was of course true that many large firms maintained substantial research and development divisions, favoured to some extent by the structure of the tax system. Nevertheless, the overall picture for the nation as a whole was, if not one of weakness, at least one of a disquieting patchiness. What the federal government had to do, if the picture was to be improved, was to do what governments did – whatever their disclaimers – in Japan and most Western European countries: get deeply involved in the business of financing and encouraging research and development, education and training – the seed-corn of economic growth.

By the beginning of 1990 – and with these considerations very much in mind – the President was once again face to face with the iron arithmetic of the budget problem. If America was not to slip behind in the international economic race, it had to spend more on research and development, training and education. If it was not to risk deepening civil unrest and mounting urban violence, it had to take active measures to reduce unemployment, and spend more – much more – on relieving poverty. But all this called for more government expenditure at a time when the budget deficit was already much too large.

That the time had finally come when the budget deficit must be cut, and cut hard, the President had no doubt. Any further delay would risk not only a sharp new resurgence of interest rates which would hit investment and knock the emergent economic recovery on the head, but also the possibility of a crisis of confidence in the financial and foreign exchange markets which could endanger the whole of his economic programme. The logic of the situation was ugly, but inescapable: there would have to be substantial reductions in expenditure, or substantial increases in taxation; and perhaps both.

But by now, early in 1990, the honeymoon period with Congress was over, and the window of opportunity, if not closed, was at any rate closing. Uneasily, the President recalled what Lyndon Johnson had told his special counsel, Harry McPherson: 'Doesn't matter what kind of majority you come in with. You've got just one year when they treat you right, and before they start worrying about themselves.' He was now coming up against some of the basic truths about the workings of the American political system.

Some political scientists had long taken the view that in modern America party labels meant nothing. The President did not share this view. Indeed it seemed to him that if anything they meant rather more than they had done twenty or thirty years ago. For since the 1960s – and more particularly since the Presidential election of 1972, when Nixon had taken the whole of the South – there had been a realignment which had ended the anomaly which had existed since the Civil War, whereby conservative Southerners had supported and voted for the Democratic Party. Nowadays – to essay a heroic but illuminating generalization – the Republicans were the party of white, particularly upper- and middle-class, America, and the Democrats were the party of everybody else. It was no doubt true that the reason why Democratic and Republican congressmen were always anxious that their party, and not the other, should control the Senate and the House owed less to their concern to implement their party's policies than to the fact that it was the majority party that appointed the chairmen of powerful committees and sub-committees. Nevertheless, it was also true that on a great many important issues party affiliation was likely to be a better guide to the line a member of Congress would take than any other single factor. That said, however, it was undeniable that solidarity with one's party in the American Congress was only a pale shadow of what it was in the parliaments of Western Europe. More than one president had been known to remark that what he faced was not two political parties, but 535: 435 in the House of Representatives, and 100 more in the Senate. It did not make for an easy life for the nation's Chief Executive.

Ruminating on this general theme, the President reflected in more detail on its particular application to the present state of affairs in his own party. There were essentially three, fluid and overlapping, but nonetheless distinguishable groupings among the Democrats. First, there was a conservative wing to the party. Many of these members of Congress came from the South (though more of them came from the West and South-west), but they were quite different from the old Southern Democrats – younger, much better educated, and entirely free from racial bigotry. While eschewing much of the ideology of the Reagan Administration, they attached considerable importance to market forces, low taxation, strong defence and the need to devolve power down from Washington to the individual states and localities. Secondly, there was the liberal wing of the party, composed of the Congressional Black Caucus and a variety of others, mainly representing the big cities and the states of the North and East, and including a fair number of people still faithful to the ideals of the Kennedy-Johnson era and, in a few cases, to the vision incorporated in Roosevelt's New Deal. By and large, these senators and representatives favoured interventionist action by the federal government to deal with economic and social problems, believed that low taxation must take second place to the need for more government expenditure to relieve poverty and improve environmental conditions, and took the view that the real threat to the security of the American people lay not so much in Soviet military expansionism as in the tensions within America itself. And in between these two groupings – the conservative and liberal – lay the third grouping: difficult to categorize, composed of individuals whose position on any given issue was frequently impossible to predict, but whose support was often essential to building a coalition that would get particular pieces of legislation through the Congress and on to the President's desk for signature.

And as if all this did not present quite enough of a problem for an administration trying to grapple with the assorted difficulties and dangers that confronted the nation, there was, in addition, the plethora of powerfully organized lobbies and special interest groups, whose financial support was often crucial to the prospects of individual members of Congress wishing to get re-elected. The military-industrial complex of which President Eisenhower had so graphically warned upon leaving office had not gone away; and since those far-off, relatively innocent days, a number of other powerful pressure groups had come into being, many of them able, other than in the most exceptional of circumstances, to block any change, however desirable it might be in a wider context or a longer time-frame, that ran counter to their own interests.

Of these other pressure groups, the old age or 'senior citizen' lobby was perhaps the most powerful. There had been a time when to be old was probably to be poor; but not any more. Roosevelt had introduced Social Security in 1935, and Johnson had introduced Medicare thirty years later. In the early 1970s Social Security benefits had been raised by about 50 per cent within a couple of years and then indexed to inflation; the result was that over the twenty years since 1970 the standard of living of the elderly had held up considerably better than that of most working people, and Social Security benefits were now costing the nation nearly $250 billion a year. As for Medicare, benefits had been worth less than $10 billion in 1970, but were now running at an annual rate of nearly $100 billion. Of course, much of this increase reflected the rising costs of hospital care and the near-scandalous level of many doctors' earnings, not to mention the cost of their liability insurance; but it also reflected a much-improved level of medical services for the elderly. And this – callous though it might seem even to think about it – meant that the old lived longer, increasing the total cost of Social Security and Medicare.

And what was the fundamental reason for all this? The President hardly needed to have it explained to him, but at a meeting of his closest colleagues in the Oval Office early in 1990 his brash and relatively youthful Treasury Secretary explained it to him anyway. 'Listen,' said this tough-minded realist, perhaps forgetting that one of the President's parents, and both of his own, were still alive, 'there are 40 million of these old passengers out there, and boy, are they organized! They make the Teamsters look like amateur night. They nearly all belong to one or other of 150 different organizations and pressure groups. They have easily the highest voting turnout of any age group in the country, and they know exactly what's going on. You're a congressman, you're a senator, you're a *president* even, you try and chop them back, you're dead.' And of course – however vernacular his language – he was right. Ronald Reagan, for a long time the most popular President in modern American history – and, ironically, the oldest – had been sniping at Social

Security for more than twenty years before taking office; but –
despite the rolling-back of the frontiers of the welfare state to
which he was so deeply committed – it had taken him less than
six months to surrender completely and rule Social Security off
limits for cuts. And of course the new President's own attempt
to cut back COLAs last year had got nowhere.

Together, defence expenditure, Social Security and Medicare
accounted for almost 60 per cent of the federal budget. Nearly
another 20 per cent represented interest payments on the
National Debt – one item which, short of the American
government actually defaulting on its contractual obligations,
was obviously inviolable. And that only left another 20 per cent
of the budget, most of which represented the various programmes directed at alleviating poverty and improving environmental conditions – housing assistance, supplementary social
insurance, food stamps, aid to families with dependent children,
Medicaid, and so on – together with federal funding of training,
research and development, on all of which the President, in line
with his campaign commitments, had taken steps to increase
expenditure, not reduce it.

'That leaves the other side of the ledger,' the Treasury
Secretary said helpfully. 'Tax increases.' But this was hardly a
bed of roses, either. In fiscal matters, as in many other matters,
the American people and their elected representatives were
deeply conservative. It was very difficult to get them to accept
even *reductions* in taxation. President Kennedy, convinced by
Keynesian advisers early in his period of office that the sluggish
American economy needed a tax reduction to get demand and
output rising again, had found it impossible to get Congress to
agree. Only the shock of Kennedy's assassination, and the
long-practised manipulative skills of his successor, Lyndon
Johnson, had got the tax cut put into effect. Similarly, despite all
the supply-side, tax-cutting rhetoric with which the Reagan
Administration had taken office in January 1981, it was crystal
clear, within a couple of months, that Congress was simply not
going to pass more than the most minimal of tax reductions, if
that. It was only after the almost-successful attempt on the
President's life at the end of March that everything had changed
– 'are you for Ronald Reagan, or against him', the White House
had dramatically asked the Congress and the country after the

assassination attempt, and of course the favourable response had been overwhelming.

'I get the message,' the President now grunted to the small group that surrounded him in the Oval Office. 'A man's gotta do what a man's gotta do. But if it takes a dead or near-dead President to get a tax *reduction*, what in hell does it take to get a tax *increase*?' And the answer, unfortunately, was far from clear. In the mid-1960s, as the Vietnam War built up and the American economy started to show inflationary strains, Johnson had tried to reverse himself and increase taxes. He had failed. In the mid-1980s the more intelligent members of Congress, though not the President, had realized that a tax increase was needed to bring down the huge budget deficits that were the consequences of Reagan's fiscal policies. In spite of the famous Gramm-Rudman legislation of 1985–6, which made it mandatory for the budget deficit to be steadily reduced to zero by fiscal 1991 (the fiscal year due to begin in about eight months' time), but a key clause of which had been ruled by the Supreme Court to be unconstitutional, nothing much had really happened. And things looked little better now.

Nevertheless, to good Americans – and the President was one of the best of Americans – a problem had always been something to be solved, not merely discussed or regretted. The political and business classes in the United States had been accustomed for a number of years to cast their eyes eastward across the Atlantic and discern something they described as Europessimism. There was not going to be anything like that here, they told each other. Sure, we have problems. But we can lick them. And it was in this spirit that the President now put together a budget package which would do what he had promised to do in his State of the Union Address a year before: it would bring down and soon eliminate the budget deficit, permitting interest rates to fall and investment, output and employment to revive; it would do this while improving the lot of the unemployed, the hungry and the homeless, and at the same time preserving the real strength of America's defences. Within a year or two America would be back in top gear, leading the world. The temporary protectionist measures could be removed as exports surged and imports were replaced by more competitive domestic production, and the nation could look forward to entering the 21st century strong, free and more prosperous than ever.

The budget package he proposed was an impressive and skilful one, genuinely measuring up to the nation's needs: in private, all but the President's most virulent critics conceded that. It contained a number of attractive but inexpensive sweeteners designed to buy off some of the most aggressive special interest groups, and incorporated an element of overkill that would permit some further concessions to be made during its passage through the House and the Senate without jeopardizing its overall impact. Stripped of detail, it contained three main proposals.

First – and despite the Treasury Secretary's misgivings – the Social Security bull was taken by the horns. People believed that they were 'entitled' to Social Security benefits because they had 'paid for' them; but actuarially, this was far from the case. On average, beneficiaries lived for seventeen years from the date of their retirement. However, the total lifetime contributions made to the Social Security fund by the employee and his employer, together with the notional accrued interest on these contributions since they first started to be made, provided benefits, at the current level, for less than four years. The remaining thirteen years of benefits represented, in their entirety, a subsidy to the retired person from the rest of society. And, with the steady rise in the number of old people as a proportion of the population, and the still-increasing life-expectancy of people upon retirement, the problem was getting worse every year. Accordingly, the President proposed a two-pronged approach. Social Security benefits, which had not been taxed at all until the mid-1980s, and were even now taxed only in the case of recipients with income in excess of $30,000 a year, would be taxed in the same way as any other kind of income; and, on the other side of the account, the Social Security payroll taxes of those in employment would be increased by approximately 10 per cent. Together, these measures, which would be phased in over a two-year period, would reduce the budget deficit by about a half, though a small part of these savings would be channelled back to retired people by improving the benefits available under Medicare to cover catastrophic illness.

Secondly, defence expenditure would be cut, and by considerably more than the modest amount proposed – and for the most part resisted by Congress – the previous year. In the interim, on the President's orders, the most exhaustive study of the Pentagon since the days of Robert McNamara nearly thirty years earlier had been conducted by as high-powered a team as could be assembled, and this had established what the President had always suspected: that the colossal military build-up of the 1980s, which had raised the real level of defence expenditure by more than half within five or six years, had done very little to increase the nation's genuine security. All it had done was to equip the four arms of the nation's military establishment with vast amounts of overlapping and overpriced hardware that – if some of the last decade's military adventures in the Caribbean and the Middle East were anything to go by – could not even communicate with each other properly in time of battle. Expenditure on equipment would now be cut back by 5 per cent a year, in real terms, for each of the next three years. But this would not be enough: half the defence budget now consisted of pay and pensions. Accordingly, the total size of the armed forces would be reduced by 5 per cent a year for each of the next three years, most of the reduction taking place in the personnel stationed – at disproportionate expense – in bases in Europe and South-east Asia; and steps would be taken to reduce the effective value of military pensions in line with the post-tax cuts made in Social Security benefits.

Finally, there would be tax increases. If the recipients of Social Security – most of whom, while far from destitute, were not particularly well off – were to have their benefits taxed, then equity demanded that the people at the top of the tree should bear a heavier burden as well. Those in the top 5 or 10 per cent of the income distribution had done exceedingly well out of the tax cuts of the Reagan years, and although the President had succeeded in taking a small bite out of them last year, they were still lightly taxed by international standards. The threshold at which the top rate of income tax became payable would, therefore, be lowered, the rate itself would be increased, as would the rate of capital gains tax, and various exemptions and loopholes which still existed would be stopped. However, while desirable as a way of demonstrating that burdens were being

47

fairly shared, the extra revenue that would accrue from these income tax changes hardly amounted to a row of beans. To eliminate the budget deficit, something much bigger was needed.

Accordingly, the President turned to indirect taxes. By European standards, he pointed out, in a televised address to the nation, excise taxes on gasoline, alcohol and tobacco were very low. There was some justification for this in the case of gasoline, because America was a big country, and people needed to drive long distances. But it was preposterous that taxes on alcohol, which had brought in 10 per cent of the total federal revenue in 1941, should have been allowed to be so eroded by inflation that they brought in less than 1 per cent; and it was ludicrous that the nation's biggest avoidable killer – tobacco – should be taxed so lightly. He therefore proposed sharp federal tax increases on alcohol and tobacco, and a modest one on gasoline. But even this would not be enough to bring the budget back into balance. Accordingly, he called for the introduction of a European-style value-added tax (VAT), at a rate of 5 per cent. This would bring in a substantial amount of revenue without producing any severe distortionary effects.

The severity of the weaknesses and imbalances afflicting the American economy at this time was well understood by a number of leading members of both political parties. The budget and balance of payments deficits were still much too large. Unemployment was too high, yet the underlying inflation rate was creeping up. Productivity was stagnating, and poverty, hunger and homelessness were much more widespread than a decade earlier. There were certainly differences of view about how much priority should be attached to different objectives – reducing unemployment, for example, compared with keeping down inflation; and about the means to be employed – defence cuts compared with tax increases, for example, as ways of balancing the budget. But on the broad thrust of what needed to be done, there was no great disagreement.

The President's budget proposals represented a clear and coherent set of measures designed to do what was needed. It is tempting to imagine how they might have been received in a rational world. There would have been well-briefed and carefully organized meetings of the House Budget Committee and the

House Ways and Means Committee, of the Senate Budget Committee and the Senate Finance Committee. Thoughtful, well-informed deliberations would take place. Staff members and researchers would write papers assessing the overall impact of the income tax changes on the post-tax distribution of income. Academic experts would be called in to testify on the likely effects of the proposed value-added tax. Would it be inflationary? Would it be regressive? Should items like food and housing be exempt? Would VAT help the balance of trade, as some economists averred, because it would be levied on imports and rebated on exports; or would it, as other economists claimed, simply result in a small compensating change in exchange rates? And so on and so forth. Eventually all this wisdom would be distilled into a budget package that would be even better than the President's – even fairer, even more effective. Both Houses of Congress would approve it by large bipartisan majorities, and the President would sign it in front of a battery of microphones and television cameras.

And indeed, on the surface and up to a point, that is what happened. But beyond that point, and beneath the surface, a lot else happened as well. The 40-million-strong Social Security lobby was mobilized. The defence contractors needed no mobilization: they were on every Congressional doorstep already. The rich warned vociferously of the severe disincentive effects of higher rates of income tax. Business claimed that VAT was unworkable, and states and localities complained that it would cause impossible complications for their local sales taxes. Scores of congressmen were unceremoniously reminded by brewers, distillers, wine-makers and tobacco growers where much of their campaign funding had come from. And everybody hated the gasoline tax.

And so, as a wet winter turned into the brief but magical Washington spring and the spring into a hot and humid summer, the President, his Administration, and his staunchest supporters on the Hill fought a brave but losing battle. There would be a brief foray here; a bit of ground would be taken there; once or twice there were fierce and sustained counterattacks. But the general pattern was one of retreat. As the weeks went by and the mid-term elections loomed ever-closer, the politicians became increasingly reluctant to be seen to be hurting the interests of their constituents in the name of benefiting that elusive abstraction, the national interest. The President's own party, the Democrats, acutely sensitive to the old charge of being the party of 'tax and spend', and ever-mindful of the way that its candidate, Walter Mondale, had been obliterated in the 1984 Presidential election after saying that tax increases were necessary, was particularly resistant to the idea that it should support the proposed tax increases. And so, in the end, not much got done. The only significant success the President achieved was in cutting the number of overseas bases and the number of American servicemen stationed overseas. The chronic Japanese trade surpluses, and what was portrayed by the US media as the rising tide of neutralism in Western Europe, had strengthened the American public's dislike of paying out large sums of money to protect countries that were apparently unwilling to spend enough to protect themselves; and the huge and in many ways wasteful military build-up under the Reagan Administration had weakened the public's sympathy for the anguished cries predictably issuing from the Pentagon.

And that was about the extent of the President's achievement. Every American politician is attuned to the idea that half a loaf is better than no bread; but the President had not got half a loaf – no more than a slice or two. Essentially, he found his administration powerless to do what any other democratic government could expect to do as a matter of course: decide on the right balance between public expenditure and taxation, and then implement the decision. It did not surprise close students of American politics to observe the President, in the summer of 1990, starting to do what all Presidents started to do at some point during their term of office: devote an increasing amount of time to foreign affairs. Foreign policy problems might be intractable and foreign politicians impossible; but they were a welcome change from trying to get anything done in Washington.

CHAPTER II

Western Europe: Action Against Unemployment

The rise in unemployment in the United States after 1987 was paralleled by a similar rise in much of Western Europe. This was hardly surprising: the world was now so interdependent that developments in the great economic power blocs of North America, Western Europe and Japan had large and immediate repercussions on each other. As the US economy moved into recession, output and employment were hit in Western Europe, and this in turn had further adverse effects on the United States, as well as on other countries.

This logic applied even to the largest and strongest economy in Europe, West Germany. For a good many years now, conservative governments in Germany had been pursuing cautious and orthodox policies designed to promote steady growth of the economy without permitting any rise in the very low inflation rate. But these policies had been less successful than had been expected. Although inflation had stayed at a low level, so had the growth of the economy. The reasons for this had been pointed out on a number of occasions, both by foreign governments critical of what they saw as the unhelpful role that Germany was playing in the task of sustaining a reasonable rate of world economic growth, and by the economists at the Paris-based Organization for Economic Co-operation and Development (OECD), the body composed of the twenty-four advanced nations of North America, Western Europe and the Pacific. As these critics saw it, successive German governments had done too little in recent years to offset the depressing effects

51

on the economy of certain adverse developments. One of these was the big appreciation of the Deutschemark in 1985–6, which had hit German exports (though not nearly enough to eliminate its large balance of payments surplus); another was the slump in investment, which had been discouraged by the fall in exports and the continued high level of real interest rates. The German government and central bank should have followed more expansionary fiscal and monetary policies, the critics claimed, to offset these contractionary influences.

These claims were vigorously resisted by the German government, which pointed to a number of cuts in personal taxation over the past few years, which had stimulated some rise in personal consumption. They also pointed out that the strong Deutschemark had led to a big increase in imports as well as a fall in exports, so that other countries' industries had benefited from exporting more to the large German market. Even more fiercely, the government argued that the post-war German economic miracle had been based on prudent and orthodox fiscal and monetary policies – keeping budget deficits to a minimum, and permitting only a slow and steady increase in the money supply. It was other countries, they claimed – particularly the Anglo-Saxon countries in the 1960s and 1970s – which had tried to expand their economies artificially by adopting lax fiscal and monetary policies, which had got into trouble. Germany had not made that kind of mistake in the past, and was not going to make it now.

And so the argument raged. What could not be argued about, however, was the incontestable fact that over the past few years the growth of the German economy had been very slow, and that unemployment had in consequence risen sharply. The unemployment rate had been around 8 per cent in the mid-1980s; by the beginning of 1989, despite some cosmetic changes in the method of measurement, it was over 10 per cent, and rising.

In these circumstances the protectionist legislation signed by the new US President in February 1989 came as a distinctly unwelcome development. Although the target of the legislation was principally Japan and the South-east Asian NICs, it was obvious that these countries would respond by switching exports from the US to Germany and other European countries, and to these countries' export markets in the rest of the world. One consequence would almost certainly be a further rise in German unemployment. At the economic summit of the seven major industrial countries held in Paris in May, the German Chancellor was one of those most critical of the American protectionist measures, but was told bluntly by the US President that Germany's slow growth and chronic balance of payments surpluses had been an important cause of the world economic imbalances which the American measures were aiming to cure.

Three weeks after the May summit, Germany's five leading economic research institutes – in Berlin, Hamburg, Essen, Kiel and Munich – published one of their periodic reports, forecasting that during the next year unemployment would rise to about 12 per cent, or an absolute figure of over 3 million. The report created an unexpected furore. For the best part of a decade now, Germany, like most of the rest of Western Europe, had suffered with apparent equanimity a rate of unemployment that would have been regarded as intolerable in the 1960s and 1970s. Various explanations had been offered as to why this high unemployment had been acquiesced in, and had had so little effect on election results. One was simply that with 90 per cent or so of the labour force in a job, what the other 10 per cent thought did not matter much. Another – particularly plausible in the case of Germany, with its chilling folk-memory of the hyperinflation that had destroyed the German middle class in the early 1920s – was that the nation was prepared to pay the price of high unemployment in return for the benefit of low inflation. Yet another explanation was that unemployment was tolerated in Germany, even by the unemployed themselves, because it reflected the masochism and *angst* buried deep in the German soul: it satisfied the need to expiate guilt through suffering. (This explanation, needless to say, was more popular among Germany's foreign critics than among Germans themselves.)

Whatever the validity of these various explanations, they now ceased to be of more than academic interest, for in the summer of 1989 the phenomenon they were directed at – the passive acceptance of high unemployment – rapidly disappeared. Why it disappeared so rapidly is, perhaps, as puzzling as why it persisted so long in the first place. Possibly the figure of 3 million unemployed contained in the five institutes' forecast, with its association with the conditions that had brought Hitler to power, triggered off a reaction strong enough to outweigh the traditional anxiety about inflation: after all, if what happened in Germany in the 1920s was bad, what happened in the 1930s was infinitely worse.

Initially, at any rate, the reaction to the institutes' forecasts took an orderly and legitimate form, but the government was left in little doubt about the extent of the nation's concern. Newspapers were inundated with letters; television programmes about the outlook for the economy and the plight of the unemployed, which a year or two before would have attracted only tiny audiences, were now watched by millions; and protest meetings and demonstrations erupted all over the country. A mass march of the unemployed, organized by the environmental Green party, but with participants from more than two-thirds of the political spectrum, arrived in Bonn to coincide with a debate in the Bundestag on a motion of no confidence in the government tabled by the official opposition. The government survived the vote, albeit by a majority eroded by a number of abstentions on its own side, and with the onset of the summer holiday season the agitation in the country died down. But this proved to be no more than a lull. In September, as schools and universities reassembled, there was a series of demonstrations by students increasingly concerned about their future job prospects; and in October, much more seriously, IG Metall, the engineering workers' union with more than 2.5 million members, started a series of selective strikes.

There was nothing new about IG Metall's disenchantment with the conservative policies German governments had been pursuing since the Christian Democrats had regained power in 1982. In 1984, convinced that a reduction in the length of the working week was an essential step in reducing unemployment, the union had engaged in extensive strike action in a bid to reduce working hours from 40 to 35. The strike, bitterly opposed by employers, had lasted for seven weeks and ended in more of a victory for the employers than for the union, with a cut in weekly working hours only to 38.5 without loss of pay. Modest further gains had been made by the union a few years later, but the goal of a 35-hour week was still some way from

54

achievement. In the new situation that now existed in the autumn of 1989, in which an already high rate of unemployment was expected to become higher, the union took the view that a major cut in standard working hours was now essential in order to create more jobs. The employers, by contrast, argued that since the union was not offering to accept any cut in pay in return for shorter hours of work, the demand for a shorter working week was no more or less than a concealed pay demand, and one which, in the highly competitive economic environment which now faced German industry, simply could not be afforded. A strike became inevitable.

The government's philosophy had always been that strikes in the private sector were none of its concern: it was for employers and workers to resolve their differences in line with their own perceived self-interest. In the present case, moreover, the government had received quiet assurances from leading employers that the strike would crumble within a few weeks, as most workers were unhappy about taking industrial action at a time of rising unemployment and falling profit margins. The government, accordingly, did nothing.

The employers, however, had misread the workers' mood. As the strike entered its second month, attitudes on the union side were growing harder rather than softer, and ministers began to feel some alarm. Not even the most complacently *laissez-faire* government could long remain indifferent to a situation in which tens of thousands of workers, in plants of strategic importance to the economy, were on strike, and tens of thousands more were being laid off every week as the supply of materials and components dried up and industry after industry ground slowly to a halt. Discreetly at first, and then more openly, the government started to put pressure on the employers to settle. But as the strike had progressed, the employers' attitude, too, had hardened, and leading employers, and those who spoke for them in the federal parliament, began to accuse the government of cowardice and betrayal. Things came to a head with a rowdy and bitter debate in the Bundestag and a vote of censure on the government's attitude towards the strike, in which a fatally large number of its own supporters abstained. Amid recriminations and disarray, the government fell. With very little warning, the nation found itself plunged into an election campaign.

The outcome of this election reminded observers with long memories and a general interest in European politics of the very similar circumstances surrounding the British general election of February 1974. There, too, a protracted strike in a major industry – in that case the coal industry – had led to the resignation of a Conservative government. In Britain the opposition Labour Party, while failing to win an overall majority in the House of Commons, had won the largest number of seats, and had taken office as a minority government with the support of the third main party represented in Parliament, the Liberals. Now, in Germany in 1989, the Social Democrats won the largest number of seats in the Bundestag, but not enough to command an overall majority. The only difference was that whereas the Liberals in 1974 had not entered into a formal coalition with the Labour Party, the third party represented in the Bundestag, the Greens, did – after furious internal debate – enter into a coalition with the SPD, albeit as a very junior partner. And, just as the new British Labour government had in 1974 taken swift steps to settle the coal strike by conceding virtually all the miners' demands, the new SPD-Green coalition now exerted itself to persuade IG Metall to accept minor and cosmetic concessions in order to put pressure on the employers to settle on terms favourable to the union.

Although some employers wanted to stand firm, others – particularly those in the automobile industry, acutely concerned that shortfalls in production were threatening a permanent loss of market share both in Germany and elsewhere – were anxious for a settlement, and it was these who won the day, agreeing, under pressure from the new government, to concede most of the union's demands. Privately, however, as later became clear, they resolved to react to the cost of the settlement partly by raising prices – where the traffic would bear it – and partly by making some workers redundant: something which the previous government's legislation had made much less costly to employers than it used to be. Both effects – higher prices and increased unemployment – could then be blamed on the new SPD-Green coalition.

The strike settled, the government, despite the small size of its overall majority, moved boldly to redeem the SPD's pledge to effect a big reduction in unemployment within a year of

56

taking office. An expansionary fiscal policy was adopted, consisting partly in tax cuts for lower income groups, but mainly in increased expenditure on social and economic infrastructure, especially on the energy front. The Green members of the coalition were not going to allow the SPD to forget the pledge it had given in 1986, in the wake of the nuclear disaster at Chernobyl, to phase out all nuclear power stations within ten years, and if this objective was to be achieved, rapid progress on energy conservation and the development of new sources of energy was essential. The government would also have liked to pursue a more expansionary monetary policy, arguing that interest rates were too high and were inhibiting investment. But here it came up against the fact that the central bank, which under the constitution was responsible for the conduct of monetary policy, was not only independent of the government, but highly conservative in its outlook. Despite private pressure and public criticism from the government, the Bundesbank, alarmed by the inflationary expectations it believed had been aroused by the election of the Social Democrats and the settlement of the IG Metall strike on terms favourable to the union, stuck to its guns, holding down the growth of the money supply by keeping interest rates high.

As if its economic policies were not controversial enough, the SPD-Green government also started to press ahead with its policy of improved relations with the countries on the other side of the Iron Curtain – the so-called Ostpolitik first unveiled by the former SPD Chancellor, Willy Brandt, at the beginning of the 1970s. In particular, it set its sights on a much closer relationship with East Germany. In economic terms, this relationship had been growing ever closer for a decade or more, but politically it was a different story: reunification of the two Germanies seemed little nearer than it had been forty years ago. Nevertheless, as 1990 dawned, observers of the German scene were increasingly asking how long the historic and deep-seated Russian distrust of Germany could continue to outweigh the equally historic and deep-seated desire of the Germans to be one nation. The Soviet empire, after all, struggling with internal pressures for greater democracy and more regional autonomy, and at the same time enmeshed in a confused transition from a planned economy to a system more reliant on the operation of market forces, had problems enough of its own.

The SPD government knew that it had to tread carefully in this minefield. Many of its own members and supporters – not to mention their present coalition partners, the Greens – had long dreamed of a united Germany, independent of both East and West. On the other hand many of those in the centre of the political spectrum, as well as those on the right, were deeply distrustful of the idea of any political rapprochement with the East. The government approached this conundrum with skill, not to say cunning. At the Olympic Games held in Seoul in 1988, even though these were the first attended by the athletes of both superpowers since 1976, the gold medal tally of East Germany and West Germany had, when added together, exceeded that of any other country. If only they had been competing as one nation! What a triumph that would have been! German superiority would have been demonstrated to the world, in the most widely televised event in history! This was a potential trick that the SPD was not going to miss. The new sports minister was given unlimited funds, and relieved of all other duties, in order to work behind the scenes on the Soviet and East German governments, and on individual members of the International Olympic Committee. In the early spring of 1990, to the surprise of those who had argued that the Russians would never agree to the idea – on athletic as well as geo-political grounds – these efforts paid off. Perhaps this was because the Russians wanted to boost the influence in Germany of the SPD, which they regarded as a much more co-operative force for long-term nuclear detente in Europe than the CDU; or perhaps the memory still rankled in Moscow of the comparison the then Christian Democratic Chancellor, Helmut Kohl, had drawn in 1986 between the Soviet leader Mr Gorbachev and the late Dr Goebbels. For whatever reasons, it was announced in Lausanne that at the Olympic Games to be held in Barcelona in 1992 athletes from East and West Germany would compete as one national team. A week later, an opinion poll taken in West Germany gave the SPD the highest rating for more than ten years.

All in all, the government was cock-a-hoop. The demoralization of the Social Democrats, which had seemed almost terminal only a few years ago, was over. The economy was expanding, and unemployment was beginning to fall. The balance of payments remained in surplus, and the Deutschemark remained about the hardest currency in the world. And the great post-war dragon of inflation, which had terrorized and ravaged so many other countries, was surely not going to dare to show its face in Germany.

In France, as in West Germany, the main economic problem in 1989 was the high and rising level of unemployment – the only difference being that whereas in Germany unemployment was only just over 10 per cent, in France the figure was almost 14 per cent. This high figure mainly reflected the policy of privatization and cuts in state subsidies to the public sector which the conservative government had been pursuing since 1986, which had resulted in redundancies in the older industries on a scale which the expansion of the high-tech and service sectors had been unable to absorb. A second factor, too, had been at work: the French inflation rate over the last few years, though low by historical standards, had been considerably higher than the inflation rate in West Germany. In order to prevent this from leading to what it would have regarded as a politically damaging devaluation of the franc against the Deutschemark in the European Monetary System (EMS), the government had kept interest rates quite high; and this had had a depressing effect on investment and on output and employment in the construction industry.

During much of the past decade public opinion in France had been, if anything, even more indifferent to chronically high levels of unemployment than in other Western European countries; but in the early part of 1989 this began to change.

The main catalyst of this change was a series of violent racial clashes in some of the outer Paris suburbs and a number of towns in the south-west of the country. In the main, these clashes were provoked by the activities of the National Front, which organized a series of marches, in areas where Frenchmen's industrial jobs had been lost or were under threat, to demand repatriation of foreigners, and particularly the deportation back to North Africa of the millions of 'Mahgrebians' who were living in France. Although the logic of the National Front's demands was characteristically confused – in one breath it attacked the Mahgrebians for taking jobs away from Frenchmen, and in the next it attacked them for being work-shy and living in comfort on social security benefits paid for by the French taxpayer – the actions its members took displayed little ambiguity. Ostensibly peaceful marches of unemployed French workers were re-routed at the last moment through the heart of North African immigrant residential areas, and swiftly degenerated into an orgy of attacks on person and property. Occasionally, well-armed groups of North African youths ambushed these marches, and much bloodshed resulted. The police were widely criticized, and not only by the left-wing press, for doing little or nothing to protect the immigrant communities from the effects of large-scale, well-publicized marches or the activities of roving bands of young National Front thugs. On the few occasions when the paramilitary riot police (the CRS) intervened in confrontations between French nationals and immigrants, it was noticeable that the number of immigrants admitted to hospital casualty wards far exceeded the number of French nationals admitted.

All this was bad enough, but a sinister new twist was given to the spiral of violence early in June – very soon after the economic summit meeting in Paris – when a huge car bomb exploded outside a CRS command post in central Paris, killing seven riot policemen and injuring a dozen more. Paris had experienced this kind of urban terrorism before, most recently in the mid-1980s as a result of extreme left-wing activities and of a byzantine secret war then being conducted against certain groups of fanatics based in the Middle East. But responsibility for the present attack was immediately claimed by a hitherto unknown organization styling itself the Movement for the Protection of Foreign Political Refugees resident in France. The French public, proud of the country's long-standing tradition of providing asylum to genuine refugees from political tyranny in other countries, was almost as incensed by the implication that such political refugees were now under deliberate attack by their hosts as it was by the slaughter itself. Connoisseurs of paradox were not slow to point out that the effect of this outrage was the opposite of what had presumably been intended, since the government's reaction during the following few weeks was to round up and expel from the country several hundred immigrants from North and Central Africa who might conceivably have been involved in the bombing, some of whom were undoubtedly innocent political refugees. More cynical observers suggested that the bomb had in fact been planted by the National Front; and certainly one of the immediate effects of the incident was a big increase in the support for the National Front demonstrated in the opinion polls.

Among the responsible political parties, the deteriorating racial situation aroused mounting concern. This was true even of the Communist Party, hopelessly torn between its ideological commitment to racial equality and the brotherhood of man on the one hand, and its extreme reluctance to see industrial workers weaned off into the National Front on the other. But the Communist Party's doctrinal difficulties over the issue, while affording much amusement to the party's many enemies, were as nothing compared with the practical difficulties the matter posed for the governing coalition. Not only did the coalition encompass a wide range of opinion on how the problem should be dealt with, and even on what the problem was; but the one aspect of the matter on which there was widespread agreement pointed a dagger at the heart of the coalition itself.

There was widespread agreement that the fundamental cause of the escalating racial tension was the high and rising level of unemployment. Without this, French industrial workers, students, North African immigrants and others involved in the demonstrations and violence would have better things to do with their time; and the National Front, instead of commanding the support – according to the latest opinion polls – of more than 20 per cent of the electorate, would be just one more small group on the lunatic fringe. But agreement on this diagnosis, so far from leading to an agreed prescription, served only to reveal a fundamental division between two different groups within the coalition.

One of these groups had always strongly supported the strict control of the money supply, the cuts in taxation and public expenditure, and the privatization and deregulation which had constituted the main thrust of the government's economic policies since 1986. Although these Thatcherite or Reaganite policies had enjoyed no more than mixed success in Britain and the United States, and had been attended in France itself by rising unemployment and increasing inequality, the group in the government which supported them nevertheless continued to take the view that the fruits of their success, in terms of improved efficiency and a more dynamic economy, were now not far away, and that it was essential to persist with the policies until these fruits could be fully enjoyed.

The other group, enthusiastic enough about these policies when they were first adopted by the new conservative government in 1986, had become gradually disillusioned. Tax cuts had not made the economy more dynamic, they suggested; they had merely made the rich richer. Public expenditure cuts had not made the public sector more efficient; they had merely led to a deterioration in the quality of service. The same was true of much of the programme of privatization and deregulation, which had done little more than substitute private monopolies for public monopolies. Above all, the growth of the economy had been slow, and the rise in unemployment had been rapid. The present high level of unemployment, they argued, which was still getting worse and not better, posed a grave threat not only to the prospects of the conservative parties in the National Assembly elections due in less than two years' time but also, perhaps, to the political stability of the nation. Urgent and substantial measures must now be adopted to bring unemployment down, even if this meant departing for a time from the coalition's basic philosophy of less public expenditure and less government intervention.

By the late autumn of 1989 this division had become unbridgeable. The actual occasion of the breakup of the coalition came with the victory in two by-elections of left-wing candidates in what had been safe conservative seats, and the subsequent defection in a crucial National Assembly vote of a number of moderate conservative deputies. A highly confused few days followed. The political climate was so volatile and unpredictable that few of the parties represented in parliament wanted to risk an immediate general election. On the other hand it seemed for a short time that the only alternative to a dissolution might be a right-wing coalition government supported by the National Front, which had some thirty-five deputies. It soon became clear, however, that such a coalition would not be able to command a majority in the National Assembly, and would be opposed by a significant majority in the country; and the threat faded.

Out of the confusion emerged a centre-left coalition. This was something of an irony, since this was rather the kind of government President Mitterrand had hoped for when he introduced proportional representation in 1985; but such a government would now inevitably be short-lived, since future elections would be fought under the old two-round, winner-take-all system, and such coalitions would be correspondingly much less likely. To what extent this was really a bad thing, however, became a matter of lively discussion over the next few months, since the new coalition failed to take radical or decisive action on anything like the scale that the situation seemed to demand. Expenditure on some large public sector construction projects was accelerated, interest rates were reduced a little, and a very modest downward realignment of the franc against the Deutschemark was negotiated in the European Monetary System (EMS); but none of this seemed likely to make much difference to the level of unemployment, at any rate within the next twelve months. The truth was that all the political parties were now jockeying for position in advance of the next Assembly elections, due to be held early in 1991. Until these elections were over, economics would have to take second place to politics.

Britain differed from most of the other main industrial countries at the beginning of 1989 in one important respect; unemployment in Britain was falling. It was falling quite slowly, and in percentage terms was still very high – not as high as in France, but higher than in Germany. Nevertheless, at least the trend was in the right direction.

The main reason for the declining trend of unemployment lay in the electoral politics of 1987 and 1988, and the struggle for power not only between the political parties, but within them. Mrs Thatcher had won the 1983 general election on the strength partly of the 'Falklands factor', and partly of the fatal division of the anti-Thatcherite vote between the Labour Party and the SDP-Liberal Alliance. The Conservatives, while hoping to benefit from the second of these factors again in the next general election, could hardly count on a repeat of the first. And by the mid-1980s the Conservative government's economic policies had become unpopular. There was widespread public concern over unemployment, which totalled some 3 million, or 13 per cent – and which, according to the critics, would have been closer to 16 per cent if the government had not changed the definition of unemployment in various ways over the past few years. As late as the autumn of 1986 – more than seven years after Mrs Thatcher had first taken office – this unemployment showed few signs of coming down. Moreover, this huge number of people without work coexisted with massive evidence of work crying out to be done: decaying inner cities, rotting council house estates, crumbling roads and sewers, overcrowded school classrooms and lengthening hospital queues.

All this had begun to pose a growing threat to the prospects of a third consecutive Conservative victory. The moderate (or 'wet') wing of the party started, however cautiously and belatedly, to assert itself, and even many of those Members of Parliament on the right of the party, who had for years been crying for even tighter control of the money supply and even bigger cuts in public expenditure, suddenly started to explain to their bemused but gratified constituents that whereas all that had been required *yesterday, today* was different, and easier monetary conditions and increased government spending on a wide variety of desirable things were what the economy needed now. Thus large public expenditure increases were announced by the Chancellor of the Exchequer in November 1986, and more goodies were handed out in the 1987 Budget. Economic expansion was very much the name of the game, and a reduction in unemployment the object of it.

Much of this expansionary action was of the kind constantly demanded over the last five years by the Labour Party and the other main political parties, and they could hardly object to it now that their clothes had been so neatly stolen by the Conservative government. All they could do was claim that the action was inadequate, and insufficiently addressed to the main priorities; and this they did. Well before the second general election of the 1980s took place, therefore, it was obvious to perceptive observers that the nation was being faced by less of a choice than at the first. Whether the next government was

Conservative, Labour or a coalition involving the SDP-Liberal Alliance, it would almost certainly be bound to continue with expansionary policies, and to give top priority to reducing unemployment, at least for some time to come. The only possible qualification to this scenario would arise if the Thatcherite wing of the party forcefully reasserted itself within a new Conservative government; and, such was the extent to which the hardline monetarist and expenditure-slashing policies of the early Thatcherite period had been discredited and abandoned, this now looked very unlikely. It seemed much more likely, in fact, that before long Mrs Thatcher would cease to be leader of the Conservative Party whether or not it won the election; and this, of course, is exactly what happened.

The instincts of Mrs Thatcher's successor as Prime Minister, and of most of his Cabinet, were thoroughly expansionist. The new Prime Minister believed in economic growth, and in a flexible, high-wage, high-productivity economy. But unlike Mrs Thatcher – who would have said she believed in all those things too – he did not think that they would just happen by themselves; in his view, they would happen only if the government's economic policies were actively interventionist, and directed specifically at creating and maintaining full employment, and stimulating soundly based, non-inflationary growth.

Full employment was, in the circumstances of early 1989, the key objective to be aimed at. The Prime Minister knew that 'full employment' no longer meant what it had done during those two and a half golden decades – as they now seemed – after the war, when unemployment had averaged less than 2 per cent. Too much had changed, in the British economy and in the world economy as a whole. Indeed he had noticed that his economic advisers never used the term 'full employment', preferring to talk of a mysterious animal called the NAIRU, which apparently stood for 'non-accelerating inflation rate of unemployment', which they thought was the right object of economic policy, and which, when prodded hard, they suggested was an unemployment rate of perhaps 8–10 per cent, or possibly a little more. The Prime Minister was a politician, not an economist, and would have none of this pessimistic academic shilly-shallying. Although he was careful never to give a precise figure for what he meant by full employment, what he had in mind was an unemployment rate of something like 5 or 6 per cent at most. By this measure, the figure of 11 per cent, or 2.75 million, to which unemployment had been reduced by early 1989, was still far too high. It represented an unforgiveable waste of resources in a country, and a world, in which desperate needs remained unsatisfied. Even worse, it represented failed hopes and stunted lives, particularly of young people who left school or college and found that nobody wanted to employ them. Short-term make-work expedients and phoney training schemes of the kind the Conservative government had been prolific at inventing earlier in the decade were no substitute for proper jobs.

The Prime Minister had sometimes been accused of bourgeois sentimentality when he spoke passionately, as he often did, about these matters; and it was true that there was a streak of sentimentality in his make-up. But that was not really it; he was moved by a much deeper concern. He had been surprised by the docile, almost apathetic, way that very high levels of unemployment had been tolerated for the best part of a decade in the north of the country, among young people generally, and among young blacks in the urban areas in particular. For in parts of the country, and among these groups, unemployment was far above the national average, in some cases reaching 25–30 per cent or even more. But such docility and apathy would not last for ever. For more than a year now, despite the gentle downward trend of unemployment, the Prime Minister had sensed that the country's tolerance was wearing thin. Unless unemployment was kept moving on a steady and convincing downward path, there might be serious trouble. History afforded plenty of examples of what could happen to a society that signally and chronically failed to provide work for its people.

The very high priority the Prime Minister attached to bringing down the unemployment rate on a substantial scale was widely welcomed in the country as a whole. There were, of course, many critics on the left of the political spectrum who claimed that unemployment should have been reduced much more rapidly since the new Prime Minister took office, if not indeed eliminated altogether. But as long as the trend was downwards, these critics posed no threat. The Prime Minister was much more concerned about critics on the right. These critics argued that in the interests of bringing down unemployment the government was trying to expand the economy much too fast, and by doing so was taking risks with inflation. The great gains of the Thatcher era, they claimed, when inflation was brought down from double figures to a rate of only 2 or 3 per cent a year, were in danger of being dissipated by irresponsible policies. These critics found a ready ear in the great financial markets in London, New York and Tokyo, and nobody doubted any longer the ability of the financial markets to sabotage the economic policies of middle-ranking industrial countries once they lost confidence in them. The most-quoted example in the 1980s was the way that a loss of confidence in the financial markets had forced President Mitterrand of France, in 1982, to abandon the expansionary policies he had embarked on in 1981. The Prime Minister did not fancy becoming the most-quoted example of the same thing in the 1990s.

There was, he knew, a real problem. Ever since the war, periodic attempts to expand the British economy in order to get output rising fast enough to bring down unemployment had run into balance of payments problems, or inflation problems, or both. To some extent this was bound to happen in any economy that expanded rapidly: rising demand would run into shortages and bottlenecks in certain sectors, and this would drive up prices and wages, and suck in extra imports. But – the Prime Minister thought of the short-lived booms of 1959–60, 1963–4 and 1972–3 – the process seemed to happen much faster in Britain than in most other countries, no doubt because of the inflexibility of the British economy and the power and recalcitrance of British trade unions. In consequence, deflationary action soon had to be taken, through tax increases, higher interest rates and public expenditure cuts, in order to prevent inflation or the balance of payments deficit from getting out of hand. It was no accident that the phrase 'stop-go' had been coined in Britain as a description of British economic policies in the 1960s and 1970s.

Mrs Thatcher, of course, was supposed to have put an end to the stop-go cycle, but all she had really done was to extend the 'stop' period – during which unemployment rose – for very much longer than usual. The 'go' phase had been inaugurated in 1986, and carried further in 1987. The fact that it was still in progress in 1989 did not mean that the stop-go cycle had been eliminated.

The length of the 'go' phase did owe something, no doubt, to the curbs Mrs Thatcher had imposed on the rights and activities of the trade unions, which had weakened their bargaining power in wage negotiations. But the fact that inflationary and balance of payments difficulties had not so far become acute enough to force the government to rein back the growth of the economy was more the consequence of two other factors. One was the low rate of inflation – due mainly to the collapse of world commodity prices in the early 1980s – from which the present expansionary phase had begun. The other was the large balance of payments cushion that Britain had achieved as a result of the big current account surpluses the country had enjoyed during the first half of the 1980s, thanks to North Sea oil.

But if these two factors were favourable to the possibility of continued expansion without critical inflationary or balance of payments problems, there was another development, on the other side of the ledger, which gave acute grounds for concern. This was the devastating rundown over the past decade of Britain's manufacturing industry. Caused by an overvalued exchange rate at the beginning of the decade, depressed market conditions at home, high interest rates and various other factors, this rundown had not only been responsible for much of the rise in unemployment in the Midlands and the north, but now threatened, in 1989, to play a critical role in aborting the economy's expansion. Far too many of the consumer goods, capital goods, materials and components that rising incomes and output were crying out for were no longer produced in Britain at competitive prices, or indeed at all, and had to be imported from abroad. In spite of the large external assets that the country had built up over the last decade out of the proceeds of North Sea oil, and in spite of the underpinning of sterling now provided by its membership of the EMS, the prospects of an old-fashioned balance of payments crisis looked much less remote than the Prime Minister would have liked. As he surveyed the future, at the beginning of 1989, he thought that he had better keep his fingers crossed.

Perhaps this time-honoured method of warding off bad luck worked – at any rate for a while. As 1989 unfolded, there were a number of developments, both at home and abroad, which were favourable to the government and its economic strategy. In

February one of the largest and most powerful unions settled for a much smaller pay increase than had been generally expected. Hardened labour correspondents pointed out that this settlement had a great deal to do with a labyrinthine power struggle that was going on inside the union, and that much of the membership was very unhappy with the size of the wage increase; it could certainly not be taken as a sign that the pay restraint the government had been calling for ever since taking office was really being exercised. Nevertheless, it was reckoned that the moderate size of this wage increase would do something to strengthen the hands of employers in other industries, and the settlement was widely taken as evidence that inflationary forces were being kept at bay.

A second favourable development was the announcement in May that a British engineering and construction consortium had won an enormous contract to build and equip a huge new industrial complex in China, defeating in the process aggressive bids from France, Japan and South Korea. This was good for national morale, and seemed to be support for the line that Mrs Thatcher used to take, that those who decried the state of British industry and British entrepreneurship were no more than carping and ill-informed Jeremiahs. In the present instance, as far as British entrepreneurship was concerned, the point was perhaps well taken: it transpired a couple of years later that for once the British had been even more unscrupulous than their foreign rivals, securing the contract only because of the number and size of the Swiss bank accounts they secretly established for the relevant Chinese officials. But that revelation lay in the future; what was widely observed in 1989 was a British consortium successfully competing with the best in the world.

There was a bit of luck, too, for the government – albeit of a somewhat grim kind – in a by-election held in June. This was occasioned when the 34-year-old MP for the constituency, who was a junior member of the government, died of Aids. He had won the seat at the last election by only a small majority, and the general expectation was that the usual mid-term swing against the government would cause it to lose the seat. In fact, probably helped a little by a sympathy vote, and undoubtedly helped a lot by a bizarre sex scandal which broke over the head of the main opposition candidate only a week before polling day, the government held the seat with a much increased majority. This was another instance where special circumstances were largely overlooked, particularly by foreign financial opinion; what was perceived was – always a plus point in the financial markets – a government still commanding the confidence of the nation.

Abroad, too, some developments in 1989 were helpful to the government's economic strategy. The inauguration in January of an expansionist-minded American President, determined to pull the US economy out of recession and to get unemployment down, was a hopeful sign, as were the political developments in France and Germany towards the end of the year, which promised more expansionary policies in those countries, which would in turn help to pull the rest of Europe out of recession too. The result should be faster growth in world output and trade in 1990 and beyond, and this would benefit Britain's exports and balance of payments.

There were, however, some unfavourable developments as well. Most notable among these, of course, was the imposition in February of American import controls. Although these were defined in such a way as to hit imports from Japan and some other South-east Asian countries rather than imports from Europe – indeed, by a displacement effect, imports into the US from Europe might actually rise – the indirect effects of the American restrictions were more problematical. The German Chancellor, for one, was convinced that the Japanese would respond by launching a new onslaught on Europe's markets, both in Europe itself and abroad, and the bitterness with which he attacked the American President at the Paris summit in May had reflected this alarm. The Prime Minister was somewhat less gloomy about the situation, at any rate as far as Britain was concerned. In recent years, in furtherance of their strategy of insuring themselves as far as possible against the dangers of protectionist measures against their exports, the Japanese had undertaken an ever-increasing programme of direct investment overseas, buying and building factories in the countries which were their best actual or potential markets. Within Europe, Britain had been one of their favourite locations. This had surprised many people, who wondered why the Japanese should want to set up in Britain, with its notorious reputation for strikes, bad labour relations and low productivity, when it could set up in such countries as West Germany, Holland or Denmark, and still have access to the entire EEC market.

But the Japanese had known what they were doing. Almost without exception, Japanese-owned and managed plants in Britain had demonstrated an impeccable record of industrial relations, and for the most part a level of productivity, wages and profits much higher than in comparable British-owned and managed firms. Just why this should be, nobody was quite sure, though it was often suggested that it sprang from something as basic as the fact that Japanese managers, unlike their British counterparts, clocked on at the same time in the morning as their workers, and used the same canteens and washrooms. Whatever the reason, it was another piece of evidence on the side of those who argued that what was wrong with British industry was its management, not its workforce. The consequence of this growing Japanese takeover of British industry was that output and employment in some parts of Britain now tended to benefit, rather than suffer, when Japanese firms mounted a sales drive on the EEC market, and in present circumstances this effect seemed likely at any rate to moderate any adverse effect on Britain of the American import restrictions.

These were among the considerations in the minds of the Prime Minister and his Cabinet as they met early in 1990 to review the economic outlook, and to consider what should be the broad thrust of the budget that the Chancellor of the Exchequer would be introducing in the House of Commons in two or three months' time. The basic objectives were clear enough: to keep expansion going, and unemployment falling, while avoiding any further deterioration in the balance of payments and any rise in the inflation rate. But the question which must have nagged at the minds of many of those present was whether these objectives were really all compatible with each other.

The Chancellor opened the discussion with a statement of the importance of reducing unemployment that was so strong, and went on for so long, that one or two of his more cynical colleagues rapidly became convinced that all this was a mere prelude to a second section in the Chancellor's statement, which would begin with the word 'however'. And so indeed it proved.

However, the Chancellor went on, the Cabinet had to face the fact that over the past few months inflationary pressures had increased. The low wage settlement achieved in a key industry just under a year ago, and widely lauded at the time, had proved a flash in the pan. Higher wage increases than that had been conceded in most other industries and, as unemployment had fallen and shortages of various kinds of skilled labour had started to become acute, wage negotiations at local and plant level had often led to pay rises much bigger than had been anticipated, or than could be justified by the underlying growth of productivity. If wage increases continued at this kind of rate, the Chancellor insisted, the government's whole economic strategy would be undermined. It was imperative that ministers continue to emphasize in their speeches – more than some of them had been doing – the importance of moderate pay settlements to the nation's economic recovery. He, for his part, was determined to stick to the central feature of his fiscal and monetary policy, which was the strict control of the growth of 'money GDP'.

At this mention of money GDP, the Prime Minister noticed, the eyes of many of his colleagues began to glaze over; but he thought it right to let the Chancellor continue.

The money GDP, the Chancellor reminded the meeting, was the total output of the British economy, at current prices. Thus if output was rising, in real terms, by 4 per cent a year, and the inflation rate was 3 per cent a year, money GDP would rise by 7 per cent a year. Of course the ideal situation would be one in which output in real terms rose at the fastest possible rate (which he reckoned to be about 4–5 per cent a year at the moment, given the amount of unemployment and spare capacity that still existed in the economy), and the inflation rate was zero. In that case, money GDP would rise at the same rate as real GDP – by 4–5 per cent. But to hope for that was a bit Utopian. Over the past year the money GDP had risen by about 9 per cent – real output had risen by roughly 4 per cent, and prices by 5 per cent. This figure of 9 per cent was greater than he had had in mind at the time of the last budget, when he had forecast a rise of only 7 per cent, made up of a 4 per cent rise in output and only a 3 per cent rise in prices. In short, the government had failed, albeit by only 2 per cent, to hold down the growth of inflation, and hence the money GDP, to what it had intended.

Conscious of increasing restiveness around him, the Chancellor hurried on to his conclusion. The point of adopting a target for money GDP, and sticking to it, he said, was this: you were announcing to the nation that the lower the level of pay settlements, and thus the lower the inflation rate, the faster would be the rise in real output, and therefore living standards, and the faster would be the fall in unemployment. Suppose that one announced a target of 8 per cent for the growth of money GDP, and used all the instruments of fiscal and monetary policy to achieve it. If wage settlements and price increases were moderate, and inflation was kept down to 3 per cent, then output would rise by 5 per cent, and unemployment would fall significantly. But if people exercised little or no restraint in their wage bargaining and price-setting, and the inflation rate came out at 7 per cent, real output would only rise by 1 per cent, and unemployment would almost certainly increase. Announcing and sticking to a target for the growth of money GDP, therefore, was a way of putting fairly and squarely before the nation the choice between low inflation and low unemployment on the one hand, and high inflation and high unemployment on the other. For this reason he proposed, in his forthcoming budget, to name a target rate of growth for money GDP, and do everything possible to stick to it. Last year's target of 7 per cent, he conceded, had been over-ambitious, and unrealistically low. But the 9 per cent figure experienced over the past year should also be the target chosen for next year. He hoped that this would lead to the inflation rate being stabilized at about 5 per cent, thus permitting output to continue growing at about 4 per cent, and unemployment to keep coming steadily down.

One of the few of the Chancellor's colleagues who had not permitted his mind to wander to pleasanter matters during this disquisition now intervened, putting his finger on what he saw as a fatal flaw in the argument.

If, he said, the nation was a single person, it would certainly act in the way the Chancellor was hoping for, since it was obviously better to have 4 per cent real growth and a 5 per cent inflation rate than, say, 1 per cent real growth and an 8 per cent inflation rate. But the nation was not a single person. It consisted of some 55 million persons, half of whom were workers – or would be, if they could find a job – whose aim was

73

to improve the living standard of themselves and their families. While it would benefit these 25 million workers *collectively* to exercise pay restraint, so as to maximize the growth of national output and minimize the inflation rate, their interests *individually* were quite different. It would make sense for any individual worker, or group of workers in a particular industry or occupation, to bargain for the biggest pay increase they could possibly get. This would have little or no effect on the price level as a whole, so that any increase in money income they could secure would represent an equivalent increase in real income. The rational thing for any individual or group to do, therefore, was to hope that everyone else would exercise pay restraint, but not to exercise any itself. But what if no one else exercised any restraint either? In that case it would be, if anything, even more irrational for the individual to exercise restraint, for by doing so he would be acquiescing in a fall in his living standard in relation to everyone else. In short, it was impossible, in logic, for the Chancellor's announced target for the growth of money GDP to have the favourable effect on inflation that he claimed for it, since it would be completely illogical for any individual or group to behave in the way that was required for the thesis to be valid.

The Chancellor retorted that if everyone's actions were always dictated by short-term self-interest, his colleague's argument would be correct, but that fortunately this was not the case. However, before he could develop this point, the Prime Minister, foreseeing the discussion degenerating into the sterile kind of point-scoring that too often characterized political dialogue, intervened. He had been told by his own economic adviser, he said, that as a result of various developments on the wage and price front that had already happened, it was inevitable that over the next twelve months inflation would be at least 7 per cent. However undesirable this prospect might be, there was nothing that could now be done about it. In this situation, sticking to the Chancellor's 9 per cent target for money GDP would surely mean that real output would rise by 2 per cent or less; and the implication of this was that unemployment would stop falling and might even rise.

The Chancellor was forced to admit, after much hedging and qualification, that this was so. Other members of the Cabinet, who had understood little or nothing of the discussion so far, grasped the basic point that if the Chancellor got his way unemployment might start rising again; and if that happened the government – not to mention their ministerial jobs – were probably doomed. It quickly became clear that the Chancellor was in a small minority. The meeting agreed – what the Prime Minister had intended all along – that the budget speech should contain no mention of a target rate of growth for money GDP, but should stress that the objective was to keep total output, or GDP in real terms, growing at a rate of 4 per cent, and unemployment on a steady downward trend. The budget itself, and other fiscal and monetary decisions, would be geared to ensuring that effective demand in the economy rose fast enough to achieve these objectives.

As the meeting broke up, and his colleagues filed out of the Cabinet Room, the Prime Minister, left alone in his chair at the centre of the long oval table, admitted to himself that he was no longer keeping his fingers crossed; he was now, metaphorically speaking, biting his fingernails.

He was very conscious that by continuing to give top priority to reducing unemployment, he was taking risks with both inflation and the balance of payments. But he saw no real alternative. He was now more convinced than ever that, however belatedly, and for whatever reason, the mood of the country had changed, and that a continuation of the present relatively high rate of unemployment – let alone a return to the even higher levels of a few years ago – would simply not be tolerated. And a failure to bring down unemployment would not just constitute a threat to the chances of his party at the next election: it was not simply a matter, as some of his colleagues seemed to imagine, of losing their ministerial jobs or their parliamentary seats. The threat, the Prime Minister believed, was to parliamentary democracy itself.

You did not need to be a genius, he thought, to see that the viability of a political system that could only keep inflation down to a low and stable level by suffering endless high and even rising unemployment must sooner or later come into question. If none of the orthodox political parties could solve the problem of reconciling low inflation with low unemployment, then people would increasingly turn to parties that claimed they could.

There were plenty of these on the extreme left of the political spectrum, and the Prime Minister, as ultimate head of the intelligence and security services, was in an almost unique position to know how much progress these groups had made in the last few years in radicalizing the working class. An increasing number of young people – middle class as well as working class – were becoming convinced that, in Marx's words, parliamentary government was no more than the executive committee of the bourgeoisie, and that effective economic and social change could only be brought about in Britain through revolutionary action. Thank goodness, the Prime Minister often said to his closest colleagues, that these assorted groups of Marxists, Trotskyists, anarchists, revolutionary socialists, syndicalists, militants and what have you seemed to hate each other nearly as much as they all hated the bourgeois state. If they were ever to get their act together, and agree on a common programme and a common leadership, they would constitute a very dangerous enemy.

As things stood at the moment, however, it was not from this quarter that the Prime Minister expected the real threat to democracy to come. It was typical of the security services, he thought, with their obsession with reds under the bed (despite the enormous irony that communist penetration of the security services up to the very highest level was a scandal that had been making newspaper headlines for the past forty years) that although they had provided him with countless reports on the activities of these left-wing extremist groups, they had provided him with virtually no information about the man he was really worried about.

It was in a sombre mood that the Prime Minister got up and left the Cabinet Room. One of the private secretaries, coming in a few minutes later to tidy up, found himself staring in puzzlement at something written on the pad in the Prime Minister's place. It was a name: Olaf D. Le Rith.

CHAPTER III

The United States: Hopes Frustrated

The results of the mid-term Congressional elections in November 1990 came as a blow to the President, though not a wholly unexpected one. The Democrats lost control of the Senate, albeit by only three seats; and while they retained a majority in the House of Representatives, a number of Democratic congressmen well known for their support of the President were defeated. Partly for this reason, the election results, while of course reflecting the influence of a variety of personalities and local issues, were widely perceived as an adverse verdict on the record of the President himself.

He had, as it happened, had one piece of bad luck. During the fortnight immediately before election day, there had been two appalling air crashes in the United States, in which a total of more than 400 people had been killed. There had been much speculation in the popular media about terrorist bombs and inadequate security at airports, and the Administration had got the blame. Ironically, official enquiries subsequently established that one crash was the consequence of faulty engine maintenance, and the other the result of a mistake by an inexperienced air traffic controller. If any Administration should get the blame for this, it was the previous one. President Reagan had fired 11,000 striking air traffic controllers in 1981, and even a decade later the Federal Aviation Administration had failed to replace all these men with properly trained substitutes; and the intense competition engendered by airline deregulation in the late 1970s and early 1980s, combined with budget cuts by the Reagan Administration which sharply reduced the number of federal safety inspectors, had led to a

77

situation in which many airlines routinely cut corners on maintenance operations. Unfortunately for the present Administration, the results of the official enquiries into the two crashes only became available after election day.

The main reasons for the President's electoral setback, however, lay elsewhere. There seem to have been two of them. First, many of those – including white liberals, blacks, and members of other minorities – who had voted for the President in 1988 in the hope that he would rapidly reduce unemployment and make big inroads into the poverty problem, were disappointed by the progress actually achieved. And it was true that, although the President's protectionist measures had led to a considerable fall in unemployment in some areas, retaliation and other adverse factors had raised it in others, and the improvement in the overall picture had not been very great. As for poverty, urban deprivation and related problems, many additional resources had been provided, but the difficulties were intractable and deep-seated, and so far visible results were sparse.

Second, there was a widespread feeling in the country at large that the President had not succeeded in getting the grip on the nation's problems that he had promised two years ago. The budget deficit was still much too big, and the National Debt had risen to nearly $3 trillion. The balance of payments was still in deficit, and the nation's net external debt was now well over $500 billion – bigger than that of the whole of Latin America. The inflation rate, which had risen to around 7 per cent after the imposition of protectionist measures early the previous year, showed no sign of falling back. And, more generally, the uneasy perception was spreading that America was beginning to slip behind some of its main rivals in terms of investment, research and development, education and training, and that the Administration, however good its intentions, had failed to do enough about it.

The President, sitting with a few aides and close colleagues in the Oval Office, watching the election results on television, was well aware of all this. He could see, too, that it was now going to be more difficult than ever to assemble a coalition in Congress that would permit him to do the things he was convinced were necessary. But he saw something else, as well: something he had never before discerned as clearly as he did now. If he was to complete his four-year term of office with a feeling of pride in what he had managed to do – let alone stand a chance of being re-elected for a second one in 1992 – he must now make a decisive choice between two courses of action. For all the uncertainties and ambiguities in political life, all the concessions and compromises and trade-offs, there had to be an overriding sense of direction if anything of real significance were to be achieved. The President knew that he had now reached a fork in the road. He had to go in one direction or the other; there was no middle way. Each road led to a desirable destination; but each was fraught with specific hazards.

The first course was to go boldly for rapid economic growth, which would substantially reduce unemployment and make available the resources to close the balance of payments gap, help to fund the war on poverty in America – not to mention in the Third World – and still permit the average American citizen to enjoy rising prosperity. Of course, as President he could only propose: in the last resort it was bodies over which he had little or no control, such as the Congress and the Federal Reserve Board, which would dispose. But there was nothing much he could do about that. At least, by choosing to travel this road, he would be directing his efforts towards the ultimate objective of economic policy – maximizing the living standards of the people. The risk attendant upon this course of action was that it would reignite inflation. The inflation rate – now stable, if at a higher level than desirable – might rise and go on rising. No democratic society could tolerate for long this kind of accelerating inflation; and bringing it under control again might prove even more difficult and unpleasant than it had in the early 1980s.

The second course of action, therefore, was to assign top priority to preventing any rise in the inflation rate, and if possible to reducing it. This was undoubtedly what a large proportion of those with jobs and savings would most favour; and these people constituted a majority of the electorate, and an even bigger majority of those who actually voted. Moreover a programme whose overriding concern was the control and reduction of inflation would reassure overseas holders of dollar assets, as well as Americans themselves, that the real value of these assets would be preserved; and now that the US had become such a huge external debtor this consideration was much more important than it used to be. But there were risks involved in this course of action as well. If reducing, or even stabilizing, the inflation rate required restrictive fiscal and monetary policies that would slow down or halt the growth of the economy, and keep unemployment high or even increase it, then there could be real trouble. Programmes for alleviating urban deprivation would have to be cut at a time of worsening inner city unemployment, and the combination could be explosive. Federal funding of education and training, and research and development, would come under attack, weakening the economy in the longer term; and this would be the effect, too, of the likely slump in business investment in the face of a slowing economy and high rates of interest.

Even as he debated this central choice with himself, and a little later with his advisers, the President knew what his decision had to be. His own beliefs and values, modified but not fundamentally changed by the experience of nearly thirty years in public life, meant that when the chips were down he had no real choice. There was only one road he could take. Of course it was important to prevent the inflation rate from rising again. But what really mattered was not what happened to prices, but what happened to employment and output. If you halved or doubled the *price* of everything, you would soon halve or double everyone's money income: it would make no real difference to anyone. But if you halved or doubled the *output* of everything, it made a colossal difference to everyone. Of course it wasn't quite as simple as that; but that was what it all boiled down to in the end. There were times, it was true, when inflationary expectations got a firm hold, and took on a life of their own. Then the hold had to be broken. The beginning of the 1980s – after the second oil shock – had been such a time, and the President considered that the restrictive monetary policy pursued after October 1979 by the Federal Reserve Board under its chairman, Paul Volcker, had been necessary. Regrettably, in the President's view, the policy had been overdone: the desire on the part of many politicians and bankers to drive the inflation rate down towards zero had become obsessive, and an unduly severe recession had been the result. But at least it had broken inflationary expectations, at any rate for the foreseeable future.

80

Now, at the end of 1990, the dragon was not inflation; it was unemployment, poverty and static or even falling living standards. It was the dangers of failing to get sustained economic growth and falling unemployment that the country really had to worry about.

In the weeks and months that followed the mid-term elections, the President's decisions and actions, and his responses to unfolding events, were to reflect this fundamental priority. And this was particularly true in the case of his attitude to monetary policy.

To the President, monetary policy had always been, at bottom, a matter of interest rates, rather than of the money supply. He recognized that there was a correlation between the growth of the money supply and the inflation rate, but was sceptical about how far a faster growth of the money supply *caused* a faster rate of inflation, as opposed to merely reflecting it. On the whole he accepted the views of those of his advisers who argued that the Federal Reserve Board (the Fed) – or any central bank – could not control the money supply in the way one can control the flow of water out of a tap. In an economy in which most of the money supply consists of bank deposits, and banks are trying to increase these deposits in order to maximize their profits, the *supply* of money is largely determined by the *demand* for money (i.e. people's desire to hold their assets in the form of bank balances, rather than in shares or securities), and the demand for money is mainly determined by interest rates, and by the level of economic activity. Essentially what the Fed did, therefore, in conducting its monetary policy, was to manipulate the level and pattern of interest rates. What was vital at the present time, the President was convinced, was that *real* interest rates should be kept as low as possible – to no more than 2 or 3 per cent at most. Given that the inflation rate was about 7 per cent, this meant that *nominal* interest rates should not be allowed to rise above the 8–10 per cent range.

Although the President's main reason for wishing to see interest rates kept low was his desire to keep the recovery going, and in particular to stimulate the productive investment so necessary to future growth and rising living standards, he had other reasons as well. One was the need to minimize the cost of servicing the national debt. Debt interest now cost the Federal government over $220 billion a year – not far off 20 per cent of the entire budget. Much of this debt was of short maturity, and the cost of re-financing it was determined by the prevailing level of interest rates. Even more serious was the fact that several hundred billion dollars' worth of US government debt was now held by foreigners – the result of all the large budget and balance of payments deficits since the early 1980s – and much of this debt was very short-term, too. In the days when the United States had been a creditor nation, it had benefited from high interest rates. Now that it was by far the world's biggest net debtor, it suffered. Since the nation's net external debt was now in excess of $500 billion, a 2 or 3 per cent rise in US interest rates would in itself worsen the balance of payments on current account by $10–15 billion a year.

But what was true of the United States was even more true of other debtor countries. The US external debt might be huge in absolute terms, but servicing it still cost only about 1 per cent of GNP. For many developing and newly-industrializing countries, debt service now accounted for between 5 and 10 per cent of GNP, pre-empting a third or more of their entire earnings from exports. And, with repayments of principal often in abeyance, and most of the debt contracted at floating rates of interest, changes in interest rates had a highly-geared effect on the cost of servicing these countries' debt.

The developing countries' debt had largely been contracted in the 1970s, as Western banks rushed to lend them money so they could pay the higher oil prices which followed the 1973 oil shock. For a few years all had been sunshine and roses; but by the early 1980s there had been another oil shock, and repayments had started to fall due. US interest rates, as a result of the Fed's determination to squeeze inflation out of the US economy by operating a very tight monetary policy, had rocketed upwards in 1979 and stayed at very high levels for several years; and this had doubled the interest rates developing countries had to pay. These countries' problems had been exacerbated by the US recession of the early 1980s, the slow world growth and depressed commodity prices that had persisted throughout much of the decade, and the rising protectionism of recent years. The President was surprised that the whole ramshackle edifice of international debt was still standing. Mexico, after all, had come close to total default in August 1982, and even closer on two occasions since; indeed it was arguable that Mexico already had, on any realistic definition of the term, defaulted, and that only the fact that nobody wanted to be the first to point out that the emperor had no clothes prevented this from being explicitly acknowledged. And a number of other countries had already travelled varying distances down the same path as Mexico. To the President's mind, a sharp rise in US interest rates now might be the pebble that started the avalanche, setting in motion a series of defaults so explicit and so numerous that all pretence that the situation was under control would have to be abandoned.

There were, therefore, compelling internal and external reasons why US interest rates should not be allowed to rise. Unfortunately, as the President was forced to point out to three Latin American presidents who cornered him at a meeting of the Organization of American States in the early spring of 1991, he had no control over interest rates. No one had much doubt that in Britain or France, for example, the head of government could, if he chose, exercise considerable influence over the central bank's monetary policy. But in the United States – as in Germany – this was simply not the case. Monetary policy was determined by the independent Federal Reserve Board – or, more precisely, by the Federal Open Market Committee, which consisted of the seven governors of the Board plus five regional bank presidents. The Fed had been established by Congress, and in the last resort, in some arcane constitutional sense, was answerable to it. But it was certainly not answerable to the President.

There was, however, one power which the President did possess: the power to appoint the members of the Federal Reserve Board, including its chairman. And, by a fortunate coincidence ('compensates for the timing of those air crashes,' as the President observed to his Chief of Staff), the present chairman's four-year term of office was due to expire in August 1991. The knowledge that this was so was not only a significant element in Washington's political manoeuvrings and social gossip-mongering during late 1990 and early 1991; it also had a powerful influence on the behaviour of the present chairman, who was eligible for reappointment.

The present chairman, although a less commanding figure than Paul Volcker had been, had nevertheless established a considerable degree of control over the Fed's policies: his views were usually supported by a majority of the members of the Board itself, and always by a majority of the larger Federal Open Market Committee. Like most central bankers, he regarded himself as the ultimate guardian of the integrity of the nation's currency, detached from the vagaries of short-term political expediency. Specifically, he saw his job as being to control the money supply in the interests of, at the very least, preventing any rise in the inflation rate, and if possible of reducing inflation to zero. At the same time, like any sensible central banker, he knew that he could not behave as though he lived in a vacuum. In a democracy, the will of the people was represented by the results of free elections, and where such elections gave a political leader a clear mandate for a particular programme – as the 1988 Presidential election had done – the programme could not simply be ignored. For this reason the present chairman had so far leaned, if unenthusiastically, in the direction of keeping the Fed's monetary policy consistent with the requirements of the Administration's economic and social objectives. And, as the date of the President's decision on his reappointment drew closer, he had a further reason for continuing to do so – quite apart from the dictates of personal ambition. If the Fed's monetary policies came to seem in flagrant contradiction to the President's economic priorities, he would certainly be replaced, probably by someone less responsible and less independent. But if he did his best, within the limits his conscience allowed, to accommodate the President, he would live to fight – should it be necessary – another day.

But by February or March 1991 the strain of doing this had become too great. The staff of the Federal Reserve Board argued about the precise weight of different factors – past declines in the value of the dollar, protectionism, the fall, albeit modest, in unemployment – but the basic fact could not be ignored: the inflation rate was beginning to accelerate. Many economists in the private sector were predicting that it would be running at 9 or 10 per cent by the end of the year, and the Fed staff's own forecasts were even more pessimistic. The chairman, however reluctantly, did what he conceived it to be his duty to do, and persuaded the Board to raise the discount rate by a full percentage point. The signal to the financial markets was unmistakable: monetary policy was being tightened. The chairman may have hoped that the rise in the discount rate would be big enough to knock inflationary expectations on the head, for the moment at least, while being moderate enough to persuade the President that he was sufficiently in tune with the Administration's priorities to merit reappointment. If so, he would have been less sanguine had he been able to foresee two events that were to occur before the President had to make a decision on his reappointment in June.

The first event was a rocket attack on New York's Waldorf Astoria hotel. In an anonymous telephone call to the *New York Times*, responsibility for the attack, which had been launched from a stationary vehicle on the other side of Park Avenue, was claimed by a group which described itself as 'Islamic Justice'. The caller confirmed that the target had been a reception being held in the hotel by an organization named The Success Club, which consisted exclusively of men and women – mainly Wall Street investment bankers and bond traders – who had made 5 million dollars and were still under thirty. The membership of this exclusive club was, regrettably, reduced by over a third by this incident: one rocket penetrated a window of the room where the reception was being held, killing seven people and injuring many more. The New York Police Commissioner saw the attack in terms of a lapse in local patrolling arrangements, the Mayor of New York in terms of anti-Semitism and the Arab-Israeli conflict, and the Director of the FBI in terms of the growth of Islamic fundamentalism among certain groups in America. While not disputing these various assessments, the President's eye was on something else: the fact that the outrage had been greeted with little short of glee in the poorer parts of New York, and beyond. It could be seen as a message to the haves from the have-nots. It confirmed to the President the urgency of stimulating growth, reducing unemployment, and sharing the fruits of economic expansion less unfairly among the population.

The second event, which occurred early in May, was one of the things the President had long feared. Whether or not the rise in American interest rates a few weeks earlier was the last straw on the camel's back was a matter of acrimonious dispute between the White House staff and the staff of the Fed. The fact, however, was inescapable. The presidents of the five biggest Latin American debtor nations announced, at a joint press conference in Rio de Janeiro, that a two-year moratorium would be imposed, with immediate effect, on the servicing of all external debt. Interest payments due during this period would be added on to the total of principal outstanding; and normal interest payments would be resumed at the end of the two years. The five leaders said that they had decided on this step with the utmost reluctance, but that they had been left with no other choice. The global recessionary conditions of recent years, the prolonged weakness of commodity prices, the relatively high level of interest rates, and the spread of protectionism, had together made it impossible to earn enough foreign exchange to service their external debt without cutting their essential imports not just to the bone, but beyond. They were all convinced that if violent political upheaval in their countries was to be avoided, they could no longer afford to use a third or a half of their foreign exchange earnings to service external debt, at any rate until there was a substantial improvement in world economic conditions.

The effect that this unilateral moratorium would have on world trade and the world economy immediately became the main item of discussion in Washington and other capitals around the globe. It was, in fact, very difficult to calculate. On the one hand, if the five countries' export earnings remained unchanged, they would be able to buy more imports than before, and this would have a stimulative effect on world trade. On the other hand, if the American and European banks affected by the moratorium cut off trade credits or succeeded in seizing the Latin American countries' overseas assets, these countries might not be able to pay for even their previous volume of imports. As opposed to this, counter-trade, or barter-trade agreements, now accounted for such a large proportion of these countries' foreign trade that their vulnerability to such action might prove to be limited. And so the arguments went on. The President's most immediate concern was not, however, with any of this; it was with the effects of the moratorium on the American banking system.

In the early 1980s most of America's biggest banks and many of its smaller ones found themselves, as a result of a decade or so of ill-informed and unco-ordinated overseas lending, grossly over-exposed, particularly in Latin America. For some of these banks, the book value of their loans to Latin America alone was twice the size of their capital base – meaning that if only half these loans had to be written off, the banks would become insolvent. (It was for this reason, as the President was well aware, that so much ingenuity had been devoted in recent years to avoiding the step of classifying many highly questionable loans as 'non-performing'.) Now, in 1991, the degree of exposure was very much smaller. Over the past decade the banks had consistently refused to make further 'new money' available to Latin America, and the growth of their other business, and the building up of their capital base out of undistributed profits, meant that their outstanding loans to Latin America were now much smaller as a proportion of their total assets, and in relation to the size of their capital base. This refusal to make new money available, the President had once pointed out to a meeting of the American Bankers' Association, was just as irresponsible as the bout of imprudent lending that had got them into trouble in the first place, since it denied the Latin American countries the foreign exchange they needed to finance investment and growth, and made default on their outstanding debt considerably more likely. The bankers had retorted, predictably, that there was no point in throwing good money after bad, that they had their shareholders to think about, and that if default did come, they would at least be in much better shape to cope with it.

'So, default has come,' the President said to a meeting of relevant Cabinet officers and economic advisers. 'Because this isn't a moratorium – they're not going to resume interest payments in two years' time, or at any time. It's a default. So what does it mean for us, and what do we do about it?'

The Secretary of the Treasury set out the position as he saw it. Although the banks' exposure was considerably less than it had been, the writing-off of assets now required by bank regulators, and by prudent banking practice, would be equivalent to a reduction of about 20 per cent in these banks' capital base. Given the accepted requirement that the capital base should

87

form at least 6 per cent of total assets, this meant that the banks must reduce their deposits, in total, by several hundred billion dollars. There would have to be huge reductions in loans to businesses and consumers. As credit contracted, interest rates would skyrocket. Some banks would have to close their doors, and many businesses would go bankrupt. Even some of the country's biggest corporations would be threatened, because the orgy of leveraged buyouts financed by the issue of junk bonds in the mid-1980s had left them very highly geared, and committed to servicing large amounts of high-interest debt. Share prices would collapse, output would plummet, and unemployment would soar.

The President listened to this catalogue of disaster with growing incredulity, and then exploded. What was this Dooms-day Machine they were talking about, he demanded. They weren't living in the Middle Ages, or even in 1929. What on earth was the Federal Reserve Board for? It must take immediate steps to offset the decline in the banks' capital base, resulting from the default, by increasing the banks' liquid reserves. The idea that a few strokes of the pen by a bunch of Latin American politicians must lead to a huge recession in the United States was the purest case of voodoo economics he had ever come across, and he wouldn't hear another word about it. The Fed must step into the breach, and fast.

The President's point of view did not, however, commend itself to the Fed. Testifying before a House of Representatives sub-committee two days later, the chairman of the Fed said that increasing the liquid reserves of the banking system would increase the money supply, and that this in turn would lead to a rise in inflation. Told by an exasperated Congressman that he was not being asked to increase the money supply, but merely to stop it from violently contracting, the chairman demurred, arguing that any 'artificial' increase in the monetary base that was not matched by higher output was bound to have inflationary results. As the discussion became more arcane and more confused, one thing emerged with complete clarity: if the President wanted to get his way, he would first have to get himself a new chairman of the Fed. And so, in due course, he did. The new chairman was a less distinguished banker than his predecessor, and the President had some difficulty in securing approval of his appointment from the Republican-controlled Senate. But at least he knew some economics, and agreed with the President that there was no reason to suppose that action by the Fed to offset the potentially contractionary effects on the economy of the Latin American default would be inflationary.

Nor, in a rational world, would it have been. But inflationary expectations do not always have the rationality attributed to them in the textbooks. What many people in the financial and business community, and indeed some ordinary people on the street, derived from this episode was the simple if distorted perception that someone who was against inflation had been replaced as head of the Fed by someone who was less against it. They thus came to expect that the inflation rate would probably rise. And this very expectation made such a rise more likely.

There were, however, other, more solid, reasons why inflation was now accelerating, and had reached double figures before the end of 1991. One of these was the persistence of an excessive budget deficit. For nearly a decade now there had been deadlock between the President and Congress over the expenditure cuts and tax increases needed to eliminate the deficit. Some action had been taken, but not enough. The budget deficit, together with investment in the private sector, still considerably exceeded the amount the country was saving, so that a large part of the budget deficit was still being financed by borrowing from abroad. Until the later 1980s foreigners had lent to the US willingly, even eagerly, letting any doubts they might have about the wisdom of America's economic policies be submerged by their faith in the underlying strength of the American economy and the stability of its political institutions. But over the last few years doubts had increasingly set in, and foreign investors became less and less willing to commit funds to American government securities except at much higher interest rates than those currently prevailing. The President's determination to avoid any rise in interest rates, and if possible to reduce them, thus meant that over the past two years an increasing part of the budget deficit had had to be financed by borrowing from the domestic banking system; and this increased the money supply. Whatever the President's own scepticism on the subject, some of his economic advisers took the view that this had unquestionably been a factor behind the rise in the inflation rate.

There was another, and perhaps even more serious, consequence of the jaundiced view that many overseas investors were now taking of the desirability of dollar-denominated assets. Some of these investors were not merely unwilling to add to their dollar portfolios; they wanted to liquidate those they already had. During the first half of the 1980s these investors had prospered mightily: not only had the dollar soared in relation to all other currencies, but dollar interest rates had been very high as well. But after 1985 it had been a different story. The dollar had fallen a long way, particularly in relation to the Deutschemark and the yen. There had, to be sure, been occasional sharp rallies – one of them prolonged – as the Germans and Japanese intervened to try to stem the appreciation of their currencies, and as the markets suddenly decided that the fall of the dollar had been overdone. But the longer-term trend had been downward. And not only had the dollar lost much of its value against the other major currencies; over the last few years American interest rates had been relatively low, and not even the increase in the discount rate in April 1991 had done much to change the picture. All in all, then, American Treasury bills and government bonds were much less attractive assets than they had been in some years before, and many foreign investors wanted to get out. But there was a Catch-22 to the situation. The more they sold dollar assets, the more the dollar would fall, and the more the dollar fell the more the value of their remaining dollar assets would be reduced. In a sense, therefore, they were locked in, and this fact had so far prevented the fall in the dollar – and the impact on the American inflation rate – from being as large as it might have been. But it was an unstable equilibrium. Foreign exchange markets, like stock markets, can panic. If anything happened to make foreigners decide that they must get out of dollars at any price, the dollar could go into free fall.

Early in 1992, something did. The basic underlying reason for what happened, when analysed by his staff, came as something of a surprise to the President, well-informed on most matters though he was.

Over the past thirty years the US had created more than forty million new jobs. This staggering total represented an increase in employment of nearly 60 per cent – a percentage exceeded, among major industrial countries, only in Canada. The contrast with Western Europe could hardly have been starker: in the European Community, over the same thirty-year period, employment had grown by barely 5 per cent. It was perhaps not surprising that in meetings with their European counterparts American officials and businessmen had long been accustomed to boast about the growth and dynamism of the American economy, contrasting this with the torpor and inertia of Western Europe, and its manifest inability to create new jobs and bring down unemployment. And certainly no sane observer could deny that it was better for people to be employed than unemployed.

There was a reverse side to the coin, nevertheless. One aspect of this was that a very large part of the increase in employment in the United States had been among women, the majority of them married, and often on a part-time basis. Because of the relative decline of agriculture, mining and particularly manufacturing, jobs for men had been much more difficult to find, and this was reflected in the high unemployment rates among older men, and among those in the 16–25-year-old age group. Another aspect was that the rise in employment had been entirely accounted for – indeed more than accounted for – by the growth of the service sector.

Output, and therefore productivity, is notoriously difficult to measure in the service sector, and the chief statistician on the President's staff admitted that his findings must be hedged around with qualifications. Nevertheless, the basic conclusion was difficult to argue with. The productivity of many of the new service jobs was very low. ('I'll say it is,' the President is understood to have grunted at this point. 'If you ask me, the productivity of most of those people in the financial services sector – those Wall Street investment analysts and bond traders – isn't so much low as negative.' The chief statistician respectfully pointed out that, on the basis of marginal productivity theory and national income accounting conventions, the value of the output of workers in the service sector is usually assumed to be equal to their income, and that therefore the productivity of investment analysts and bond tranders was worth a million

91

dollars a year or more; it was the productivity of teenagers who worked in McDonalds that was very low. Not wishing, understandably, to hear what the President's opinion of this way of doing things might be, the chief statistician hurriedly reverted to his main point.) Because the productivity of many of the new service jobs was so low – much lower than in the declining manufacturing sector, for example – the productivity of the American economy as a whole had grown very little over the past twenty or thirty years. In other words, properly measured, the total output of the economy had not grown much faster than total employment.

One implication of this fact struck the President immediately. It was that whereas households where there were now two earners, because the wife was going out to work, were probably doing pretty well, the standard of living of households with only one earner could not, on average, be much higher than it had been twenty or thirty years ago. Was this, he wanted to know, correct? The statistician confirmed that it was, adding that for the bulk of one-income households the position was worse than this: because of the shift in the structure of the national income from wages to profits which had taken place during the Reagan years, the average industrial wage, in real, inflation-adjusted terms was no higher now than it had been in the 1960s, and in many parts of the service sector, even for adult males, real wages were lower still.

There was an ominous longer-term dimension to this, which confirmed the concern the President had often expressed – and had tried to act on since taking office – about America's lagging performance on innovation, research and development, education and training. If real wages were low, why should American employers invest in new, labour-saving techniques of production? And if they did not, how could labour productivity grow? And if labour productivity did not grow, how could real wages increase? It sounded like one of those vicious circles so beloved of economists and so depressing for politicians who wanted to get things done.

It was not these longer-term implications of stagnant real wages that were causing the President particular anxiety early in 1992, however, but a much more immediate problem. The discontent felt by many workers about the failure of their living

92

standards to rise over a long period of time was now being aggravated by the sight of rapidly rising prices, and the ever-tighter constraints on household budgets. Pressure for large wage increases, which had been building up in some industries for several months, now erupted in the form of strike action first in one plant, then in another, first in one industry, then in another. The solidarity of the labour movement, which had been in abeyance since the failure of other unions to support the air traffic controllers in 1981, seemed suddenly to have been re-born. In many industries employers, lulled into a false sense of security by a decade or more of relative peace on the labour front, were caught off guard, with low inventories of finished goods and no plans for coping with a prolonged strike. In many cases the lesser evil seemed to be to concede large wage increases and hope that the protectionist measures taken in 1989, and for the most part still in force, would permit them to pass these wage increases on in higher prices without much loss of market share. And so, during the first three or four months of 1992, wages rose, prices rose, and a further sharp twist was given to the inflationary spiral.

The financial markets reacted unfavourably to this latest development, and another familiar vicious circle was re-created. Share and bond prices fell, and foreigners decided the time had come to sell and get out. Their efforts to move their assets into other currencies depressed the value of the dollar, and this fall in the dollar raised the expected inflation rate, leading in turn to a further fall in the price of shares and, in particular, of government bonds. And this in turn led to a further flight from the dollar, and a further fall in its value on the foreign exchanges, towards an exchange rate of only 100 yen and 1.2 Deutschemarks. Within a few weeks the Administration was facing a foreign exchange crisis of a kind more usually associated with Britain or France, and not experienced in the United States since October 1978, under the last Democratic President, Jimmy Carter. But the situation now was very different. In 1978 the United States had been the world's largest creditor, with overseas assets that greatly exceeded overseas liabilities, and the crisis had essentially been one of liquidity. Now, the US was a net debtor to the rest of the world to the tune of many hundreds of billions of dollars, and what was at issue was something that looked uncomfortably close to national solvency.

While Congress – blissfully unaware, or seemingly so, of the responsibility its own actions, or inaction, over the years bore for the present situation – called for immediate steps to halt the decline in the dollar and restore confidence, the President, the Secretary of the Treasury, and the chairman of the Federal Reserve Board held a series of urgent and secret meetings. There was no disagreement about the immediate objective: to halt, and later to reverse, the fall in the dollar. The first step must be for the Federal Reserve Board to support the dollar at its existing level by intervening to buy, with Deutschemarks and yen, whatever amounts of dollars people wanted to sell. But the US itself did not have enough of these currencies to intervene in this way. The only solution was for the governments and central banks of Germany and Japan to agree to lend the US whatever quantities of their own currencies were needed for the purpose.

Although both Germany and Japan were unhappy about the appreciation of their currencies, and hence the threat to their export performance, implicit in the decline in the dollar, it proved more difficult to get their agreement to this arrangement than the President had anticipated. The Japanese had not forgotten the protectionist measures the American Administration had aimed at them three years earlier; and public opinion in Germany, as in other Western European countries, was increasingly being infected by the anti-American attitudes of the Europe First Movement (*see* chapter IV). A deal was struck; but it was a tough one. Germany and Japan, under the aegis of the Bank for International Settlements, would lend the US whatever quantity of their currencies was required to stabilize the value of the dollar; but the loan would only run for three months, and would not be renewed unless the United States had by then concluded an agreement with the International Monetary Fund to adopt whatever measures the IMF deemed necessary to bring the US economy, and particularly its balance of payments, back into reasonable equilibrium. These, the Treasury Secretary and the chairman of the Fed informed the President, at the end of intense and prolonged negotiations with their counterparts in Germany and Japan, were the best terms they could get.

The President was appalled. The United States had been the

dominant partner, with Britain, in establishing the IMF nearly half a century ago, and since then had largely dictated the Fund's basic approach to those of its members who wished to borrow from it. Over the years, and with the approval of the US Administration of the day, countless developing countries, and indeed a number of Western European countries, had been required to cut public expenditure, reduce government borrowing, abolish food subsidies, increase taxes, devalue their currencies and suffer other painful adjustments as the price of obtaining IMF assistance. And now this medicine was to be applied to the United States itself! In some objective and cosmic sense, the President admitted to himself, it was just. For the best part of a decade the US had been running budget and balance of payments deficits with a profligacy that no developing country would dream of, and had got away with it simply because of the size of the US economy, the prestige of the dollar, and the fact that America was a superpower. And now the day of reckoning had come. Congress would not like it, and neither would the country. But there seemed to be no alternative.

Congress did not like it, and made the fact clear, as soon as the terms of the three-month arrangement with Germany and Japan were made public, in a hundred television interviews. Public opinion polls showed the country heavily against it, too. Was the US to go cap in hand to the IMF? It was unthinkable. A draft Letter of Intent from the Administration to the Managing Director of the IMF, promising expenditure cuts, reductions in government borrowing, the removal of import restrictions and various other measures in return for a large drawing on the Fund, was rejected out of hand by the Senate. The President was back at Square One. As so often, Congress had prevented the Administration from taking appropriate action, without itself proposing alternative action that would achieve the desired objective.

What, then, was to be done? The problem, as the President saw it, had two aspects: accelerating inflation, and the falling dollar. These were intimately related to each other, and indeed fed on each other: the rising inflation rate led to a loss of confidence in the dollar, so that more and more people dumped dollars on the market, and its value declined; and the declining dollar aggravated inflationary expectations in the US, causing further increases in prices and wages. In theory, one might be able to break this vicious spiral by attacking one or other aspect on its own, but the situation was now so serious that if possible vigorous action should be addressed to both aspects simultaneously. How, the President now enquired of the distinguished academic economist who was the chairman of his Council of Economic Advisers, might this be done?

The chairman of the CEA produced a paper within twenty-four hours; no doubt it had been sitting in the top drawer of his desk, awaiting this moment. The only way to bring inflation under immediate control, this paper argued, was for the President to impose a freeze on all wages and prices for a period of six months, in much the same way as President Nixon had done in 1971. In a market economy, in which the flexibility of prices and wages constitutes the very essence of the process of resource allocation, such a freeze could only be temporary; but in the short run it could stop inflation in its tracks, and in doing so could administer a sharp rebuff to inflationary expectations in the medium term. As for the declining dollar, the obvious step here was the imposition of exchange controls. Until relatively recently, countries such as Britain and France had used exchange controls to prevent or at any rate to moderate runs on their currencies, and there was in principle no reason why the United States should not do the same. It would, to be sure, be a wholly unprecedented step for the US to impose exchange controls; but the country was facing an unprecedented crisis.

Whether the President had the power to order a wage and price freeze and to impose exchange controls was unclear. The President's legal counsel, citing the Nixon measures, took the view that he had. But even if Congress challenged the President's executive action, the orders would probably remain in force until the Supreme Court had ruled on the matter, and that would take several months. By that time, the bleeding would have been stopped, at any rate for the moment.

However, just how things might have worked out will never be known. Both the Secretary of the Treasury and the chairman of the Federal Reserve Board expressed their total opposition to any notion of controls over wages, prices or foreign exchange movements. Within a matter not of months but of weeks, they argued, a wage and price freeze would produce a myriad cases of businesses going bankrupt because they could not pass on past cost increases in higher prices, or because they could not retain labour by offering higher wages; and the Federal government had no existing capacity to evaluate or pronounce on applications for exemption from the freeze on the grounds of acute distress. And even if the freeze could be maintained intact for three months (or, impossibly, six months), there would just be a leap in prices and wages when it was removed. The President would probably have incurred great unpopularity without having any real achievement to show for it. As for exchange controls, in contemporary circumstances the notion was simply farcical. Nowadays there was a 24 hour a day global marketplace for currency dealings, with hundreds of billions of dollars' worth of currencies changing hands every day. Even if it were made illegal for American citizens to sell dollars for other currencies without central bank authorization (the essence of the exchange control systems operated in the past by Britain and France) it would make no difference – even supposing the arrangement could be policed – since thousands of billions of dollars were held by people who were not American citizens. In short, the dollar was falling because more people were trying to sell it than buy it, and there was no conceivable way in which this process could be halted by the announced imposition of exchange controls.

Although he was not completely convinced by these arguments, one thing at least was plain to the President: he was not going to get exchange controls or wage and price controls out of this Fed chairman or this Treasury Secretary. He could do nothing about the Fed chairman, whose term of office had another three years to run; and in view of the jittery state of the world's currency and stock markets, this was hardly the time to replace his Treasury Secretary. 'So what,' he asked them, 'is the alternative?'

There was only one alternative, the chairman of the Fed replied. He was reluctant to adopt it, because he shared both the President's desire to keep the American economy growing, and the President's fear that a new recession in the United States could bring both external and internal dangers that he would prefer to avoid. But in the face of the accelerating inflation rate and declining dollar with which they were now confronted, these considerations had become academic. The only answer was a big rise in interest rates. The rate of return on dollars must be made attractive enough to make people want to hold them again: this was the only way to stop the dollar's slide. As for inflationary expectations, the only way of knocking them on the head was to re-establish very strict control of the money supply. Interest rates must be raised enough to reduce the demand for money, and thus the growth of the money supply, to the extent necessary to bring the inflation rate back down, over a period of a couple of years, to the low single figures enjoyed in the mid-1980s.

To the President, this came as a bitter blow. Two years of tight monetary policy and high interest rates would finally put paid to his ambition of getting America back to rapid economic growth, to his hopes of securing a big fall in unemployment, and to his plans for allocating more resources to education and training, the alleviation of poverty and the improvement of conditions in the big cities. Indeed he seems to have felt that this U-turn in economic policy which was now being forced on him by accelerating inflation and the slide in the dollar might represent the death-knell not only of his own Administration, but of the whole liberal approach to America's economic and social problems.

But, as his Inaugural Address three and a half years ago had indicated, the President was a realist as well as an idealist, and he listened calmly enough to the Fed chairman's private forewarning that the Fed would now be adopting a much tighter monetary policy. 'Well at least,' the President is reported to have said, 'it doesn't need the approval of Congress. And,' he added with a certain satisfaction, 'we're still doing a hell of a lot better than they are in Britain and France.' And it was certainly true that in Britain, France and a number of other European countries the economic and political situation had deteriorated markedly over the past two years.

CHAPTER IV

Western Europe: Growing Strains

In Britain, by the autumn of 1990, the economic picture was beginning to darken ominously. There was a large budget deficit, the balance of payments deficit had increased, and the inflation rate was rising. Unemployment, it was true, was falling, but the fall had been much smaller than the Chancellor had forecast in his budget speech six months earlier.

Some of the reasons for this could be traced to the protectionist measures the new US administration had taken the previous year, which, as widely predicted, had had the effect of diverting the Japanese export offensive to Europe, and to Europe's markets overseas. Although Japanese subsidiaries in Britain had benefited from this process, Britain overall had suffered more than most European countries, because of its declining competitiveness. Prices and wages had risen faster than in other European countries over the past couple of years, and the normal remedy for this – some depreciation of the exchange rate – was politically much more difficult now that sterling was in the EMS, and the British government pledged to maintain its value against the other main European currencies. Because at this time the EMS currencies as a whole were appreciating against the dollar, this meant that Britain found it more difficult to export not only to Europe, but to the US and other countries whose currencies were linked to the dollar; and, correspondingly, imports from all these countries found it easier to penetrate the British market.

Britain's relatively high inflation rate, therefore, contributed to its worsening balance of payments situation. But the same thing threatened to happen in reverse as well. Increasingly, the financial markets took the view that Britain's balance of

99

payments could only be put right by a substantial depreciation of sterling; and when this happened it would, by jacking up import prices, worsen the inflation outlook. Altogether, the view about sterling became steadily more bearish. In the belief that devaluation of the currency within the EMS was becoming inevitable, investors and traders sold sterling in ever-increasing quantities in both spot and forward markets. The Bank of England, assisted by the other European central banks, supported the currency, but it rapidly became clear that only a massive rise in British interest rates – of perhaps 3 or 4 per cent – could prevent this official support being overwhelmed by the sheer weight of money moving out of sterling in the world's financial markets. Despite pleas from the Governor of the Bank of England, the government held firm: it would permit a 1 per cent rise in bank base rates, the Chancellor told him, but no more: anything else would abort the nation's economic recovery and plunge it back into an unacceptable situation of stagnant output and rising unemployment. A downward realignment of sterling in the EMS, said the Chancellor, though exceedingly undesirable, would be the lesser of two evils. And so it was done. After a feverish weekend of negotiations which began in Frankfurt, moved to Paris, then to London, and then back to Frankfurt, agreement was reached on a realignment of currencies within the EMS, the main feature of which was a devaluation of sterling of about 12 per cent against the average of other European currencies.

The first effect of this devaluation, as of most devaluations, was to worsen Britain's balance of payments even further, because of the so-called 'J-curve' effect: in sterling terms, the country's import prices, and therefore total import bill, rose more or less overnight, whereas it would take time for the country's improved competitiveness to show up in terms of higher exports. Nevertheless, pressure in the foreign exchange markets eased immediately, as financial opinion took the view that Britain had bitten the bullet and done what was necessary to restore the balance of payments to health in the medium term. The effect on output and employment of the country's improved competitiveness was also favourable, and unemployment continued, if somewhat erratically, to move down.

The effect on the price level of the devaluation and of the

inflationary expectations which it aroused was, however, much more worrying. By the beginning of 1991 inflation, at an annual rate, was running at over 10 per cent, and economists in both the Treasury and the City were forecasting that it would be running at 15 per cent by the end of the year. A particular feature of this inflation was that house prices, after the sharp setback they had suffered in the late 1980s, had taken off again. Once again people were becoming convinced, as they had been in the early 1970s, that bricks and mortar were the only sure hedge against inflation. The rise in house prices was, however, far greater in the south of the country than in the north, thus increasing the already large differential in house values between the two parts of the country. A crucial consequence of this, as the Secretary of State for Employment often complained bitterly to the Chancellor, was that workers in the north, where unemployment was still high, found it impossible to move down south, where unemployment was now quite low and unfilled vacancies growing rapidly: even if they owned their houses in the north, they could afford neither to buy nor to rent accommodation in the south. Consequently market forces, of the kind Mrs Thatcher had been so accustomed to laud, hardly worked at all in this crucial sector of the economy: unemployment stayed high in the north, and labour shortages intensified inflationary pressures in the south.

By early 1991 British public opinion was becoming distinctly restive – a fact remarked upon particularly by those foreign press correspondents who did not confine their research to lunches and dinner parties in central London, but who travelled regularly around the country. A series of articles in the *New York Times*, entitled 'What was it all for, then?' captured the mood of the country well. In essence, the complaint was that the nation had put up with high unemployment, and increasing poverty for those at the bottom of the scale, throughout the 1980s in order to slay the dragon of inflation once and for all, and now, with unemployment still too high, inflation was beginning to rocket upwards again. One East Ender was quoted at some length in the paper – which, perhaps with dim memories of the smashing success in New York of *My Fair Lady* three or four decades earlier, was clearly determined to convey to its readers the full flavour of the cockney vernacular. 'We put up wiv that bleedin' Maggie Thatcher for all those years,' this character was represented as saying, 'and she said she was going to stop rising prices an' that, an' now look at where we are. Even 'ere in London 'arf the kids leave school and can't get no proper job, and up north where my bruvver lives it's just bleedin' 'opeless. An' prices are going froo the bleedin' roof again. What's the point of it all, eh? Fair makes you sick. All that lot dahn in Westminster is as bad as each other. Sack the 'ole bleedin' lot, if you ask me. What we need is some bloke oo'll come in and sort the 'ole bleedin' thing out proper.' Asked whether he had anyone particular in mind, this down-to-earth citizen apparently replied, 'I dunno. 'Ow about that bloke Le Rif? 'E was on the telly the uvver night. Bit weird, o' course. But 'e 'ad some good ideas. Couldn't do no worse than that lot dahn in Parleyment, could 'e?' True to its tradition of not leaving its readers in ignorance of any aspect of any story it was running, the paper accompanied this article with a lengthy feature explaining who Le Rith was.

Olaf D. Le Rith was the son of a German-Swedish father and a French mother, who had been educated at schools in England and Italy, and had been to University at the Sorbonne. No doubt because of his background, and because he was fluent in all four of the major European languages, he thought of himself as a European; and, perhaps because of the nature of the education he had received, he had developed a profound and unshakeable respect for what he saw as the superior quality of European culture. None of this, however, helped him to find a job when he left university in the early 1970s – a problem compounded by a personality which often made people uneasy. The headmaster of his English school had written that he was 'not an easy boy to get to know. He is very relaxed and self-confident, but there is a reserve about him that is impossible to penetrate. He has a strong personality and great leadership potential, but gives people the impression that he is coolly calculating their usefulness to him, and has no other interest in them.'

Eventually, through the good offices of one of his former professors at the Sorbonne (a man who had once been suspected, though never found guilty, of being a collaborator during the war) Le Rith was awarded a travelling scholarship to the United States, and spent a year at university in California. Whether he suffered some particular traumatic experience during that year, as has sometimes been alleged, remains unclear; but he came back with a deep and abiding contempt for Americans and what he was accustomed to call 'American non-culture and American non-civilization'. Back in Paris, he got a job as an assistant catering manager in a hotel chain, but lost it when the chain was taken over by the Saudis. For a while he scraped a living as a cab driver, but could not compete with the Algerians who were willing to work very long hours for very low pay, and soon found himself on the street again. Neither of these experiences was calculated to increase his liking for non-Europeans. What he lived on for the next few years remains obscure, though there is some evidence that before long he was adopted by a wealthy patron who was attracted by his ideas. And it was these ideas, brooded on and developed over the best part of a decade, that formed the substance of the book Le Rith published in the mid-1980s, entitled *Europe First*.

The argument of the book was essentially simple: Europe had a proud history and a culture superior to the rest of the world's, but it was being denied its pride of place in the world, and its opportunity to solve its economic problems, by the hegemony of two of the most ignorant and uncouth players ever to strut the global stage – America and Russia. This state of affairs had only come about because of the folly, weakness and petty national jealousies of the 'old' politicians who had allowed Europe to tear itself apart in two continental wars. Hitler had been right to see the danger of communism, and of political and economic arrangements imposed on Europe by Americans and other 'alien elements', but wrong to try to build a response to these threats on a purely German rather than a Europe-wide foundation. Today's problems – unemployment, inflation, foreign immigration and Russo-American global domination, to say nothing of Arab terrorism, dependence on imported materials and energy supplies, the erosion of European civilization and values by the onslaught of a culture whose highest attainments were represented by rock music, Coca-Cola, and the hamburger, and the need to liberate fellow Europeans trapped behind the iron curtain – these problems could only be solved if Europe seized control of its own destiny and its own resources, made its own political decisions, deployed its own military forces and confronted the other superpowers, not just with an equal

103

population and an equal economy, but also with an equally strong and well-equipped central executive.

But the road to this solution was blocked, the book argued, by the parochial preoccupations of the 'old' politicians based in the 'old' national capitals, and their refusal to concede any genuine measure of sovereignty to the supposedly supra-national institutions of the EEC. Nothing illustrated this more clearly than the ludicrous and outrageous history of the Common Agricultural Policy (CAP) which, in the process of producing and storing vast unwanted food surpluses, had for many years been swallowing two-thirds of the EEC budget, and thus pre-empting funds which should have been spent on research and development, on education and training, and on regional and industrial regeneration. No wonder Europe was falling so badly behind not just Japan and the super NICs, but even an increasingly inefficient and divided United States as well. The Commission and the rest of the Brussels bureaucracy were a farce: exceedingly expensive, but completely impotent. There was only one answer, and this lay in the direct election to the European Parliament of 'Europe First' candidates drawn from every EEC country, who would then form an effective 'European' government, seizing and forging the powers needed to do the job that had to be done – much as English Parliamentarians had done in the 17th century, and as Franklin D. Roosevelt had done in establishing his New Deal in America in the 1930s. The whole ramshackle, incompetent, faint-hearted and corrupt *galère* of the 'old' politicians and bureaucrats in Brussels, and the 'old' myopic, narrow-minded, parish-pump governments in the 'old' national capitals would be swept away. Under a new European government a new Europe would arise, united and powerful, in the vanguard of technological progress, and soon to resume its rightful place of predominance over an America racked by racial tensions and rotted by political corruption, and a Soviet Union enervated by ethnic rivalries and enfeebled by economic inefficiency.

The book had not been taken seriously by the sophisticated political world when it first appeared, nor even when it was translated into one European language after another, and began to circulate more persistently – a process helped by its short, punchy title, not only easily translatable, but neatly side-stepping the vexed terrain of the old class and religious battles which had plagued the continent for centuries. But after a while the media, ever hungry for novelty, and faintly amused by Le Rith's robust defiance of the conventional decencies of post-war political thinking, began to give him air-time. By early 1988, with his commanding presence, simple message, intellectual nimbleness and multilingual fluency, he was becoming a familiar figure on television current affairs programmes and chat-shows in many European countries. Later that year, when he founded the Europe First Movement (EFM), it became apparent that Le Rith's talents were not confined to writing and talking. EFM 'national sections' were established in each of the twelve member states of the European Community, all of them generously funded, but all of them tightly controlled by the executive committee of the Europe First Movement, of which Le Rith himself was chairman. These EFM national sections quickly began to attract a wide measure of support from both ends of the conventionally defined political spectrum – both classically extreme right-wing bodies and various populist protest groups, including some of those associated with environmental campaigns.

Progress varied, of course, from country to country. It was very slow at first in France, where some of the territory Le Rith had mapped out was already occupied by the National Front. In Italy, it was much more rapid, the EFM appealing to former supporters of the extreme right-wing Italian Social Movement (MSI) and to many communists as well: both groups, it seemed, saw the EFM as a vehicle which might enable them to break out of the impotence they suffered within the confines of their national electoral scene, and build a real power base in the vacuum that was the European Parliament. Progress was also good in parts of Germany – particularly Bavaria – and in Spain. Only in Britain, where the EFM was initially greeted with massive indifference, and in Denmark, where from the start it met with outright hostility, was the response discouraging. But, as Le Rith was in the habit of saying, it was early days yet.

It was, indeed, too early for the Europe First Movement to make a major impact in the 1989 elections to the European Parliament, though it polled remarkably strongly in a number of countries. But Le Rith's eyes were on the Euro-elections of 1994. Between now and then his strategy would be to appeal to the electors of Europe over the heads of the old, discredited, national political parties, convincing them that only a Europe-wide solution to their problems made sense, and that only the EFM was capable of delivering such a solution. In the meantime, although he had no interest in trying to penetrate or take over national parliaments, and the EFM did not want to squander resources fighting general elections in individual European countries, national sections would be encouraged to fight parliamentary by-elections whenever these seemed likely to provide the Movement with extensive publicity. And it was this part of Le Rith's strategy that led to the British government receiving a bloody nose in the early spring of 1991.

On 14 March – a day that came to be known in government circles as 'Black Thursday' – there were three by-elections in Britain, all of them in seats held by the government. The government retained one of them by a narrow majority – no great source of consolation, since in the last general election it had had the third largest majority in the country. It lost the second to the candidate of the main opposition party. But the real sensation came in the third. It was the only seat in which the EFM fielded a candidate, and the EFM candidate won.

Some of the Prime Minister's colleagues were disposed to shrug this result off, talking of protest votes, funny things happening in by-elections, and the like. The Prime Minister himself took the matter far more seriously: he had felt the ground shifting beneath his feet. The victory of an EFM candidate, he informed the Cabinet bleakly, was a sign not just of a loss of faith in the government, but a loss of faith in the working of the country's parliamentary democracy. 'The people,' he said, 'the people of Britain and the people of Europe, no longer have confidence in the world we built after 1945. The deadly combination of inflation and unemployment – "stagflation", if you like – is destroying people's faith in the ability of parliamentary democracy and traditional politics to make the economy work properly, or indeed work at all. If we, and our fellow governments in France and Germany and Italy fail once again to square the circle of higher employment and stable prices, then we face the prospect of a fundamental withdrawal, not merely of support, but of any kind of tolerance or benefit of the doubt, by the electorate.'

The Prime Minister paused, but he had not finished. 'Don't make the mistake of underestimating Le Rith. We may speak privately of his "white trash" politics: but he is not a fool. He has seen the weakness of the "old" European parliamentary democracies. They can't make the economy work; and they count for nothing in global politics. He has also seen his opportunity – the yawning vacuum of the directly elected European Parliament, that we all went along with so casually without a thought to the potential for irresponsible power that we were creating.'

The Prime Minister paused again, and there was a long silence. 'Martin Luther King had a dream,' he went on. 'I have a nightmare. It is that the people of Europe will turn away from a political system that seems incapable of providing them with jobs or of guaranteeing the value of their savings from year to year or even month to month. They will turn to Le Rith, with his promise that all will be well if Europe looks inward, and rejects the outside world. But Le Rith is not just a crude chauvinist and xenophobe; he is much more than that. He knows that he must secure power by democratic means; but he is not a democrat. Unless we can pull ourselves together, and provide our people with the modest degree of economic success they are demanding, the ultimate consequences do not bear thinking about.'

Having delivered himself of these darker reflections, the Prime Minister moved the meeting briskly back to business. Inflation was already running at more than 10 per cent, and the forecasters were saying that by the end of the year it would be 15 per cent. That must simply not be allowed to happen; indeed in his judgment it was politically imperative that by the end of the year inflation should have been brought down to single figures. But this must be achieved without stopping the decline in unemployment, or at the very least without allowing unemployment to rise. How was this circle to be squared? There was only one answer, he said, and however much they might dislike it, all of his colleagues knew what it was: a statutory pay and price freeze.

This pronouncement drew immediate protests from a number of those seated around the Cabinet table, particularly the Secretary of State for Employment and the Secretary of State for Trade and Industry, both of whom foresaw a pay freeze rapidly leading to extensive strikes and industrial disruption. The idea had been tried before, they said, in the 1960s and 1970s, and had only had a short-term effect: when the thaw came, the flood-gates had burst open, and things had been worse than ever. Other members of the Cabinet, however, pointed out that when six-month pay and price freezes had been imposed in the past they had not only sharply checked rising inflation, but had actually proved popular, since in the short-term people seemed more impressed by the fact that everyone else's pay was being frozen than the fact that theirs was too. As time went on, it was true, this feeling dissipated, and people became increasingly restive at the constraints the policy imposed on themselves. But in the meantime the bleeding had been staunched, and there had been time to work out a more flexible and viable longer-term incomes policy. It was true that these policies had always broken down in the end, but not before they had reduced inflation, sometimes by quite a lot. The incomes policy imposed by the Labour government in 1975, for example, had brought the inflation rate down from 26 per cent to 8 or 9 per cent within three or four years, and although it had ended in the notorious 'winter of discontent' in 1978–9, it could be argued that this had not been an inevitable result of the policy itself, but mainly the consequence of clumsy handling of its later stages.

The argument went on for a considerable time, but it gradually became clear that those who regarded a freeze as essential substantially outnumbered those who regarded it as impossible. Accordingly, the Prime Minister said that the following day, in the House of Commons, he would announce a general pay and price freeze. The freeze, which would last for ninety days in the first instance, would become effective immediately for all government employees, including local authority and other public sector employees whose pay was indirectly financed by the government. Legislation freezing private sector pay and prices would be rushed through Parliament as rapidly as possible. In 1972, the Prime Minister reminded the Cabinet, Ted Heath had got his Counter-Inflation (Temporary Provisions) Bill on to the statute book in three and a half weeks, and he hoped, by reconvening Parliament immediately after Easter, in just over a week's time, to do even better. There might, in the interim, be some rushed last-minute pay and price increases in the private sector, but the total effect would not be serious.

The Prime Minister had, however, seriously overestimated Parliament's willingness to respond to the gravity of the situation. Some of his own backbenchers tabled wrecking amendments to the legislation in the Committee stage of the bill, and it became apparent that approval by the House of Lords would come very slowly, if at all. Early in May the Prime Minister was forced to throw in his hand. The pay and price freeze would not be statutory, he announced, but the government strongly urged employers in the private sector to comply with the provisions of the bill on a voluntary basis in the interests of securing a rapid reduction in the inflation rate. For its part, the government would continue to operate a public sector pay freeze for the remainder of the initial ninety-day period, and would urgently consult with its own employees, and with employers and unions in the private sector, with a view to reaching agreement on flexible anti-inflation arrangements to be brought into operation later on.

They were brave words, but they could hardly conceal the fact that the government had suffered a humiliating defeat. In normal circumstances, the forced abandonment of legislation which the government itself had claimed was essential to the country's economic progress would have led to a massive run on the pound. But the Prime Minister was lucky in his timing. Only the day before his announcement, there had come the bombshell from Rio, when five Latin American presidents issued a joint statement announcing a two-year moratorium on their external debt payments. Financial opinion around the world took the view that it was the American banking system that was most vulnerable to this *de facto* default, and there was a large movement of funds out of the dollar. Although few of these funds went directly into sterling, the currency, as a member of the EMS, benefited from the backwash of the flow of funds into the Deutschemark, and the abandonment of the British government's attempt to impose a pay and price freeze got largely overlooked in the general turbulence. But the reprieve was shortlived. Bad trade and inflation figures in August and

109

September led to a major erosion of confidence in the financial markets, and despite support from the central banks of other EMS members it soon became apparent that the sterling exchange rate could not be held unless drastic action was taken.

Late in September the Cabinet assembled to hear what the Chancellor had to say. It was even worse than most ministers had expected; and it came at the worst possible time, just as the annual party conference season was getting under way – almost certainly the last party conferences to be held before the next general election. The Chancellor was terse and to the point. Although unemployment was still unacceptably high, he said, it was the rising inflation rate that people were really becoming agitated about. If the party was to stand any chance of winning the next election – and if the deeper horrors the Prime Minister had spoken of at their meeting in March were to be avoided – it was absolutely essential that the inflation rate be stabilized and then brought down. In these circumstances, any further devaluation of sterling within the European Monetary System was out of the question. But this could only be avoided if firm action were taken – and seen to be taken – to reduce the budget deficit and cut back the growth of the money supply. Accordingly, he was proposing to announce a package of cuts in public expenditure and increases in both direct and indirect taxes; and he was instructing the Governor of the Bank of England to take whatever action was necessary to ensure that bank base rates were raised from 11 per cent to 14 per cent. In addition, he was proposing to introduce an immediate, though temporary, surcharge on all imports of manufactured goods, which had reached intolerable levels in consequence of the Japanese and super-NIC onslaught on the European market following the American government's earlier imposition of import controls. This surcharge would unfortunately have to apply to imports from the rest of the EEC as well as from other countries if it was to be effective, despite the legal problems which would ensue; but the surcharge on imports from the EEC would be only half that on other imports, and would be removed at an earlier date. This temporary surcharge was needed not only to help close the yawning gap on the balance of payments, but also to help cushion the impact on employment and domestic manufacturing industry of the restrictive measures he had been forced to take.

110

Finally, the public sector pay freeze would be extended for another three months.

If MPs were stunned by the announcement of these measures at a press conference the following day, and the immediate recall of Parliament to debate them, the initial reaction of the country as a whole was simply one of bafflement. The run-up to an election was traditionally the time when taxes were cut, public expenditure increased, and interest rates reduced: witness, for example, what had happened under Mrs Thatcher in 1986–7. And now exactly the opposite was happening. Of course some economists had been saying for years that when North Sea oil production started to fall rapidly away, and when the government ran out of things to privatize, then the country would find itself facing huge budget deficits and acute balance of payments problems; but no one had taken much notice. Had they, perhaps, been right? Had the moment of truth finally arrived?

As the autumn progressed, the full implications of what had happened began to sink in. At a time when unemployment was still unacceptably high, inflation had taken off again. From the figures of 3 or 4 per cent experienced in the mid-1980s, it had risen to well over 10 per cent, and by some accounts would be closer to 20 per cent before long. The government had tried to stem the inflationary tide with a pay freeze, but no one was going to stand for that, and it had soon backed off. Now it had clobbered the economy with a great package of spending cuts and tax increases, and mortgage interest rates had gone through the roof. There was no assurance that any of this was going to bring down the inflation rate, but it was absolutely certain that it would put up the unemployment rate, probably by quite a lot. High inflation and high unemployment – was that all that was on offer?

To the surprise of some observers, the winter of 1991–2 passed off relatively calmly. There were a few strikes in the engineering industry; a number of demonstrations by teachers and nurses, whose pending salary increases had been blocked by the government's continuing public sector pay freeze; and a large rally of the unemployed, which, having assembled peaceably in Hyde Park but then defied police instructions by marching on the Palace of Westminster, had led to a good deal of fighting and several hundred arrests. But considering the severity of the September measures, and the increasing hardship now being experienced by millions of households, the mildness of the public's reaction was remarkable.

Some commentators attributed this to the fact that the lifetime of the present Parliament was drawing to a close, and that people were consciously storing up their resentment in order to inflict a savage thrashing on the government at the polls. Others were not so sure. They sensed that in a confused and inarticulate way the British people were beginning to go through some process of soul-searching, of fundamental reappraisal of their attitudes towards the political and economic system under which they lived. In a tentative and muddled way, objectives and institutions which had always been taken for granted were starting to come into question. What it meant, and what it might portend, nobody knew. But acute observers had a strong feeling, as 1991 ended and 1992 began, that something was going on; something was in the wind.

In Germany, by early 1991, strains of various kinds were beginning to appear.

Part of the trouble was political. Although, after the last election, the Greens had agreed to enter a coalition government with the SPD, they had done so reluctantly, and only after a bitter internal debate. The majority took the view that an SPD government would be bound to pursue more environmentally sound policies than the possible alternatives – a minority CDU-CSU government, under its abrasive new leader, or some kind of CDU-SPD coalition – and that it would be irresponsible for the Greens not to guarantee the SPD a solid and reliable overall majority in the Bundestag. And if they were going to provide the government with consistent support, they might as well form part of it and influence its policies directly.

A sizeable minority among the Greens, however, took a much more radical view. To these people, it was not enough that the government was pledged to phase out civil nuclear power, or promote energy conservation, or take tougher action to reduce acid rain. Over the last decade they had become progressively more alienated from the conventional assumptions and values of post-war German society – the consensus between

112

government and industry, the obsession with material comfort and – as it seemed to the critics – the conviction that what most mattered in life was making money and spending it on the fast cars, expensive clothes and a thousand and one other artefacts so incessantly paraded and advertised on television and in the ubiquitous glossy magazines.

There was, of course, nothing specifically German about the insistence with which a luxurious life-style was held up as something to be envied and emulated, or about the contempt felt for the whole thing by a minority, particularly among the young: these phenomena were to be observed in most Western European countries. What was, however, particularly pronounced in the German case was the vigour with which this minority rejected any notion of collaboration with the bourgeois state, and the lengths to which a small number of people – a minority within the minority – were willing to go in order to effect the destruction of that state. By the beginning of the 1990s, to a greater extent than in Italy, where the Red Brigades had been largely destroyed a decade before, or even in France, where *Action Directe* and other extreme left-wing groups were still in evidence, the Red Army Faction and various breakaway organizations were increasingly engaging in acts of terrorism. In the second half of 1990 alone, three prominent politicians and industrialists had been assassinated, and several more had been the targets of assassination attempts. Slowly but perceptibly, a climate of fear was beginning to spread among the large number of people who had reason to believe that they might soon be in the sights of these extremist death squads.

Meanwhile, on the economic front, too, there was accumulating evidence that all was not well. By the beginning of 1991, as the expansionary measures initiated by the government a year earlier gathered pace, a number of weaknesses in the German economy were starting to become apparent.

The first problem was a marked increase in the inflation rate, compared with a year or two earlier. Although this came as a surprise to those who had believed that Germany had somehow solved the problem of maintaining a low and stable inflation rate, there were good reasons for it. Initially, there had been a degree of consensus between the trade unions and the new SPD-Green government. If the government's policies to bring down unemployment were to work, it was agreed, there had to be a fair measure of pay restraint on the part of the unions. But this consensus had soon broken down as employers pushed up prices to cover the extra costs of the IG Metall settlement, and similar settlements in other industries, and as a decline in the unemployment figures began to enhance the bargaining power of labour, and particularly skilled labour. And a more general and pervasive factor was in evidence, too: in recent years, real wages had risen very little in Germany, the benefits of rising output having gone largely into the earnings of highly paid executives, into profits, and into the balance of payments surplus. Now that *their* government was in power, many voters evidently felt, it was time for *them* to benefit. And so prices rose, and wages rose: and as each rose, it provided a justification for a further rise in the other. By the spring of 1991 prices were rising at an annual rate of about 6 per cent. This was not particularly rapid by comparison with what was happening in Britain and France, and even the United States; but it was rapid enough to cause considerable concern.

It was not, however, the rise in the inflation rate, in itself, that was most exercising close observers of the German scene in early 1991. It was another development, which was certainly a factor behind the rising inflation rate, but which was deeply worrying in its own right. This was the accumulating evidence that the decade of virtual recession after 1979 had taken a heavy toll of the underlying strength of the German economy. Those who talked in terms of irreversible damage having been done to the basic fabric of the most powerful economy in Europe were initially dismissed as being absurdly alarmist; but the case they were making soon began to be widely talked about.

There were, in essence, three particular reasons for concern. The first was the low level of investment over the past decade, which had prevented the nation's stock of industrial capital from increasing in the way it should have done, and meant that much of the existing capital stock was obsolescent, at any rate by comparison with that of Japan and the major newly-industrializing countries. The second reason was the erosion that had taken place in the skilled labour force, in consequence of the widespread redundancies and lack of job opportunities that had characterized the last ten years. Although the situation

114

was still far better than in, say, Britain, where the failure to train and re-train labour on an adequate scale had been a national scandal for decades, it was nevertheless serious by comparison with the state of affairs in Germany in the 1960s and 1970s. And the combination of these two factors – inadequate capacity and an inadequate supply of skilled labour – meant that before long the expansion of the economy which got under way early in 1990 started running into bottlenecks and scarcities of many different kinds. Production schedules were disrupted, and in some sectors inflationary pressures became acute.

The third reason for concern was the most serious of all. In addition to the failure to invest or to train skilled labour on an adequate scale, it was becoming increasingly apparent that at a deeper level the German economy had been failing to adapt to some of the fundamental changes that were taking place in the world economy. As comparative advantage in the production of ships, steel, chemicals and engineering goods of many kinds had shifted to Japan and the newly-industrializing countries of South-east Asia and Latin America, Germany should have adapted, moving resources into the new, high-tech, knowledge-intensive industries. And to some extent – more than in Britain and several other European countries – it had done so; but not enough.

Behind this failure to adapt lay an interesting paradox. One of the great strengths of German industry had always lain in its ability to obtain low-cost, long-term finance from the banking system – a situation which also existed in Japan, but which was in sharp contrast to the usual method of financing industrial investment in Britain and the US. In consequence German firms, like Japanese ones, had been able to adopt long time-horizons in their investment planning, and stick to their basic long-term strategy in the face of short-term setbacks. American and British firms, on the other hand, too frequently obsessed by the effect that annual or even quarterly turnover and profit figures might have on their stock market quotations, were much less likely to take a long-term view.

Now, however, this seemed to have changed. Banks in Germany which in the past had been happy to put up large quantities of long-term capital to finance the construction of visible and tangible investments like shipyards, steel mills, engineering works and petrochemical complexes, were much more wary about backing ventures in the emerging new information-based technologies of the 1980s. Where the collateral for their loans would consist not of largely immobile plant and machinery, but of such assets as computer software and highly mobile skilled and educated individuals, the banks proved much less supportive. In consequence, the climate for the emergence of new technologies in Germany in the 1980s was a relatively unfavourable one, and many of the younger and more dynamic people who would have been at the forefront of progress in this field found a much warmer welcome abroad, mainly in the United States.

For all these reasons, the economic outlook in Germany was much less rosy in the early 1990s than it had been a decade or two before. Despite the mainly successful efforts of the Bundesbank to control the growth of the money supply, the inflation rate was rising ominously – a phenomenon explained by the economists in terms of 'a rise in the velocity of circulation'. The fall in unemployment was relatively slow, partly because, ironically, shortages of skilled labour were holding up the expansion of production and thus the demand for less skilled kinds of labour. In many sectors, demand for high-tech goods and services had to be met by imports, limiting the growth of domestic output and eroding the time-honoured German export surplus. All in all, the complacency which had been such a marked feature of the German scene only a few years before was beginning to give way to worry and self-doubt.

In France, meanwhile, those who had hoped that the rather ineffectual left-centre coalition which had taken office at the end of 1989 would be replaced in due course by a socialist government with a clear majority – like that elected in 1981 – were doomed to disappointment. The outcome of the National Assembly elections held a little over a year later, early in 1991, was a decisive win for the right.

The main reason for this lay in the country's deteriorating economic situation, for which the left-centre coalition – not entirely fairly – got most of the blame. Under the market-oriented conservative government of 1986–9, the unions had fared badly, failing to secure wage increases even in line with inflation, and suffering widespread redundancies among their members in the older industries. Wages and salaries in the public sector, particularly, had fallen markedly behind. With the formation of the new centre-left coalition at the end of 1989 the unions had seen their chance, and had demanded large wage increases, an end to mass redundancies, a big boost to public expenditure, and a stepping-up of subsidies to industries and regions that were suffering most from recession and unemployment. Although the government had resisted these demands for a time, an extensive campaign of strikes and mass demonstrations, organized by the socialist unions and the increasingly confident Communist Party – glad to be able for a while to divert attention from the tricky racial issue – soon forced the government to back down, and most of the unions' demands were conceded.

Although labour unrest quickly died down, the high cost of these concessions soon started to become apparent. The inflation rate rose, as employers in both public and private sectors moved to increase prices in order to cover higher costs; the budget deficit soared, and was mainly financed by increases in the money supply; and, as extra imports were sucked in by the higher expenditures workers were now able to pay for out of their fatter wage packets, the balance of payments plunged heavily into the red. A majority of the electorate viewed these developments with mounting unease, and registered its disapproval in the 1991 election.

The complexion of the new National Assembly was markedly different from that of the old one, not merely because of the electorate's shift to the right, but because the proportional representation system operative at the time of the last National Assembly elections in 1986 had subsequently been discarded, and replaced by the former two-round, first-past-the-post system introduced by President de Gaulle in 1958. The main casualty of this change was the extreme right-wing National Front, which had won thirty-five seats in 1986, but this time won none. Any rejoicing over this by moderate opinion would, however, have been naive. The National Front leader, Jean-Marie Le Pen, had long since seen the problem coming, and had taken good care to ensure that – in return for his pledge to urge his supporters to vote for RPR candidates on the second ballot –

many of those who stood for election under the RPR label were broadly sympathetic to his point of view. In consequence, the new government and its supporters in the National Assembly were even more right-wing and hardline than they appeared to be.

There was, however, another consequence of the composition of the new Assembly, which was to play a key role in the events of the next few years, not just in France, but in Europe as a whole. The Euro-elections of 1989 had been fought in France under the same proportional representation system as those of 1984, and the National Front, taking advantage of the anti-immigrant feeling in the country in 1989, had increased its representation in the European Parliament from ten seats to eighteen. The eighteen MEPs, suddenly bereft, in a formal sense, of their home base by the results of the 1991 National Assembly elections, now started to suffer what an unsympathetic British Labour MEP described as a 'severe identity crisis, which with luck will soon have them crawling back into the holes they came out of'.

Olaf D. Le Rith had other plans for them. Flushed with the success of a Europe First candidate in winning a seat in the British by-election held three days before the second round of voting in the French National Assembly elections, he moved swiftly and surely into the vacuum. This would, to be sure, have been more difficult but for the demise a short time earlier, and in mysterious circumstances, of the National Front leader, Jean-Marie Le Pen. If, for Le Rith, this was a great stroke of luck (and there were those who hinted that it was too convenient to be luck), that was fair enough: no one succeeds in politics without a measure of luck, and Le Rith was no exception. Now, within a matter of weeks, he had convinced all but a handful of the French National Front Euro-MPs that their basic objective – a strong and prosperous France, free of alien influences and undesirable immigrants – could only be achieved by action on a fully European scale, and that their historic contribution to the fulfilment of Europe's true destiny was to discard their National Front label, and form the nucleus of the Europe First Movement's representation in the European Parliament. Accordingly, by April 1991, the EFM could claim that it had fifteen seats in the European Parliament. It was only a toehold – only 3 per cent of the total number of seats. But it was a beginning.

Many of those in various parts of Europe who had been watching Le Rith's activities with some apprehension were delighted by this new development. By overtly absorbing the French National Front MEPs into his Europe First Movement, they chortled, the man had come out in his true colours. He is basically a fascist, and everyone can now see it. He is finished.

Such rejoicing was premature. For neither the first nor the last time, Le Rith proved to have a much better understanding of the seismic forces moving under the surface of Europe than his critics had. Most Europeans neither knew nor cared that the handful of EFM Members of the European Parliament had previously represented the French National Front, or were being described as 'fascists' by the political experts. Most Europeans, indeed, had very little idea of what a fascist was, linking the word, if anything, to a jowly, bemedalled, strutting Italian called Mussomething-or-other who, at any rate from the safe distance of fifty years, looked a comic rather than a sinister figure. What most Europeans saw – and Le Rith's highly organized publicity machine ensured that they saw it quite a lot – was a group of men drumming home the message that Europe's economic problems, and particularly its crippling combination of high unemployment and high inflation, could only be solved on a Europe-wide basis; and only the Europe First Movement had this Europe-wide approach. The fact that all these EFM Members of the European Parliament were French was, admittedly, not an unmixed blessing: in Britain, particularly, which had entertained a healthy distrust of France for a thousand years or so, it tended to put people off. But, as Le Rith would repeat, it was early days yet. The increasing awareness, from the Atlantic to the Elbe and beyond, from the North Sea to the Mediterranean, of the existence of the EFM and of the views being expressed by its spokesmen in the European Parliament was further evidence to Le Rith of the way that the currents of opinion within Europe were shifting, and of how the old divisions and distinctions were becoming irrelevant as there emerged a growing and hardening consciousness of the potential of a new and powerful European entity.

Meanwhile, the newly formed French government got down to work. Although the political philosophy of the new Prime Minister and his colleagues was considerably to the right of that

119

of the incumbent President, it had become widely accepted since the experiment in 'cohabitation' had been launched in 1986 that it was only in foreign and defence matters that the President had the ultimate authority; in the area of domestic economic and social policy it was the Prime Minister who called the tune. Accordingly, the new government went ahead with a series of hardline measures designed to eliminate the budget and balance of payments deficits, and bring inflation down from the 12 per cent rate at which it was currently running to 'low single figures'. Indirect taxes were increased, and large cuts were made in a wide range of government expenditures, including welfare payments and subsidies to agriculture, industry and the transport system. In addition, the soaring growth of the money supply was to be reined back hard, even if this meant a temporary period of very high interest rates. All this, it was hoped, would restore confidence in the franc – sadly eroded in recent months – and permit the balance of payments to be brought under control without recourse to a humiliating and inflation-enhancing devaluation. Nevertheless, certain surreptitious steps were also taken to make the lot of importers a more difficult one; and six months later, when the British government imposed 'temporary' import controls, the French government immediately seized the opportunity of imposing 'temporary' import controls of its own. By the end of 1991 both the favourable and unfavourable consequences of these policies were beginning to be widely felt. Inflation had fallen to just under 10 per cent, and the balance of payments had improved. But unemployment had risen by nearly half a million, and with the squeeze on real incomes and the cutbacks in state support of various kinds, life for a majority of the population was becoming very hard, and discontent was deepening.

In many other European countries, too, there was much concern by the end of 1991 about the economic outlook; and in some cases this was compounded by mounting anxiety about the stability of the political system.

Sweden was one of the few exceptions to the rule – 'because it's not in the EEC', some critical citizens of the European Community said enviously, but probably inaccurately. Sweden was benefiting from a broadly consensual approach to the problem of pay restraint, from a continuation of its long-established procedures for training and re-training people for new jobs on a very large scale, and from its policy of finding jobs for people – particularly married women – in the public service sector of the economy. The result was a relatively low level of productivity, as conventionally measured, and a high level of taxation; but another result was a comfortable average level of family income, low unemployment, and an inflation rate that was pretty much under control.

The Low Countries were doing less well. Holland was still struggling with the legacy of the sudden wealth brought by the development of the natural gas fields more than twenty years ago, much of which had been used to create an over-generous system of welfare payments which, though subsequently much eroded, were still more than the country could really afford. The Dutch economy was so tied to the German economy that the inflation rate was still fairly low; but unemployment was high, and mutual animosity between those who had jobs and those who did not was more marked than in most other European countries. In Belgium, too, a corrosive degree of mutual animosity was much in evidence, but in this case it was between the Dutch-speaking Flemings of the north and the French-speaking Walloons of the south. Although there had been a substantial measure of devolution of power to the two regions of Flanders and Wallonia in the early 1970s, the language issue had flared up from time to time since then, paralysing government decision-making and occasionally seeming to threaten the ultimate break-up of the state. This division was itself in part the product of economic hardship, since the French-speaking south, with its older industrial structure, had suffered more from the recession of the 1980s than the more populous, Dutch-speaking north. Now, in 1991, rising unemployment in each half of the country was prompting a search for scapegoats in the other.

In the Iberian peninsula, the benefits of entry to the EEC at the beginning of 1986 had been substantial. In Spain there had been a rapid rate of industrial growth; Portugal had benefited considerably from disbursements from the EEC's social and regional funds; and both countries had enjoyed rising exports of fruit and vegetables to the Community's markets. Nevertheless, unemployment in both countries remained very high, living

121

standards for the mass of the people were still very low and, especially in Portugal, inflation was on a rising trend. In Spain the picture was further complicated by the running sore of Basque terrorism, and the lurking fear that the organized right, backed by the still immensely powerful Civil Guard, which had suffered most from ETA terrorist attacks, might be tempted to intervene and overthrow the still youthful democracy in the name of restoring law and order and heading off the prospect of anarchy.

In Greece, sadly, it was once again becoming apparent that a country's ability to generate and nurture the world's first experiment in democracy, in 5th-century BC Athens, was no guarantee that it would be much good at operating a democracy some twenty-five centuries later. The democratic system which had replaced the colonels' military dictatorship in 1974 was still in place; but a series of disastrous economic misjudgments, following the collapse of the courageous attempt at economic stabilization in the mid-1980s, had depressed living standards, raised unemployment to the highest level in Europe, and unleashed a frightening new bout of inflation; and this in turn had re-opened the deep and bitter divisions between conservatives and communists which had plagued Greece ever since the Second World War. In bars and tavernas around the country, the question of how long the existing democratic order could last was a subject of increasingly animated discussion.

It was, however, in Italy that the most menacing signs of trouble were beginning to appear. Unemployment was the highest in Europe outside Portugal and Greece. The halcyon days of the mid-1980s, when the collapse of oil prices had briefly brought the inflation rate down to 5 per cent – the lowest for nearly twenty years – were long since gone, and prices were on a strongly rising trend. But it was the contrasts that were the most striking feature of the Italian scene at the end of 1991. This was not just a matter of the long-standing contrast between the developed north and the undeveloped south, though this remained as stark as ever. It was the contrast between those in the north who had jobs and those – mainly the young – who did not. It was the contrast between those who lived in such prosperous regions as Emilia Romagna, where a vigorous entrepreneurial culture flourished, paradoxically, under a

communist administration, and earnings were high and unemployment low; and those who did not. It was the contrast
between those who had no option but to pay high levels of
taxation because it was deducted from their wages and salaries
at source, and those in the self-employed and black sectors of
the economy who managed to evade payment of all but a
fraction of their fair share.

Underlying all this was the ever-increasing burden of a public
sector debt that was virtually out of control. Because for many
years public expenditure had been running well ahead of public
revenue, the National Debt was now significantly greater than
the GDP, and this meant that each year nearly 10 per cent of
Italy's national income was needed simply to make interest
payments on the National Debt. The fact that this operation was
to a large extent a straightforward transfer from one section of
the Italian population to another (often, in fact, the same
people) did not alter the fact that taxes had to be levied in order
to finance the payments; and this levying of taxes, like so much
else that was done by the Italian state, was done with singular
inefficiency.

The immediate reasons for the political system's seeming
inability to wrestle with this and various other urgent problems
lay in factors which often amused foreigners: Italy's plethora of
political parties and frequent changes of government, not to
mention the abiding strength of the Communists, who in the
1984 Euro-elections had polled exactly a third of the total vote –
fractionally more than the Christian Democrats – but had never
been allowed to participate in any of the country's fifty or so
post-war governments. But underneath all this lay a much
darker suspicion. Few Italians had forgotten the Gelli affair,
and the uncovering in 1981 of a secret masonic lodge, code-
named P2. Many of the thousand or so members of this lodge,
consisting of politicians and industrialists, police and army
officers, had subsequently been shown not merely to be deeply
implicated in the crime syndicates organized by the Mafia and
the Camorra, but to be involved through a process of favours,
bribery and blackmail in attempts to bypass the formal institutions and overt processes of a democratically elected government, and to set up a state within a state, with a sinister secret
agenda.

This plot had been foiled, it was said, and the villains unmasked. But was this really so? Nobody knew. Where was all that Mafia money going? How was it that the extreme left-wing Red Brigades had been virtually eliminated by police action in the early 1980s, with an efficiency that ostensibly better-organized countries like France and Germany had envied, but the Mafia was so very obviously still in business? Suspicion festered and spread in Italy during 1991, as the economic situation deteriorated. If, as close observers increasingly believed, there was going to be a real explosion in Europe as inflation mounted and attempts to bring it down simply resulted in ever-higher levels of unemployment, then Italy might well prove to be the country in which the spark was ignited.

Heads of government in the United States and other countries with fixed-term elections had often envied the British Prime Minister for being able to call a general election at a time of his own choosing, provided it was within five years of the previous one. British Prime Ministers did not always share this view. To be able to choose was to be able to make a mistake; and although this mistake sometimes became apparent only with hindsight, that never stopped your party from blaming you for it for a long time to come. So, at any rate, thought the Prime Minister early in March 1992. Not that there was a great deal of choice left to him, since the five-year limit was rapidly approaching; but he still had to choose whether to go to the country immediately, or wait a little longer in the hope that things would improve.

The possibility that things would improve, at any rate in the near future, did not, however, look particularly strong. Over the past six months unemployment had risen very little, partly because the restrictive measures taken last September had been slow to start biting, and partly because there had been some fall in unemployment in a number of the industries now protected by the temporary surcharge on imports. But the deflationary forces now mounting in the economy were powerful ones, and the rise in the unemployment trend would soon pick up speed.

Inflation, by contrast, had been rising faster than the Treasury forecasters had predicted. One reason for this lay in the boost to the price of imported goods given by the import surcharge, and

124

the opportunity this provided to domestic manufacturers to raise their prices. Another lay in the fact that although a few loyal trade union leaders were still urging their members to conform with the government's voluntary pay restraint programme in order to keep inflation down and avoid a threat to jobs, most of them were demanding that wages rise by at least enough to compensate for the 15 per cent inflation rate. Moreover, at local level, officials and plant bargainers were not even paying lip service to the idea of restraint: their idea was to screw the highest possible wage increase out of their employers before the government's deflationary measures took hold and workers' bargaining power was weakened again by falling profits and rising unemployment. And so throughout most of the private sector, despite growing employer resistance, wages rose quite strongly, and were often quickly passed on in higher prices, even in sectors not directly protected by the import surcharge. Thus although the major rise in unemployment now in prospect would no doubt start bringing the inflation rate down in the medium term, it might get worse before it got better.

All in all, the Prime Minister decided, he had better go to the country as soon as possible. And so, on 12 March, he announced that a general election would be held in exactly four weeks' time, on Thursday 9 April.

Many of those who observed and wrote about the British general election of 1992 have remarked on its strange, almost surreal, quality. Themes familiar from every election campaign of the last thirty years were solemnly wheeled out and paraded up and down. Candidates representing the right-hand part of the conventional political spectrum insisted that the top priority must be to bring down the soaring double-digit inflation rate to something closer to the 3 or 4 per cent figure enjoyed under Mrs Thatcher in the mid-1980s. A second priority, they added, must be to toughen up on law and order, and crack down hard on the crime rate, now higher than at any point in the nation's recent history. On the left-hand part of the political spectrum, by contrast, candidates insisted that the top priority must be to prevent any further rise in unemployment, which was already much too high. A second priority, they added, must be to reduce the appalling incidence of poverty and homelessness, now higher than at any point in the nation's recent history.

What struck observers of this scene was not that neither set of actors was listening to the other – for this indeed was normal – but that the audience was not paying much attention either. To the electorate it was all stale and sterile stuff; they had heard it all before, and it was no longer worth listening to. But there was one voice they did listen to: the voice of Olaf D. Le Rith.

Le Rith had calculated the odds carefully. At this time his funds (later revealed to come from a number of European engineering and chemical firms, and from an eccentric Texan billionaire called Wildcat 'Gusher' Hunk, who believed that European unity of the kind advocated by Le Rith was the only thing that would save the world from communism), though substantial, were far from unlimited; they had to be deployed to maximum effect. Le Rith authorized the British section of the Europe First Movement to fight twenty-seven seats. Although this represented less than 5 per cent of the total number of parliamentary seats, they had all been very carefully selected. They included – in order to get maximum coverage – the seats of the leaders of all the main political parties, together with other seats where local circumstances suggested that the appeal of the EFM might be particularly strong. These local candidates were backed up by a national advertising campaign that exploited every one of the media to the fullest extent permitted by the law (although no further: Le Rith was risking no lawsuits). The message conveyed by the national advertising and the local candidates was the one that was already becoming familiar to those interested in politics: the old parties had no answers to Britain's problems; what was needed was a radically new approach, Europe-wide; Europe must unite, and show its muscle; the Americans and Japanese must be confronted by another, greater economic superpower, capable of providing jobs and prosperity for all its people, and eliminating inflation once and for all by maintaining a firm control of monetary conditions and a strong and unified external currency.

Economic and political experts expressed considerable scep-ticism about all this, but people were fed up with economic and political experts. Le Rith had a new and simple message, and to a great many people it made a lot of sense. In constituencies where there was no EFM candidate, electors complained that they were being denied real freedom of choice; in constituencies where there was, electors said that when polling day came they would be showing the sitting MP what they thought of him and all that he represented.

And so they did. The result of the 1992 general election was as sensational, in its way, as any since 1945, when a disbelieving world saw Winston Churchill swept aside in a Labour landslide of unimagined proportions. Of the twenty-seven EFM candidates, fourteen were elected. One of them defeated the left-of-centre party leader most generally predicted – until now – to be the next Prime Minister but one. As the results came in, the television studio psephologists, tapping away at their computer keyboards, agreed that if the EFM had stood in every seat in the country, instead of only twenty-seven, it would certainly be the largest party in the House of Commons, and might conceivably have had an overall majority. Cooler heads among the television pundits denied this, pointing out that the EFM had deliberately chosen the most favourable seats, and would have made a much less impressive showing if it had fought on a broader front. Nevertheless, the basic point was incontrovertible: the Europe First Movement had arrived on the British political scene with a bang loud enough to be heard all over Europe.

However, although the longer-term implications of the election result might be of seismic proportions, the immediate consequence was a parliament with a majority – though not all came from the same party – of members who were well to the right of centre. Those electors who had not been able to vote for the EFM (and who had not – as many had – spoilt their ballot papers by writing in the name of Le Rith) had, it seems, decided that candidates calling for lower inflation and more law and order were to be preferred to those calling for lower unemployment and more measures to relieve poverty. And so the former Prime Minister delivered up the seals of office, and furniture vans moved into Downing Street, even as the new Prime Minister drove to Buckingham Palace to accept the Sovereign's request to form a government.

One person, at least, was in no doubt about what he thought of the new Prime Minister: the colourfully loquacious taxi driver, on whom the *New York Times* had evidently been keeping careful tabs. '''Im?' this character now demanded.

'Makes bleedin' Maggie Thatcher look like Florence Nightingale. 'E'll get inflation down, all right, an' bleedin' kill us all in the process. Law an' flippin' order? Wot does that mean? The bleedin' prisons is overflowin' already. Goin' to 'ang 'em all, is 'e? 'undreds of bleeders on Death Row, like wot you 'ave in the States? Not likely, guv, we're a *civilized* country we are, like wot that Le Rif says. We got to get together with the rest of Europe, like wot 'e says. Then we'll show you lot, all right. Nothin' personal, guv . . . oh, ta . . . very generous, guv, wish more English geezers was like you Yanks.' This point of view, or something like it, was soon to be shared by a large and growing number of people in Britain.

The new government took drastic further action to reduce public expenditure which – coming on top of the reductions imposed six months earlier by the previous government – threatened to cut the provision of most public sector services not just to the bone, but beyond, and at the same time to throw large numbers of people out of work. Interest rates were raised another 3 points so that bank base rates were now 17 per cent, and mortgage rates close to 20 per cent, in order to rein back the growth of the money supply and, it was hoped, inflation. And the cost of servicing a mortgage was also increased by a quite separate measure: in order to raise tax revenue and thus contribute to cutting the yawning budget deficit, the government grasped the nettle of the biggest and longest-standing subsidy in Britain – the tax relief enjoyed on their mortgage interest payments by more than 10 million householders. This form of tax relief, it was announced, would be completely eliminated over the next three years.

What effect all this would have on inflation remained to be seen, but there was little doubt that it would substantially increase unemployment, and cut deeply into the living standards of the vast majority of the British people, who, until now, had thought that real hardship and deprivation was something suffered only by the 10 or 15 per cent of the population at the bottom of the heap.

As Parliament broke up for the 1992 summer recess, there were scores of MPs, as well as many millions of their constituents, who were beginning to believe that perhaps it was only Le Rith who offered a solution to the nation's problems.

CHAPTER V

The United States:
The Return of 'Realism'

During the summer of 1992, as the clock ticked steadily on towards the November Presidential election, the man who had been President for three and a half years, increasingly conscious of his failure to achieve his economic and social objectives at home, surveyed the foreign scene to discern what comfort might be drawn from that. The answer was, not a great deal.

It was true that, on the greatest issue of all, some progress had been made. Negotiations with the Russians on nuclear disarmament – little more than a farce during the first six years of the Reagan Administration – had gone well: there had been a genuine 'build-down' of nuclear weapons, and a corresponding reduction in East-West tensions. There had also been some progress in the unceasing battle to prevent nuclear proliferation. But although rendering the world a slightly less unsafe place was, in the President's view, a major achievement, it was not the kind of achievement that most people noticed or rewarded you for at the ballot box. On another front – one on which a key segment of the American electorate kept a relentlessly close and critical eye – things were going much less well. The Arab-Israeli conflict was no closer to permanent resolution than it had been forty-five years ago, and the unending factional fighting between different groups of Arabs, and particularly between different extremist Islamic sects, continued to make the Middle East – still the source of more than half of the non-Soviet world's oil – a place for any sane man to steer clear of if he could. Unfortunately, many American businessmen, journalists and others could not do so, or chose not to, and the consequent catalogue of hi-jackings, kidnappings, hostage-takings and murders continued intermittently to inflame American public opinion and make rational policy-making more difficult. And, beyond the routine day-to-day atrocities, lay the ever-present possibility of what any thoughtful American President must fear above almost anything else: a new Arab-Israeli war in which Israel appeared in imminent danger of destruction by superior Arab forces.

Nor were things much better elsewhere. India was in the process of breaking up, as the richer states seceded and the fissiparous tendencies of warring castes, tribes and religions grew too strong for the central government to control. About the best that could be said of Africa was that at least the bloodbath in South Africa was finally over; but the country mourned more than a million dead, and although foreign capital was now tentatively moving back in, economic recovery would be slow and national reconciliation slower still. Throughout much of the continent, Aids was rampant and taking an appalling toll, particularly among the better educated, who offered the brightest hope for their countries' future. Apart from this, hunger, chaos and corruption, military and guerilla atrocities, political repression and tribal warfare were so endemic as to threaten to overwhelm the few countries still struggling to preserve democracy and improve the economic condition of the people.

Of far greater direct importance to America, developments in Western Europe were looking ominous. A Euro-nationalist, anti-American mood was daily gathering strength, and some of the remaining American military bases were virtually under siege, their personnel forbidden to venture beyond the perimeter fence for fear of attack. It was unclear how long the cohesion of the Atlantic partnership, on either a military or an economic front, could survive these rising tensions.

The United States' nearest neighbours, too, were in various kinds of trouble. Canada – partly in consequence of American policies – was suffering from high inflation, though growth was sluggish and unemployment heavy. To the south, from the Rio Grande to Cape Horn, 7000 miles away, Latin America was struggling with acute economic and political problems. The moratorium on interest payments declared the previous year by the five major countries – and soon copied by a number of others – had on balance done them little good. Nominally, there had been immediate foreign exchange savings at an annual rate of many tens of billions of dollars. As against this, a number of countries had soon retaliated against Latin American exports; many Latin American assets located overseas, ranging from individual bank accounts to aircraft which happened to be at foreign airports, had been impounded as soon as the moratorium announcement was made; and all forms of trade and inter-bank credit had been suspended: no one was selling anything to Latin America any more except by way of barter deals, or in exchange for cash on the nail. In the longer run Latin America, a huge continent rich in agricultural and mineral resources, and with an already extensive industrial capacity, might reasonably hope to overcome these setbacks. But in the short run these new obstacles, superimposed on the gathering world recession, the continued weakness of commodity prices, the debilitating effect on capital investment of a decade of acute foreign exchange constraints as individual countries had struggled to service their external debts – and all this against the background of rapid population growth – resulted in a further worsening of economic conditions, and a renewed squeeze on living standards. Food riots multiplied, and unrest spread. Incidents of armed confrontation between government and people became more widespread. The more authoritarian governments cracked down hard, provoking retaliation from leftist guerilla groups. In countries in which, during the past decade, democratic government had been tenuously preserved or painfully restored, the military increasingly threatened – and in some cases acted on the threat – to intervene 'to restore law and order'.

Finally, the President turned his thoughts to the Pacific – the ocean which for some decades now, as the United States' own centre of gravity moved steadily towards the West and South West, had gradually been supplanting the Atlantic as the body of water whose farther shores harboured the economic developments that really seemed to matter. Here, too, there were some disturbing trends. Australia and New Zealand, like Canada, were staunch English-speaking parliamentary democracies which had stood at the side of Britain and the United States fighting dictatorships in two world wars, but which had now been partially estranged from the US by the nuclear arrogance of the Reagan years and the adverse effects of some of America's economic policies. In particular, all these countries had lost valuable overseas markets for agricultural products as a result of the huge export subsidies with which the United States and the European Community had been competing to provide their farmers, especially since the mid-1980s. These countries feared, too, the longer-term effects on their economic independence of the increasing foreign ownership of their mineral resources and manufacturing industries, though it was true that in recent years their animus over this had been directed more at Japan than at the United States. In Australia particularly, sometimes described by unkind critics as a Third World country with First World living standards, the prolonged weakness of commodity prices had depressed real incomes and exacerbated political disagreements.

In the Philippines, the situation gave serious cause for concern. Ever since Mrs Aquino's brave experiment in democracy had been brought to an end by intervention by the military, backed by former Marcos supporters, the communist insurgency had been gaining ground. To the immense relief of the Pentagon, the Philippines military government had agreed in 1989 to a fifteen-year extension of the leases on Clark Air Base and Subic Bay Naval Base, by now the largest American bases anywhere in the world outside the continental United States. The Philippines government had assumed that renewal of the leases would act as a guarantee of United States backing for whatever steps it needed to take to eliminate the insurgency. But the action had backfired. The prospect of another fifteen years of what many Filipinos regarded as neo-colonialist occupation and exploitation boosted support for the communists, while the American people, through their elected representatives, had made it incontrovertibly clear to the hawks in the Defense Department that there was to be no question of America running the risk of being drawn into another Vietnam. The worst-case outlook, therefore – and the worst case looked increasingly probable – was that the communists, unhampered by American military intervention, would win what was by now a full-scale civil war, and the US would have to evacuate the bases. The national humiliation would be keenly felt in America, while the damage to US military capabilities in the Pacific would be even greater than that which had attended the evacuation of the Vietnam bases at Da Nang and Cam Ranh Bay in 1975.

If developments in the Philippines constituted a potential threat to America's military security, developments elsewhere in the Pacific continued to pose an increasing danger to its longer-term economic health. In particular, the so-called 'Gang of Four' super-NICS (Hong Kong, Singapore, Taiwan and South Korea – though of course other newly-industrializing countries such as India and Brazil were in many respects in this category as well) could now produce a large variety of the goods the United States could, but at a much lower price. This was fine for American consumers, but less fun for American producers – which was why some of these countries had been covered by the import controls the President had imposed soon after taking office in 1989. The real trouble, as the President had recently become acutely aware, was that productivity in these countries had largely caught up with productivity in the United States, whereas wages still lagged a long way behind. If American industry was to compete on equal terms with these countries, either its productivity would have to rise significantly – and the low rate of expenditure on investment and research and development in recent years was not a good augury here – or else real wages would have to fall by a substantial amount. Given the increasing labour unrest in the United States in the face of the failure of real wages to rise, the consequences of any significant *fall* in real wages hardly bore thinking about.

There was however one – admittedly double-edged – source of consolation in all this, the President thought. It was that Japan, too, was worried by the rise of the super-NICS. The Japanese were exercised, in particular, by what had been happening in South Korea, perhaps because of its close geographical proximity to Japan, perhaps because it was the largest and most dynamic of the Gang of Four. Since the early 1960s, after recovering from the near-total devastation of the Korean War, the country's industrial progress had been rapid, and since the mid-1980s it had been spectacular. Although left-wing opposition to the country's authoritarian and military-backed government had been steadily growing – and at one point had looked like severely disrupting the Olympic Games held in Seoul in 1988 – the rise in living standards had been rapid enough to keep discontent too muted to pose a serious threat to the regime; though – in spite of the ruthlessness with which demonstrations were sometimes suppressed – increasing militancy among groups of radical students, many of whom resented American influences and wished for reunification with the communist North, made it uncertain how long this state of affairs would last. Meanwhile, through a process of massive investment, and expenditure on research and development that, as a percentage of GNP, was equalled only in Japan, South Korea had leapt to near-developed country status. In the field of consumer electronics and cars particularly (it was now exporting two million cars a year), it had made increasing inroads into Japanese overseas markets, and even Japan itself; and it was pushing rapidly ahead in such high-tech areas as advanced ceramics and genetic engineering.

Nevertheless, Japan was by now such an economic superpower that its need to worry about competition from South Korea and other members of the Gang of Four was still not very great. What the Japanese ought to be worrying about, the President thought, was something else: a kind of schizophrenia that appeared to be emerging in the Japanese economic and social psyche.

On the one hand there were the great Japanese corporations, companies which now had a large – in some cases predominant – share of the world market for cars and consumer electronics, engineering and capital goods and, of late, even aircraft and biotechnology. An increasing share of the output of these companies came from plants located overseas, including some in the United States, so as to leapfrog the tariff and non-tariff barriers which since the early 1980s one country after another had been forced by domestic pressure to erect against Japanese imports. These companies invested continuously in new plant and machinery, spent hugely on research and development, and worked hand-in-glove with Japan's super-Ministry of International Trade and Industry to plan and implement an industrial strategy for the country which had a time horizon of at least ten years, and sometimes closer to twenty. The employees of these companies, guaranteed life-time employment and enjoying annual bonuses linked to the companies' performance, were highly trained and educated, highly motivated, and immensely hard working. They constituted the heart of the Japanese economic miracle which, for four decades now, had been the envy of much of the rest of the world.

But there was another Japan, too. This was the Japan of the inefficient small farmers, of the myriad small businesses squeezed by the monopoly powers of the big firms, of those in the older industries like textiles and shipbuilding, put out of work by foreign competition, of those employed in the large fraction of the service and distributive sector that was ill-organized and antiquated. It was the Japan of those who did not succeed in getting jobs in the big firms or the great government bureaucracies, of those who failed to get into the best universities, of those whose sense of inadequacy in the face of pressures to succeed which they began to experience as soon as they started school had given Japan almost the highest suicide rate in the world. It was the Japan of the rapidly rising number of old people, many of whom found that the provision of social security and health care fell well below what might have been expected; of the tens of millions who considered the condition of the housing stock, of the physical environment and the quality of life generally to be a near-disgrace in what was now the second richest country in the world. And, in a more diffuse and inarticulate way, it was the Japan of all those who thought that the forty years of the economic miracle – perhaps the whole century or more of industrialization – represented a journey along the wrong road, a worship of false gods, a betrayal of Japan's cultural heritage and of the unique spirituality of its traditional way of life.

No doubt these tensions had always existed in Japan, but over the past five years – partly in response to the way that other countries, including the United States itself, had been shutting out Japanese exports – they had increased alarmingly, and were taking an ever more explicit and violent form. In the 1970s and early 1980s there had been isolated occasions when groups of students and farmers, accoutred like medieval *samurai*, had fought pitched battles with the riot police to prevent agricultural land being taken over for the construction of power stations or

135

airports. Now, such incidents were far more frequent, involved much larger numbers of people, and were often directed at even more critical targets. It was clear, moreover, that the successful deployment of Japanese technology was no longer confined to those who approved of the existing political and economic order. The amateurishness of the home-made rockets with which a far-left fringe group had attempted to assassinate President Reagan during his attendance at the Tokyo summit in 1986 was a thing of the past. Highly sophisticated weapons had recently been used in a series of attacks on key government buildings and on the American embassy, and not even the most advanced security techniques had managed to prevent the assassination of several prominent figures in the political and business worlds. Perhaps inevitably, these outrages had provoked not only a repressive response from the authorities, but systematic violence aimed at known left-wing groups on the part of gangs of right-wing youths who consciously identified themselves with the nationalistic and militaristic posture the country had adopted in the 1930s. In spite of all this, life in Japan continued for the most part to go on much as usual; but many thoughtful observers viewed the future with apprehension.

It was facile, the President knew, to try to summarize in a brief generalization what was going on around the Pacific. But if he had to make the attempt, it would go something like this: while economic failure – as in the Philippines – might make violent efforts to overthrow the existing order inevitable, economic success – as in Japan, Taiwan and South Korea – did not necessarily inoculate a society against such assaults, particularly where democracy had no deep and time-tested roots, or barely existed at all. What the eventual outcome would be – whether, in such countries, the free enterprise system, unable to satisfy the deeper aspirations of the people, was ultimately doomed – only time would tell.

Meanwhile, back at home, the President was suffering from a form of Murphy's Law: everything that could go wrong, was going wrong. The Fed's tight new monetary policy had not yet had time to affect the inflation rate, which was still running in double figures. But very high interest rates were already biting hard into the construction and automobile industries, and tens of thousands of workers were being laid off every week. Most of the economic forecasts talked of an impending recession.

The President came under attack from all sides. Liberals cited his failure, after nearly four years in office, to achieve any significant reduction in unemployment, particularly among young people and blacks, or to make convincing inroads into the problems of poverty and urban degradation. Conservatives assailed his policies as having led directly to high inflation and a major weakening of America's defences. In between, tens of millions of ordinary, non-political people simply felt that the President was floundering, the country was in trouble, and that it was time for a change. Thus it was that although – such is the power of incumbency – the President succeeded in securing his party's renomination at the Democratic convention in July, all eyes were beginning to focus on the man who had emerged as the Republican candidate for the Presidency.

Political commentators at this time agreed on one thing at least: that, in spite of the débâcle of the final period of the Reagan presidency, their traumatic loss of the White House, and the recriminations and in-fighting which had subsequently plagued the party, the Republicans had now achieved something quite remarkable. They had nominated as their candidate for the Presidency a man whose mastery of television was even greater than that of Ronald Reagan in his prime. Reagan, after all, had merely graduated to television from radio and films; the new Republican candidate had made his career out of it from the beginning. One of the earliest of the television evangelists, his outstanding talents had soon drawn him well ahead of the field. He had looks, he had presence. His voice could thunder, and it could caress. He was alternately stern and friendly, tough and tender, unbending and – yes – cuddly. Above all, he knew with absolute certainty what was right and what was wrong. At first millions and later tens of millions of Christians would tune in to his television programme three times a week to be told what to do, how to behave, how to think – not just about the obvious issues of abortion and school prayer, but about everything. 'The Ayatollah Khomeini had nothing on this guy,' one veteran political reporter had once observed; and nobody seemed disposed to dispute the point.

More than 40 million people, many but by no means all of

them non-Christians, voted Democratic in the November 1992 Presidential election, and the number might have been larger but for a late-breaking corruption scandal affecting the Democratic administration in New York, which threatened to dwarf the scandals of 1986, and which probably did the party some considerable damage nationally. But nearly 60 million people voted for the Republican candidate and his party. The result was arresting. The Republican Presidential candidate won every state in the Union (though not the District of Columbia). Republicans won Governorships in eleven states previously held by Democrats, enlarged their majority in the Senate and, most remarkably of all, won clear control of the House of Representatives for the first time in 40 years. The stage was set, everyone agreed, for some real changes in the direction of American policy.

The general nature of these changes had become apparent enough during the election campaign, but it was only when the new President took office in January 1993 that the details started to become clear. In his Inaugural Address and a series of subsequent messages and pronouncements he set out his position concisely and unambiguously.

An absolute priority would be the elimination of inflation. 'Double-digit inflation,' he declared, 'will destroy this country in a few years. The Soviets and their acolytes throughout Central and Southern America are laughing themselves sick. Inflation will be eliminated by my Administration, whatever the cost. We shall do whatever it takes. Only in this way can we restore the strength of the dollar and the strength of America.' He therefore supported the tight monetary policy the Fed had belatedly introduced in the summer of 1992, and indicated that in his view it should now be tightened even further. But printing too much money was only the proximate cause of inflation. The real cause was unbalanced budgets. Budget deficits always happened under Democratic administrations, he said (conveniently overlooking the fact that the budget deficit had got out of hand only after President Reagan had taken office): look at the deficit, equivalent to nearly 3 per cent of GNP, that he had just inherited from his Democratic predecessor. Budget deficits were the work of the devil, and they would not happen under his Administration. (In private briefings he often said that there would never have been any budget deficits in America if the Democrats had not fallen for the teachings of John Maynard Keynes, who had advanced the notion that budget deficits were frequently a necessary requirement for getting a country out of a slump. Keynes, he would always add, pausing significantly, was a homosexual from the University of Cambridge, England which had produced the large number of communist spies who had risen to top jobs in Britain after World War Two, and then betrayed incalculably valuable American secrets to the Russians. Without that information, Soviet military technology would still be twenty years behind America, whereas – and partly also because of the cuts in America's defence programme under his Democratic predecessor – they were now dangerously far ahead. Intimates of the new President reported that he would sometimes go on in this vein for hours.)

Not only would budget deficits not happen under his Administration, the President said; he would make sure that they would not happen under any future Administration either. He would do his utmost to get Congress to enact a balanced budget amendment to the constitution. If only Congress had done this ten years ago – and it had come tantalizingly close – America would be in much better shape than it was. But getting the balanced budget amendment through Congress and ratified by the necessary number of states would take time. The urgent need now was to get rid of the budget deficit he had inherited.

This, he acknowledged, would not be easy. America's military security had been put at risk by his predecessor, and defence expenditure had to be increased. Income tax, despite the reductions achieved under the Reagan Administration, was still too high, and was stifling the natural enterprise and energies of good Americans. Although the budget problem meant that income tax could not be cut immediately, there was certainly no question of increasing it. He would, however, be proposing big increases in federal taxes on alcoholic drink and tobacco, evil commodities which had brought untold misery to tens of millions of American families; but the extra revenue would not be sufficient to make much of a dent in the deficit. What it came down to, then, was the need to eliminate the plethora of wasteful and useless federal government programmes. He was not proposing, he said, to touch the Social Security benefits and

139

Medicare entitlements which retired people had earned by their contributions and were now rightly enjoying. ('His knowledge of economics may be less than nil,' one Democratic senator murmured on hearing this pronouncement, 'but his knowledge of politics is sure in good working order.') But federal funding of most kinds of welfare programmes, including such items as food stamps and aid to families with dependent children, would be discontinued. Most of this assistance went to people, or the dependents of people, who were perfectly capable of working but who simply chose not to, preferring to lead a fairly comfortable existence at the expense of the federal taxpayer. If the states or localities chose to subsidize idleness, that was their affair; but they would get no help in doing so from his Administration. The same applied to many other programmes on which federal funds had been wasted in the past: grants to support education and training, or to help the unemployed get re-trained and find jobs; grants to provide or improve public housing, or to revitalize derelict urban areas; grants to promote environmental improvements; subsidies to mass transit systems and to the national railroad network; and much else besides. If those states and localities which had succumbed to decades of soft-headed liberal propaganda – propaganda often influenced by socialist or communist ideas – wanted to provide these services to their residents, that was up to them. But they themselves would have to raise the necessary revenue, out of local income or sales or property taxes, to pay for them. The federal government was going to get out of that business completely and, he hoped, for good.

This message was first spelled out, in all its starkness, in an address delivered by the President to a joint session of Congress. A liberal Democratic congressman said later that on hearing it he had 'not been so much stunned as concussed'; and his reaction was shared not only by most liberal politicians and intellectuals, but also by leaders of labour unions and a variety of other organizations, including the Leadership Conference on Civil Rights, the American Jewish Congress and the National Organization for Women. The director of the nation's most prestigious institute of poverty studies, interviewed on television shortly afterwards, was almost incoherent with shock and rage. 'Not even Reagan talked like that,' he said, 'and Reagan never knew what he was talking about anyway. This guy really means it. He *really means* it. He must be insane. But he can do it. He's just been elected by a landslide, and he controls Congress. He can do it. What am I going to do? I'm going to emigrate. It's just too bad that the poorest 20 per cent of the people in this country can't do the same.' The director was subsequently censured by the institute's board of trustees for a disgraceful lapse from accepted standards of professional conduct, but a motion to dismiss him got nowhere: too many people in the institute and the university it was linked to agreed with what he had said.

However, objections to the President's measures from the academic community, social welfare experts and the like cut little ice in Washington. In former times labour unions would have fought tenaciously to obstruct or moderate the programme, but the labour movement had never fully recovered from the demoralization it had suffered in the 1980s, and was now weak and divided, each group of workers concentrating on protecting its own interests in the face of high inflation, falling real wages and rising unemployment. One major union had just suffered a humiliating defeat in its attempts to get its members' wages linked to the consumer price index; and the most powerful union of all – the Teamsters – was an ardent supporter of the new President anyway. In Congress, where Democrats were in a minority, liberal Democrats were in an even smaller minority. Some of them, in the Senate, employed the time-honoured tactic of the filibuster in an attempt to thwart some elements of the President's programme, but they knew that the mood of the country was against them, and were gradually worn down by the volume of hate mail they received and by the tireless, evangelical fervour of their opponents.

In the House of Representatives, the loss of control of committees and sub-committees, after nearly forty years in the driving seat, had thoroughly demoralized the Democrats, and rendered them even more ineffective than might have been expected. Among the majority Republicans in both Houses there were of course many different shades of opinion, and in the Senate particularly a number of people were uneasy about the radicalism of the President's proposals. But their first loyalty was to the President and the Republican Party – many of them,

141

indeed, had been elected on the President's coat-tails – and by and large, when the chips were down, they voted for the President's proposals, turning a deaf ear both to appeals from well-meaning liberals and to the pleadings of all the special interest groups which had been so successful in emasculating the spending cuts proposed by President Reagan a decade before. 'The good people of America are behind us in this great endeavour,' the President had said in commending his proposals to the Congress; and for the most part Republican congressmen believed, or found it expedient to believe, that this was so. And thus, as the year wore on, and unemployment rose and living standards fell, the individual elements in the President's prog-ramme were slowly assembled and slotted into place. By the beginning of the new fiscal year, on 1 October 1993, the picture was complete, and the President and his hard-line supporters looked forward with undiminished faith to the day, now surely close at hand, when their shining vision of what America ought to be would be translated into reality.

On another front, however, the President was less pleased with the way things were going. In the Philippines, what had been a stalemate between the military government and the Communist insurgents during the winter of 1992–3 had suddenly erupted into a blaze of guerilla activity of a size and ferocity that was being compared with the Tet Offensive which had turned the tide in Vietnam a quarter of a century earlier. Things happened so fast that by the time the President had decided – regardless of the lessons of Vietnam – that the US must commit ground troops in support of the government, it was too late: the communists were in effective control of all the major cities, including Manila, and had issued a proclamation requiring the US to evacuate its two military bases by 31 December 1993, in eight months' time. Some of the President's advisers took the view that this was a bluff, designed simply to screw a significantly higher rent out of the United States; they pointed to the analogy of Cuba, where the Guantanomo Naval Base was still being used by the US some thirty-five years after Castro's revolution. The President disagreed. Even if the new Commun-ist government in the Philippines did turn out to be willing to sign a new agreement over the bases, it could not be trusted to stick to it. New American bases must be constructed elsewhere in the Pacific, as a matter of the highest urgency. It was typical of his predecessor's lack of concern for America's military security, the President told Congressional leaders, that this had not been done long ago: the writing had been on the wall in the Philippines for years. But it must be done now, and fast.

Another, closely related, matter was also becoming of major concern to the President and his advisers at this time. The big fall in world oil prices in the mid-1980s had brought oil drilling and exploration activities in the continental United States to a virtual standstill, and thousands of small wells, suddenly rendered hopelessly uneconomic, had stopped pumping. Analysts had warned that this would lead to a big and permanent reduction in America's oil-producing capacity, and had urged the imposition of temporary oil taxes to offset the fall in import prices and keep the domestic industry going; but President Reagan, true to his free-market philosophy, had declined to act. The costs of this inaction were now becoming apparent. High oil consumption – sharply boosted by the low prices of the mid-1980s – and diminished domestic production meant that America now had to import well over half its oil. Traditionally, most of America's oil imports had come from the Western Hemisphere, but this source of supply had been jeopardized by the repercussions of the moratorium on debt service imposed by Central and South American countries in 1991, and the increasing turbulence in the area. In consequence, the United States was becoming ever more dependent on supplies from the Middle East. Although there was little the US could realistically do to protect these supplies in the event of major hostilities in the area, the President – in contrast to some of his more experienced advisers – believed that a stronger American military presence in the region, by making clear the extent of America's determination to keep the oil flowing whatever the circumstances, would be a helpful factor. Accordingly, plans were made to expand such American military facilities as already existed in the area, and to build new bases in a number of nearby African and West Asian countries which, whatever their ideological reservations, were desperately in need of the new jobs and additional foreign exchange that such bases would bring.

However, as the President's Treasury Secretary forcibly

pointed out to him, there was a problem about all these new Pacific and Middle Eastern military bases: how were their construction and subsequent operation going to be paid for? To his considerable surprise, the President had an answer. Over the next six months, all American military personnel would be withdrawn from Western Europe, as much equipment as possible would be removed, and the outstanding leases on the bases would be sold back to the governments concerned. Redeploying these resources of manpower and *matériel* from Europe, said the President, would cover a large proportion of the cost of the new and enlarged bases in the Pacific and the Middle East.

The Treasury Secretary was just as far from being a member of the old, Europe-oriented East Coast establishment as the President was, and was conscious that he knew little of defence matters; nevertheless, he felt some qualms about the implications of a swift and unilateral withdrawal of all American troops from Europe. The President, however, was adamant. Europe, he pointed out, was becoming increasingly anti-American. The American bases there were exceedingly unpopular, and even American tourists were often jostled and insulted in the streets. If that was how the Europeans felt, then America should get out. The Russians were not about to march into Western Europe, the way many people had feared in the late 1940s and 1950s: they had too many economic and political problems of their own. And even supposing they did – so what? Western Europe had a bigger population than the Soviet Union, and if it couldn't defend itself against a Soviet conventional attack, that was just too bad for Western Europe. Forty years ago a free and democratic Europe had been vital to America's own security. That was no longer so. Europe was old and tired; perhaps finished altogether. Europe was to do with America's past; America's future lay within itself, and to the West – in the Pacific basin, which was where the real action was going to be in the 21st century. America must look to its own interests; and they no longer included doing for Europe what Europe should be doing for itself. No more American lives were going to be laid down defending Europe.

The President's decision to withdraw all American troops from Europe was duly implemented, though it did little to

144

assuage the anti-Americanism associated with the burgeoning Europe First Movement. In America, the decision saddened some of the President's own supporters – veterans who had landed at Anzio and on the Normandy beaches, who had stopped the Ardennes offensive at Bastogne, who had inched their way to the Rhine and beyond, who had survived the suicidal daylight bombing missions to the Ruhr, playing their part in liberating Europe from the Nazi yoke. But these men were now in their seventies and eighties, and their sentimental memories counted for little. More to the point were the misgivings of the liberal intellectuals, who feared the psychological impact on American opinion of the symbolic rupture with Europe represented by the troop withdrawal. The effect, they foresaw, would be to strengthen all the inward-looking, parochial, philistine, anti-intellectual tendencies in American life, reinforcing the intolerance of dissenting views which could already be seen at work in the new Administration, and increasing the acceptability of the harsh measures that might soon be needed to override the mounting opposition to the President's radical economic and social programme.

1994 was a year in which developments in America took a decisive turn for the worse. One columnist looking back, at Christmas, over the previous twelve months, was moved to suggest that 'maybe George Orwell had lousy handwriting', and the implicit reference to Big Brother and the Thought Police seemed a good deal less absurd than it would have done a few years earlier.

On one front, at least, the year had begun well. In consequence of the very tight monetary policy being operated by the Fed, of the rapidly rising unemployment rate which had kept increases in money wages at a very low level, of the fall in world commodity prices in the face of the worsening global recession, and of the surge in the value of the dollar which reflected the financial markets' confidence in the President and his policies, inflation had already fallen to quite low single figures, and seemed likely to be eliminated altogether by the end of the year. The President was well on track, in fact, to achieve his most important objective, and his own overwhelming self-confidence, and the massive support the opinion polls showed him enjoying in the country at large, were the happy rewards of his success.

There was, however, another side to the coin. The economy was beginning to snowball rapidly downhill into a severe recession. What the previous President would readily have identified as a vicious spiral was at work. High interest rates had led to a virtual collapse of investment. Men were thrown out of work, particularly in the labour-intensive construction industry; and many of the cuts in federal government expenditure ordered by the President had the same effect. As men were thrown out of work, they had to cut back on their own spending, reducing production and employment in the consumer goods and service industries, and further eroding the incentive to invest. It was, in fact, the Keynesian multiplier at work – though unfortunately the President's knowledge of Keynes's sexual proclivities does not seem to have extended to much knowledge of his economic theories.

The vicious spiral that had come into operation was not, however, simply a matter of the bloodless variables which form the substance of macroeconomic models. Many of those who lost their jobs had not been much above the poverty line; now they and their families sank below it. And at this point they started to feel the tightening noose of the President's welfare cuts. In some of the wealthier states, welfare provision was maintained by making up the shortfall in federal funding out of state revenues. But in the poorer farm states, and in most of the states where the biggest urban conglomerations were situated, this happened little, if at all. In the old industrial states of the North-east, such as New York, New Jersey, Pennsylvania, Michigan and Illinois, there was a long history of resentment in the suburbs and the small towns of the taxes levied in order to subsidize the big city ghettos, and the national mood which had put the present President into the White House was not going to permit his programme to be neutralized by action at state or local level. And in the South and the West, by and large, the hostility to welfare programmes was greater still. And so the cash grants received by the poorest section of society were cut, and the value of food stamps reduced. In many places, supplemental nutritional programmes for children and infants were discontinued. The number of homeless people in the nation – put by some unofficial surveys as high as 5 million, or one person in fifty – increased rapidly, as the public housing stock deteriorated and rents rose above many people's ability to pay. Even the provision of emergency overnight shelter was becoming increasingly inadequate, and in many big cities thousands of people – including families with young children – slept in the streets. Quite apart from their homelessness, many of these people had, quite literally, no idea where their next meal was coming from. Medicaid had virtually ceased to function in most parts of the big cities, and many hospital wards had been closed, because of the lack of funds. The number of people roaming the streets who were mentally disturbed or even deranged steadily mounted.

All these problems were at their worst among the black community, though in some areas Hispanics were nearly as badly hit. More recent immigrants, from Vietnam, Korea and other parts of Asia, were affected much less, and this led to tensions and occasional violence between Asians and other ethnic groups in some big city areas, though this was less of a problem than the hostility which existed between the blacks and Hispanics. But no one who studied the matter doubted that the heart of the problem lay in the black ghettos. Unemployment among blacks had been brought down somewhat in the 1989–93 Democratic Administration, but had remained well above the national average and – in spite of the demographic trend which had led to falling numbers in the 16–25 age group – for teenagers and young adults had never fallen below 30 per cent. Now it was rocketing upwards, and unemployment rates of 50 or 60 per cent were already commonplace in the inner cities. With jobs virtually unobtainable, and welfare payments even to the huge number of teenage unmarried mothers being reduced to subsistence level or below, the consequences should have been obvious to all. Certainly they were pithily forecast by a liberal newspaper columnist whose view of the President and his policies had always fallen well short of idolatry. 'There are millions of blacks,' he wrote at the beginning of 1994, 'who have no jobs. They have no savings. They get little or nothing, in cash or in kind, from the federal government, or from the state, or from the city. Their relatives and friends can't help them; most of them are in the same box. They're close to starvation; their illegitimate kids are close to starvation. So what do they do? What would you do? They turn to crime.'

Much of the rising wave of crime which started to gather force in the cities early in 1994 took the traditional form of shoplifting, muggings, car thefts, burglaries – economically motivated crimes designed to put the perpetrator in quick possession of money or goods. But this was small-scale stuff. To the more ambitious and enterprising, the temptation was irresistible to get involved in the biggest and most lucrative business in America – drugs. This did not primarily mean marijuana, even though unofficial estimates made at this time suggested that marijuana was now the most important single cash crop in the United States. It meant heroin and cocaine. People who got themselves hooked on these drugs simply had to have their regular fixes, and were willing to go to desperate lengths to pay for them. And this in turn meant that supplying drugs to these addicts was an exceedingly profitable business. The drug business therefore spawned two quite different types of crime: the crime of inducing people to experiment with drugs, and supplying their needs once they were hooked; and the multitude of crimes committed by addicts in order to pay for these supplies – crimes which ranged from simple street-corner muggings to the immensely sophisticated computer frauds sometimes engaged in by cocaine-addicted senior white-collar executives. (There was also, in fact, a third type of crime, consisting of murderous assaults on each other by competing groups of drug dealers; but, except when innocent bystanders got caught in the crossfire, nobody bothered too much about this.)

The problem of rising drug addiction had first aroused nation-wide concern in the early 1980s, when middle-class white parents woke up to the fact that it was not just blacks in the working-class ghettos who were getting heavily into drugs, but their own children as well; and it was no longer a question of smoking marijuana – which many people regarded as no more addictive, and probably less harmful, than tobacco – but of injecting heroin and snorting cocaine. Many adults were involved, too: the use of cocaine, particularly, had become widespread in fashionable circles by the mid-1980s. But in the later 1980s there had been a strong reaction against drug-taking among whites, occasioned perhaps by the shock effect of the appearance in the middle of the decade of a terrifyingly powerful and addictive new form of cocaine, known as crack, and of heroin, known as black tar. Moreover, drugs had been slow to establish a real foothold among the vast majority of white Americans, middle class or working class, who viewed them as an evil on a par with abortion or communism.

Thus although, in 1994, there were still plenty of white drug addicts, the problem was predominantly concentrated among blacks. And white concern about the problem was accordingly focused less immediately on the first kind of crime associated with the drug culture – the creation of new addicts – than on the second – the crimes committed by existing addicts in order to pay for their supplies. As blacks in the ghettos turned increasingly to drugs to escape the total desolation which encompassed them and the even more hopeless future which apparently awaited them, and as legitimate sources of income to finance the purchase of these drugs dried up, the crimes they committed became more numerous and more daring, and were carried out over an ever-widening area. Streets in neighbourhoods occupied by whites and middle-class blacks which had always been reasonably safe were suddenly safe no longer. Houses with routine security devices such as steel shutters and alarm systems, and even modern apartment blocks with doormen and closed-circuit television, were no longer immune to the desperation and ingenuity of drug-addicted marauders. Nor did the mounting crime wave, though economically motivated, affect property alone; murder would be committed without compunction in the furtherance of theft, and rape and serious assaults became too commonplace to report.

Over the past decade or so, successive Administrations had made various attempts to discourage young people from getting into drugs. Nancy Reagan, for example, had inaugurated a campaign directed at schoolchildren, using the slogan 'Just Say No'. Her successor as First Lady had done much the same. In the big cities, both local police forces and federal agents had been involved in undercover operations aimed at identifying and prosecuting drug pushers. But the problem was like the Hydra: you cut off one head, and two more grew in its place. Well before the end of Reagan's first term, the Administration had concluded that the only effective way to deal with the drug problem was to prevent drugs coming into the country. The United States might glory in the variety of its geological and climatic conditions; but although it might be God's Own Country – or perhaps precisely because it was – God had not bestowed upon it the right conditions for the cultivation of either opium poppies or coca plants. If heroin and cocaine could be prevented from entering the country, therefore, the scourge of drug addition could be eliminated.

There was, unfortunately, a problem about this solution. Opium poppies grew in vast profusion in Mexico; indeed their cultivation had, ironically, been encouraged by the United States during the Second World War, as a source of morphine for wounded soldiers. Coca bushes grew in large numbers in Peru, Bolivia and Colombia. The profits to be made by getting the derivatives of these plants into the United States could be measured in terms of tens of billions of dollars. The only difficulty in doing this – since few obstacles existed to smuggling coca paste from Colombia or other South American countries to Mexico – lay in getting them across the Mexican-American border, and this border was more than 1500 miles long. As the director of the Drug Enforcement Administration had put it to the former President in 1991, 'you don't have to be an economic genius to figure out why peasants in Colombia are happy that blacks in Harlem or Bedford-Stuyvesant are spaced out on crack.' And over the past few years, for two particular reasons, the problem of drug-smuggling had grown considerably worse.

The first reason lay in the increasing difficulty Central and South American countries had been experiencing in earning foreign exchange, in consequence of the weakening trend of world trade, the low level of commodity prices, the restrictions imposed by a number of European countries on Latin American exports of manufactured goods, and the effects of retaliation against the debt service moratorium of 1991. This situation had induced the governments of the countries that produced heroin and cocaine to turn an increasingly blind eye to the smuggling of these drugs into the United States, and in some cases to help actively to promote it, in return for ensuring that a proportion of the huge dollar proceeds ended up in the vaults of the central bank. (A proportion also ended up, of course, in the private bank accounts of many government officials.)

150

The second reason for increased drug-smuggling had its origins in the very high birth rate and depressed economic conditions which existed in Mexico. These factors had together produced an explosive situation, kept under the most tenuous control only by the safety-valve of migration across the Rio Grande into the United States. This immigration into the US, most of it illegal, had been going on, at a fluctuating rate, for many years. The United States authorities had made intermittent efforts to reduce it, but these efforts had usually seemed to lack serious intent. Until 1986, for example, an astonishing state of affairs had prevailed, in which it had been perfectly legal for an American employer to hire illegal immigrants to work for him, even though it was illegal for the immigrants to perform such work, or even be in the country at all. Even now, the new law was rarely invoked against employers. One did not have to be wedded to the Marxist theory of capitalist exploitation to discern in this hypocritical arrangement a source of considerable convenience for the American rich. Well-off households, particularly in the South and West, were supplied with an inexhaustible flow of cheap domestic servants. More generally – and perhaps a major factor behind the stagnation of labour productivity that the former Democratic President had been so concerned about – the large and continuous inflow of immigrants willing to work for relatively little money had exerted a strong dampening effect on the growth of American real wages, particularly in unskilled and semi-skilled occupations.

In consequence of worsening economic conditions in Mexico, increasing turmoil and political repression in some other Latin American countries where living standards were deteriorating, and the absence of effective border controls in the United States, the tide of illegal immigration had, by 1992 or 1993, become a torrent. Many of these immigrants, in the hope of starting life in the US with some money in their pockets, acted as couriers for the big drug rings, or brought in packages of heroin or cocaine on their own initiative. It was clear that, quite apart from whatever other steps might need to be taken, the supply of drugs entering the United States was not going to be brought under control until this illegal immigration was stopped, or at any rate enormously reduced. The debate on how this might be done was brought to only a momentary halt early in 1994 by an odd event.

151

A year before, immediately after taking office, the President had set up a high-level commission, chaired by a distinguished former Republican state governor, to study the entire drug problem and make recommendations. The report of this commission was now published. It recommended that the use of heroin and cocaine be de-criminalized, and that these two drugs be supplied free of charge, under medical supervision, to all addicts registered at their local hospital.

In a private interview with a near-apoplectic President shortly before the report was released, the chairman tried to explain the rationale behind these startling recommendations. 'No one is going to stop people getting hooked on these hard drugs if they want to, Mr President,' he said. 'The history of the last ten or fifteen years demonstrates that. The real problem is the crimes that these junkies commit in order to pay for their fix. It's these crimes which are beginning to terrify the country – and particularly the people who support you. If you adopt our recommendations, you solve this problem at a stroke. If addicts can get their fix for free from the local hospital, they don't need to commit these crimes. And there's another plus: the big drug rings are put out of business overnight; you can't sell someone something he can get for free. And if there's no profit in pushing, then pushing will stop, and new cases of drug addiction will start to drop off. I strongly urge you, Mr President, to adopt these recommendations.' To the President, however, what he had heard was not a powerful intellectual argument; it was the voice of the devil. And he knew that was how the tens of millions of people who had voted for him – and a great many of those who had not – would view the matter as well. The report's recommendations were rejected out of hand. The only way to deal with the drug problem, the President insisted, was to stop the stuff entering the country in the first place.

The easier, if expensive, part of this operation lay in dealing with the light planes that flew in from Mexico and the Caribbean, and the boats that made brief landfalls on the Pacific coast and in the Gulf of Mexico. Attempts had been made to deal with this problem in the mid-1980s, but on a wholly insufficient scale. Large new funds were now voted to the Customs Service and the Coastguards, a fleet of AWACS planes with a radar range of over 200 miles was kept continuously in the air, and scores of military helicopters and motorboats were kept on constant alert around the entire southern perimeter of the United States. But none of this helped much in preventing thousands of Mexicans and what were officially known as OTMs (Other Than Mexicans) crossing the land border every day. The Rio Grande was not a great natural frontier like the English Channel or the Pyrenees or the Alps. In places it was no more than a few yards wide and a few feet deep. Short of stationing half the US army along the border, or constructing a system of electrified fences and minefields that would have to be three times as long as the Iron Curtain, there was little hope of doing more than cutting, by perhaps a quarter or a third, the number of people who actually got across the border. Much of the answer, the Administration said, must lie in pouncing on these illegal immigrants once they showed up in the towns and cities, confiscating such drugs as they might be carrying, hopefully bagging some bigger operators in the drug business at the same time, deporting the more innocent fish caught in the net, and jailing the rest.

Put like that – and this is how it was put to Congress and the country – the proposed policy sounded entirely reasonable and responsible. Many people asked why it had not been done long ago. But even at the time there were plenty of observers in the liberal political tradition who suggested that the nation was looking at the thin end of a very large wedge. And so, indeed, it was to prove.

CHAPTER VI

Western Europe: Out Of
The Frying Pan . . .

The various strains and weaknesses developing in the German
economy in the early 1990s were not particularly severe by
comparison with what was happening in much of the rest of
Europe, or in the United States: some evidence of this was
provided by the fact that it was into the Deutschemark, as well
as the Japanese yen, that money poured during the dollar crisis
of the early summer of 1992. Nevertheless, inflation was rising;
German exports had been hit hard by the strength of the
Deutschemark and the protectionist measures adopted first by
the US, and later by Britain and France; and unemployment had
resumed its upward trend. There was, more generally, a
spreading climate of doubt and pessimism, and a deepening
apprehension that the days of the German economic miracle
were gone for ever.

It was against this background that an increasingly bitter and
strident debate was being conducted in Germany. The focus of
the debate was the future of nuclear power, though in a way it
was also, at a deeper level, a debate about the whole future of
German society and the German nation.

On one side of the debate was the SPD-Green coalition
government and the majority of its supporters. True to the
pledge given by the SPD in 1986, this government had stopped
all construction work on nuclear power stations and reproces-
sing facilities when it took office at the end of 1989, and had
taken various steps designed to promote energy conservation
and to increase non-nuclear electricity generation, while at the

same time spending a great deal of money on cutting down the pollution emitted by coal-fired power stations.

The thesis underlying these policies was essentially two-fold. First, nuclear power was, simply, too hideously dangerous to be tolerated. Any lingering doubts about this should have been categorically dispelled by the Chernobyl disaster in 1986, which had contaminated not only much of the Soviet Union, but large parts of Western Europe as well, with a dose of radiation that would be claiming victims for decades to come; and Chernobyl could easily have been even worse than it was. Secondly, although nuclear power might look relatively cheap, particularly in relation to the longer-term rise in oil prices that must be the result of dwindling world oil reserves, this was the consequence of wholly artificial accountancy procedures. If the full economic cost of disposing of nulcear waste, and of eventually dismantling nuclear power stations, was brought into the balance, the true cost of nuclear energy was very much higher than it appeared.

Equally strong views were held by those on the other side of the debate. It was quite unacceptable, they argued, that Germany should remain dependent – indeed, if the anti-nuclear lobby had its way, become even more dependent – on hostile or potentially hostile countries for its energy supplies. Who knew what might happen to oil supplies from the Middle East, or natural gas supplies from the Soviet Union? Nuclear power stations now accounted for only 30 per cent of Germany's electricity supplies, compared with more than 75 per cent in France. The objective must be to increase Germany's nuclear capacity. To phase it out, as the government proposed, would be suicidal, not merely vastly increasing Germany's dependence on foreign countries, but directly increasing costs throughout the economy, and dealing a severe blow to the efficiency and competitiveness of German industry.

These two positions were diametrically opposed to each other: this was not a matter on which the usual fudging and mudging of politics could get to work, blurring issues and eventually producing some sort of compromise. Either the nation phased out nuclear power, or it did not. And, roughly speaking, half the population wanted to phase it out, and the other half wanted to keep it and even extend it.

How this deadlock would have been resolved will never be

known, for in June 1992 the whole configuration of the debate was transformed by a devastating accident at the French nuclear power station at Cattenom. The accident – caused, it was subsequently established, by human error – was less severe than the one at Chernobyl, but worse than the one at Three Mile Island in Pennsylvania in 1979; and Cattenom was only 100 miles south-west (and upwind) of Bonn and Frankfurt.

Even the French public, which had always displayed a remarkable insouciance about the country's expanding nuclear power programme, was badly jolted by this incident. In Germany, the repository for most of the escaped radiation, the reaction was one of near-hysterical fear and anger. For several days, the autobahns were choked with traffic as families sought to flee from the west of the country to the south-east and the extreme north. And for the best part of a day, it was subsequently revealed, the German government debated whether to send troops across the border to occupy Cattenom by force, so that German nuclear scientists could be brought in to advise on how to control the damage. Only the fear that the radiation risk to German conscripts might prove politically explosive, it seems, stopped a course of action which would have had incalculable repercussions on Franco-German relations. Even as it was, these relations were reduced overnight to their worst state since the end of the war.

The leak of radiation was in fact quite quickly contained by the French, and it was established that the fallout in Germany and elsewhere had been less than at first feared. In a superficial sense, life in Germany was restored to normal within a couple of weeks. But at a deeper level there had been a sea-change in public opinion. Logically, the accident might be thought to have strengthened the case of those arguing for an expanded pro-gramme of nuclear power in Germany: whatever it did, Germany was obviously at risk from other countries' nuclear power stations, and by promoting nuclear power itself it might at least hope to play a part in improving safety standards throughout Europe. But logic got little of a look-in during the months after Cattenom. There was a huge swing of public opinion in favour of the SPD government, and its policy of phasing out nuclear power stations; indeed more than a quarter of those responding to opinion polls in the immediate aftermath of the disaster said that all German nuclear stations should be shut down immediately, and that Germany should impose all possible sanctions against those of its neighbours which refused to do the same. Support for the CDU and CSU, which were strongly identified with the pro-nuclear line, plummeted to its lowest level ever. Not even on the traditional law and order front did these conservative parties any longer enjoy a lead over the SPD, for the govenment's firm support for anti-terrorist action had resulted in mass arrests of members of the Red Army Faction and its offshoots, and the climate of fear engendered by the brief recrudescence of terrorism in 1990 had largely been dissipated.

A little later in the year, support for the government was boosted further by a happier event. In the Barcelona Olympic Games, the unified German team – the negotiation of which with the Russians had been one of the SPD-Green coalition's earliest triumphs – headed the gold medal table, beating the Soviet Union by a comfortable margin, and the United States by an even more substantial one. By the autumn of 1992, with the next federal elections little more than a year away, the CDU and CSU were demoralized, and fighting both among themselves and with each other; and the SPD enjoyed a majority in the opinion polls over all other parties combined.

The popularity of the SPD caused strains between the coalition partners during the first half of 1993. Although the Greens, too, had benefited from the anti-nuclear backlash from Cattenom, they were running at no more the 10–12 per cent in the opinion polls and in actual elections in some of the states. Given the weakness of the CDU and CSU, and the disappearance from the reckoning of the FDP, it seemed likely that after the next federal elections the SPD would be able to form a government on its own. Although such a government's stance on nuclear power could now be guaranteed not to waver, on other issues dear to the hearts of the Greens – the so-called 'quality of life' issues – there was much less reason to suppose that it would pursue the kind of policies the Greens would favour. Although a majority of the Greens accepted this prospect with a certain gloomy fatalism, a minority had other ideas. A plot was launched with the object of discrediting the SPD and increasing support for the CDU and CSU on a scale sufficient to deny the SPD an overall majority in the Bundestag.

157

At first, it looked as though the plot was succeeding only too well, and that the end result might actually be a CDU-CSU government. Evidence was planted that implicated a senior SPD minister as a Soviet spy, and a sensational series of leaks to the popular press suggested that a key member of the SPD Chancellor's staff was running an extensive call-girl racket from his office.

Much more serious was something organized by an extreme left-wing group with only tenuous links with the Greens – the assassination of the head of the Bundesbank. This murder, which seemed to strike at the heart of German economic and financial stability, produced a huge public outcry and a surge of support for the traditional defenders of law and order, the CDU and CSU. But the plotters had overdone it. The apartment from which the fatal shot had been fired had been rented a fortnight earlier by a man who had let slip that he worked for the SPD; and when the police searched it, they found the charred remains of some SPD literature in the waste basket. It was all a little too obvious, and within a few weeks the truth not only about the assassination, but also about the two other scandals, had all come out. The popularity of the Greens, apparently implicated in the plot, fell back sharply, but so did that of the CDU-CSU, since many people believed that somehow or other they had a hand in it as well. Once again the SPD found itself riding high; and in the Bundestag elections late in 1993 it secured a comfortable overall majority.

The most surprising feature of the election results was not, however, that the SPD had won 56 per cent of the seats, or that the Greens failed to win the 5 per cent of the total vote necessary to secure their representation in the Bundestag. The most surprising feature was that Le Rith's Europe First Movement won nearly as many seats as the CDU and CSU combined.

The news that the EFM had won more than 20 per cent of the seats in the German federal parliament opened eyes not just throughout Europe, but around the world. Suddenly, Le Rith was much more of a force to be reckoned with than most of the old-style politicians had anticipated. There was, in fact, a particular reason for the EFM's strong showing in the German elections. Le Rith had perceived clearly that a large segment of right-of-centre German opinion foresaw a long period of SPD dominance in Germany, during which time there would be all sorts of developments which it feared and distrusted. Nuclear power stations would be closed down, energy costs would soar, the inflation rate would rise, the economy would be weakened, a dangerous rapprochement would be undertaken with the Russians, and a form of creeping socialism would be unleashed, spreading insidiously throughout the land and before long destroying the vigour and strength of the German nation. With brilliant opportunism, Le Rith seized his chance, and during the year before the German elections drummed home one message, and one message only: a socialist government might be inevitable for the next ten years in Germany; in Europe, it was not. Only the EFM, Le Rith's argument went, offered the prospect of a Europe-wide government that would override the powers of the old, discredited national governments. Anyone who wanted to stop the spread of socialism in Germany should not waste their vote on the old, out-of-touch CDU or CSU, but should vote for the Europe First Movement, both in the German federal elections of late 1993 and – far more crucially – in the elections for the European Parliament in the summer of 1994.

The attractions to the German right were obvious. The EFM offered government of a non-socialist kind on a European scale, which would act as a counterbalance to the efforts of a firmly entrenched German social democratic government to push the country to the left. A more genuine Europe-wide market would be created than anything the individual member governments of the EEC had permitted, and this would be protected much more effectively than at present from the unfair competition from Japan and the newly-industrializing countries of South-east Asia and Latin America. Within this huge, protected market, German industry – still much more efficient than most of its European competitors – would do extremely well. Moreover any tendency for German trade unions to demand excessive increases in wages or reductions in hours could be trumped by recourse to the much cheaper labour available in the poorer parts of Europe – either recruiting this labour to work in Germany, or employing it in German-owned factories in their own countries.

It was not only from the conventional right, however, that Le Rith's message elicited a favourable response. Analysis of the voting figures in the Bundestag elections showed that many of those who had previously voted for the Greens had now voted for the EFM. This puzzled some of the political experts who had fallen into the simplistic trap of labelling Le Rith as a fascist, but it was not so surprising. Many Greens had long known that satisfactory control of pollution could only be achieved on a Europe-wide scale – a point that had been underlined by the Cattenom disaster; and the EFM was the only organization that offered a convincing prospect of that. And beyond this specific issue there was the much more important fact that Le Rith was offering a new vision – a vision of a Europe strong and free, no longer plagued by unemployment and ravaged by inflation, no longer at the political or economic mercy of foreign nations and alien creeds. Cynics might scoff at such a vision; but there had never been a shortage of people eager to follow a charismatic new prophet down the shining path to Utopia.

In France, the nuclear accident at Cattenom was little more than a nine-day wonder. Indeed, perhaps because the prevailing wind had dispersed most of the escaped radiation over Germany and Luxembourg and not over France, many Frenchmen regarded it as an agreeable, if brief, distraction from the increasingly grim daily struggle for existence. Although the hardline government elected in 1991 had succeeded in bringing down inflation to below 10 per cent, unemployment had soared. For the most part, wages and salaries had fallen markedly behind inflation; and higher taxes and interest rates had added to the fierce squeeze on living standards of those who did have jobs.

The rise in unemployment had been much steeper than expected. Although the import controls the government had imposed late in 1991 had helped to preserve some French jobs, French exports had fallen drastically as a result of the continuing reverberations of the American import controls of 1989, the British measures of 1991, a whole series of overt and covert restrictions imposed by other countries during this period, and the cuts in imports forced on developing countries by foreign exchange shortages due to declining world commodity prices and the repercussions of the Latin American debt moratorium of May 1991. The world economy was sliding into recession, as individual governments raised taxes and interest rates in an attempt to reduce inflation, and imposed import restrictions in an attempt to protect employment; and France was contributing to this process, and suffering from it, as much as anyone.

As unemployment in France rose, first to 3 million, then to 3.5 million, and then to 4 million, a sense of crisis slowly began to envelop the nation. At first, the government had quite an easy ride. Half the country in any case instinctively supported a government determined to curb inflation, even at the cost of high unemployment; and among the other half, industrial workers who still had jobs, and students who hoped to get them, thought it more prudent to keep quiet than to risk their position by striking or demonstrating. But as time went on, and more and more people found themselves and their relatives and friends out of work, or soon likely to be so, the mood began to change. Strikes and sit-ins at factories became more common; and students, perhaps with fond memories – or illusions – of what had been achieved in 1968 and 1986, started to march and demonstrate with increasing stridency. And against this back-ground of mainly peaceful strikes and demonstrations, a series of much uglier incidents erupted, as extreme left- and right-wing groups took advantage of the mounting turbulence. Arson attacks on the homes and businesses of immigrants multiplied, while at the same time *Action Directe* and other terrorist organizations on the left, in pursuit of their proclaimed aim of 'destroying the oppressive bourgeois state', stepped up their campaign of political assassinations.

The government showed no sign of being diverted from its chosen course by any of this activity. It had been elected, the Prime Minister was in the habit of saying, to bring down inflation and eliminate the budget deficit and the balance of payments deficit, and it intended to do exactly that. It was encouraged in this stance by the election of a right-wing government in Britain in April 1992, and by the election, in November of the same year, of a right-wing Republican President in the United States. The government had a solid majority in the National Assembly, and it made it clear that – unlike some of its predecessors – it would in no circumstances be swayed by demonstrations or riots in the streets. These tough words were backed up, when occasion demanded, by equally tough action.

The crucial test came in April 1993, when three-quarters of a million students and workers from all over France assembled in the Tuileries, the Esplanade des Invalides and the Luxembourg gardens, and then began a concerted march on the Palais Bourbon, where the National Assembly was sitting in emergency session. The government had announced that no marchers would be permitted to get within 300 metres of the Palais Bourbon, and to enforce the decision fielded a force of 40,000 riot police, themselves backed up by 10,000 paratroopers.

The result was a violent confrontation of a kind more familiar in recent years in South Korea than in France. The marchers from the Luxembourg and the Invalides, dispersed by barrages of tear gas and concentrated forays by truncheon-wielding CRS men, reassembled in the heart of the Latin quarter, and were soon joined by the marchers from the Tuileries who, forcibly prevented from crossing the Pont de la Concorde, had infiltrated back across other bridges to the left bank. Barricades of wrecked and burnt-out vehicles were erected in an attempt to seal off the area surrounding the Boulevard St Michel. CRS men who tried to dismantle these barriers came under attack from paving-stones and petrol bombs, and several of them were killed or wounded by sniper fire from surrounding buildings. It was three days before all the barricades were demolished and the area reoccupied by the police, and during that time the toll had been a heavy one. More than a dozen people – mainly students – had been killed, and many hundreds injured. The number of students and workers arrested was close to a thousand, and although the majority of these were released within a week or two, over a hundred were still being detained, under emergency legislation, three months later.

Although the nation was deeply troubled by these events, it was clear from the opinion polls, as the dust settled, that the government had won the public relations battle. Even the President, widely respected as a responsible and moderate man, had accepted the logic of the government's argument when acceding, albeit reluctantly, to the Prime Minister's request to make army units available as a backing to the CRS. If the government were to abandon its anti-inflationary stabilization programme under pressure from riots in the streets, the argument went, the economy would face collapse. Business and

financial confidence would evaporate, the franc would plummet, and the end result could easily be the kind of hyperinflation
that had destroyed the German economy in the early 1920s. 'But
is it enough to avoid hyperinflation,' the President enquired of
the Prime Minister as they made a joint tour of the devastated
areas of the Latin quarter after order had been restored, 'if the
alternative is so much unemployment that it all ends in revolution
or civil war?' Perhaps because the question was a rhetorical one,
there is no record of any reply from the Prime Minister.

As the economic and political scene grew darker, one beacon
shone ever more brightly: the future offered by the Europe First
Movement. The fifteen French Euro-MPs who now spoke for
the EFM began to prove an invaluable asset in Le Rith's
campaign for the 1994 elections to the European Parliament.
They spent far more time travelling around France than they
spent in Brussels or Strasbourg, tirelessly presenting the EFM
case in every corner of the country; and the few who were
personable as well as articulate were constantly to be seen on
television.

Their message was simple enough to be readily understood,
but not so simple as to appear superficial or naive. The heavy
unemployment in France and other European countries, they
said, was principally the result of unfair competition in the
industries where Europe ought to be self-sufficient – steel,
shipbuilding, textiles, engineering, vehicles and a number of
others – from Japan and the newly-industrializing countries of
South-east Asia and Latin America. For decades European
governments had been too weak to counter this unfair competition, and the EEC bureaucracy in Brussels, hamstrung by trying
to reconcile the conflicting demands of twelve short-sighted and
self-interested governments, had been too feeble by far to
utilize Europe's collective muscle either to keep these imports
out or to force Japan and the other NICs to open their markets
to European exports in a genuine and comprehensive way. A
European Parliament in which the EFM had a majority of seats
could and would put all this right.

Nor – the EFM argument went on – was it just a matter of the
millions of jobs that Europe had lost in the older industries.
In the rapidly-growing new industries of the present and the
future – information technology, advanced telecommunications,

163

thermonuclear fusion, biotechnology and so on – the US and Japan had been forging ahead of Europe for several decades now. This was particularly true of Japan, which for some time had been moving at a faster pace than the United States, except in the relatively limited number of areas such as space technology where its huge military procurement programmes gave the US an advantage. Generally speaking, in fact, '*le défi Americain*', which had so exercised French public opinion in the 1960s, had now been superseded by '*le défi Japonnais*'. This lagging behind in the technological race had largely been the result of Europe's failure to create a genuine Europe-wide market which permitted the most efficient firms to reap the economies of scale that American and Japanese firms could count on. It was the result, too, of the failure of either individual European governments, or the EEC Commission in Brussels, to promote research and development of the new technologies on anything like an adequate scale. This, like other aspects of European weakness, was due to parochial bickering and back-biting among the 'old' politicians and the 'old' national governments, who were now all hopelessly out of touch and out of date.

This general line of argument the EFM representatives leavened, as the occasion offered, with more specific illustrations of Europe's decline, and the need for a new start on a Europe-wide scale. French farmers, for example, increasingly prone to block roads with their tractors and to dump large quantities – depending on the part of the country they lived in – of milk, meat, grain or grapes on town hall steps in protest against low prices, were told by the EFM that these low prices were the result of American subsidies which a genuinely united Europe/of the kind the EFM was seeking to build would have the strength to put a stop to. Other special interest groups received equally reassuring messages. Even the bureaucrats in the Ministry of Finance in Paris, ever alert to the threat posed by domestic disturbances to the value of the franc, and the ultimate humiliating possibility of the need for recourse to the International Monetary Fund for a loan, were reminded that after more than forty years during which it had been taken for granted that the Managing Director of the IMF was always a European (usually, indeed, a Frenchman), the job was now occupied by a Japanese.

164

Through all the variations and all the detail the basic message shone clear: Europe's problems could only be solved by decisive action on a European scale, and only the Europe First Movement, if given a majority in the European Parliament, could take that action. True Gaullists, ever sensitive to anything which might infringe French sovereignty, did not like this message; nor did many socialists, who were more conscious than most that until recently the French EFM Euro-MPs had represented the National Front. But for every person who dismissed the Europe First Movement, there seemed to be two who showed increasing interest in what it had to say. As the 1994 Euro-elections grew closer, Le Rith surveyed the French scene with growing satisfaction.

By the beginning of 1993, unemployment in Britain was rising rapidly: within a month or two, it was estimated, it would be over the 4 million mark. This reflected the deflationary measures the government had taken in 1992, together with the multiplier effects of these measures throughout the economy. People who lost their jobs because of reductions in public expenditure had to cut back hard on their own spending; and the real incomes of those still in employment were being squeezed by rising prices and much higher mortgage costs, which were forcing them to reduce their expenditure on everything that was not essential. In spite of the public expenditure cuts, the budget deficit was still rising, partly because falling incomes and output reduced the government's revenue from income tax and VAT, but also because the resources so recklessly squandered during the 1980s had now just about run out. The state had no more assets left to privatize, and North Sea oil production had long since peaked, and was now falling fast. The state of affairs long predicted by the critics had finally come about. The furniture had all been sold to pay for the food, and the flow of foreign exchange and tax revenue from the North Sea had all but dried up. The nation was in a parlous plight.

The only positive achievement the government could point to was a decline in the inflation rate from a peak of 17 per cent the previous year to a figure of less than 8 per cent in early 1993. This achievement was a crucial one, since the decline in inflation and the very high level of interest rates were the only factors preventing the financial markets from taking fright at the country's large and increasing budget and balance of payments deficits, and getting out of sterling on a scale that could set in motion an unstoppable spiral of forced devaluation and accelerating inflation. It was because the government regarded this as the worst of all possible outcomes that it continued, despite rising unemployment and mounting hardship, to cut back on public expenditure and to maintain interest rates at a level of 20 per cent or more. This was, however, a very high-risk strategy, as the events of 1993 and early 1994 were to demonstrate.

The price of gilt-edged securities had been hit hard by the abrupt rise in interest rates in April 1992, though they had subsequently recovered a little as the inflation rate fell back into single figures. Equity shares, however, bolstered by the fact that a hardline Conservative government was now in office, had held up much better, and the *Financial Times* industrial ordinary share index, though down from the peak of 1909.7 achieved a few years earlier, had been trading around the 1700 mark since the autumn of 1992. Now, on 17 March 1993, the stock market collapsed. There was no particular reason why it should have collapsed on that day rather than some other day, just as there had been no particular reason why the Wall Street crash of 1929 should have begun on 24 October rather than some other day. Both crashes, in the light of hindsight, had been postponed for longer than seemed readily explicable, in view of the gap that had been opening up between the price of shares and the real health of the economy underlying them.

On Wednesday 17 March the FT index fell by 158 points, from 1703.4 to 1545.6 There was a slight rally on Thursday, but a plunge of another 73 points on Friday. By the end of the month the index had fallen by 30 per cent, to 1195. Six weeks later, in the middle of May, the market seemed to have stablilized, but at a level – around 900 – that represented a fall of nearly a half within a period of two months.

The stock market collapse impinged directly on a considerably larger number of people than it would have done a decade earlier. Although Mrs Thatcher's campaign to extend share ownership more widely had not been very successful – the great majority of the 'small investors' who had subscribed to shares in British Telecom, British Gas and so on had long since taken the handsome profits guaranteed by the privatization of these organizations at an issue price well below market value – there were nevertheless more individual shareholders than there had been ten years earlier; and there was also a greater awareness among the public generally that a collapse of share prices posed a real threat to the value of their pension plans and insurance policies. It was not, however, the collapse of share prices that set Britain on the road to disaster in 1993; it was the collapse of house prices.

House prices – in the southern half of the country at any rate – had risen to ridiculous levels in the mid-1980s and again, after a sharp setback, in the early 1990s. The main factor responsible was the intense competition that had developed in the home loan market between banks, building societies and other financial institutions. Conventional notions of prudence had been flung to the winds as these organizations competed for a larger share of this lucrative market, offering mortgages equivalent to the value of four or five times the borrower's annual income, and up to 100 per cent of the market value of the property. As long as incomes and house prices rose, and interest rates stayed low, this was fine. But in 1992 all that had started to change. Many workers lost their overtime payments, or were put on short-time; many others lost their jobs. At the same time, mortgage interest rates skyrocketed, and tax relief on these interest payments was cut by a third. Within a few months, the number of people who could no longer keep up their mortgage payments rose from the tens of thousands to the hundreds of thousands. By the spring of 1993 the number had risen to well over a million, and was still increasing. As these people sought to extricate themselves from their situation by selling their house and moving to cheaper accommodation, house prices plummeted, and they soon found that the value of their house – if they could find a buyer at all – was less than the outstanding amount of the mortgage, and that they were, in effect, bankrupt.

Although the lending organizations were initially sympathetic, the scale of defaults on mortgages soon forced them to repossess properties in defence of their own solvency; even so, some of the smaller building societies went bankrupt, and one of the major banks suffered losses on its housing loan account that more than swallowed up the year's profit, cutting into its capital base and forcing it to rein back its lending to other sectors of the economy. As banks and building societies tried to cut their losses by putting repossessed houses on to the market at a large discount, house prices fell even further, and more and more home owners found themselves insolvent, saddled with a debt which they could neither afford to service nor to pay off.

At first, most people economized on everything else in order to keep up mortgage payments. In better-off households, children were withdrawn from private schools and holidays abroad were cancelled. In poorer households, other bills simply remained unpaid, and as the winter of 1993–4 began, nearly 2 million households had had either gas or electricity supplies cut off, and nearly a quarter of a million had even had their water supply disconnected. But in hundreds of thousands of cases even these economies and hardships were not enough to enable mortgage commitments to be met, and the number of repossessions and evictions steadily mounted.

The traumatic effect of these repossessions and evictions can scarcely be exaggerated. It had long been accepted that unsatisfactory council house tenants sometimes faced eviction, but this, at least in the eyes of the rest of the nation, was a sanction used by local authorities only as a last resort against feckless unskilled labourers who beat their wives, harassed their neighbours, and spent all their money on drink. What was happening now was very different. Skilled workers, and members of the middle class, whose main ambition in life had been to live in a home of their own and who, through hard work and frugal living, had achieved it, now found themselves on the street, surrounded, in the most poignant cases, by nothing but those personal belongings which had not been repossessed by rental and hire purchase agencies. And these cases were numbered not in thousands or even tens of thousands, but in hundreds of thousands – soon, perhaps, in millions. It was, as a Swedish television documentary screened just before Christmas 1993 asserted, not just an appalling human tragedy, but a recipe for revolution.

Although those evicted from their homes were among the most visible and unfortunate of the victims of the economic hurricane that struck Britain in 1993–4, they were far from

168

being alone. Indeed before long virtually everyone could be reckoned a victim of one sort or another. The main cause of this was a rising tide of industrial action in the public sector of the economy. Public sector employees had had their pay frozen by the previous government in the spring of 1991, and during the ensuing eight months had fallen behind most employees in the private sector, where substantial wage increases were being conceded. There had been only the briefest of thaws during the early months of 1992, from which fewer than a quarter of public sector workers had had time to benefit, before the new Conservative government had announced that in view of the overriding importance of cutting public expenditure and reducing inflation it would concede no pay increases to any of its own employees during the next twelve months, nor permit local authorities, nationalized industries nor any other public agencies to grant any pay increases either. At a time when inflation was still running in double figures, this meant severe reductions in the real wages of workers whose living standards had already fallen during the last year or two. And when, during the spring and summer of 1993, the government did finally enter into pay negotiations, it rapidly became apparent that the pay increases it was willing to concede would be lower than the current inflation rate, so cutting living standards even further.

The patience of workers in the public sector in the face of all this had been remarkable. For years they had been represented by Conservative governments and much of the right-wing press as doing jobs of little or no value to the economy, and contrasted unfavourably with the 'wealth-creating' private sector. The fact that their work was essential to the functioning of society seemed to have been forgotten. Their increasing anger had, perhaps, been tempered by rapidly rising unemployment and a sense of gathering national crisis. But when their wrath finally erupted, in the late autumn of 1993, the results were frightening. To those who remembered it, the 1978–9 winter of discontent seemed glorious summer by comparison with the winter of fury and violence experienced in 1993–4.

At the very beginning, it was little more than a matter of minor irritations. Trains left late. Buses never came. Garbage collections became erratic. Letters took a fortnight to travel a couple of miles. Holes in the road got ever larger. Hospital visiting hours were curtailed. Schoolchildren were sent home in the middle of the morning.

But very soon the pace and scale of disruption increased, as lightning and semi-unofficial strikes and a variety of 'legitimate' forms of industrial action erupted like a rash all over the country. Railway stations, and stations on the London Underground, were closed by 'selective action'. Hospital casualty departments were closed by 'staff shortages'. Schools were closed by the 'performance of contractual duties only'. Electricity supplies, 'accidentally' cut off, could not be restored because of a 'work to rule'. And much the same kind of thing applied in other services which were no longer in the public sector, but whose workers were convinced they had had a raw deal: gas supplies, cut off 'for safety reasons', could not be restored because of 'industrial action', and telephone lines, mysteriously out of order, could not be repaired because maintenance engineers were 'working to rule'. BBC technicians went on strike and were soon joined by their ITV counterparts, so that the nation's television sets were periodically blacked out, and people at home had nothing to do. Even more explosive was the fact that frequent strikes by staff in local social security offices meant that millions of people often failed to get the social security benefits to which they were entitled; and many of the younger of them turned to crime as the only means of survival.

Most serious of all was the 'withdrawal of goodwill' by workers in the emergency services. Although the majority of men and women in these services in fact continued to do their jobs as conscientiously as ever, there were enough cases – always played up by the tabloid press – of people dying because ambulances and fire engines took their time about getting to their destination for public anger to be frequently vented on unoffending firemen and ambulance drivers. The consequence was a vicious circle, as these workers became more preoccupied with their own safety than with doing the job on hand. But it was the withdrawal of goodwill by the police that was the most fateful form of protest in 1993.

Under agreements reached in the 1970s, police pay had been largely insulated from subsequent public sector freezes and squeezes, and in recent years successive governments had seen to it that the police were, by any standards, paid exceedingly

170

well. But in 1993, under a new hardline leadership, the Police Federation, citing the increased danger to its members from the rising crime wave and the spreading social disorder, presented the government with two demands. One was for a substantial pay increase; the other was that all policemen should be armed.

The Cabinet wasted little time in rejecting the second demand. It was true that the use of firearms in the furtherance of crime had risen significantly in recent years, but this had been adequately responded to: nearly a third of all police officers now – unobtrusively – carried firearms as a matter of course. To arm the police force as a whole would, the Cabinet believed, risk escalating the use of firearms on Britain's streets to the level of inter-war Chicago or contemporary Miami.

Discussion of the police demand for a substantial pay increase was more protracted. Some ministers, while conceding that the demand was inherently unreasonable, nevertheless took the view that in the current atmosphere of mounting violence and disorder, the danger of alienating the police was simply too great to be accepted, and that the claim must be met. The Prime Minister, on the other hand, argued forcefully that, for all the disruption that was going on in the country at the moment, the economic stabilization programme was working extremely well. Thanks to the very low level of wage increases and the continuing fall in world commodity prices, the inflation rate was tumbling down. By the end of the year inflation should be close to zero – something that not even Mrs Thatcher had managed to achieve. Once that happened, and confidence in the pound had been fully restored, the government would be able to ease up on its tough monetary and fiscal policies, and an era of non-inflationary growth could be inaugurated, for the first time in more than thirty years. But all this would be jeopardized if the large police pay demand was conceded, for it would then become impossible to hold the line on a host of other public sector pay claims; employers in the private sector would follow suit; and inflation would rocket upwards again. The government was not far from the light at the end of the tunnel, the Prime Minister concluded, and must not lose its nerve now. With some misgivings, the Cabinet agreed, and the die was cast.

The immediate result of the withdrawal of police goodwill that followed the rejection of their demands was a marked rise in crime. Arguing that they were inadequately remunerated and insufficiently armed, policemen became increasingly reluctant to venture out of, or far from, their police stations and section houses. The poorer parts of most of the major cities now hardly ever saw a policeman, and became effectively no-go areas, ruled by gangs of local thugs, who burgled, looted, assaulted, raped and sometimes murdered with apparent impunity. Local residents cowered in their homes, in some instances even dying of cold or starvation rather than venturing out of doors. Racial tensions mounted and exploded into countless outbreaks of violence as blacks erupted out of the big city ghettos, and the 'black on black' crime that the middle classes had never worried about too much suddenly became 'black on white' crime that terrified them. In even the quietest and most respectable neighbourhoods people were afraid of being mugged on the streets or attacked in their own homes. Not even the rich, long insulated by their money against the rising tide of hardship around them, felt safe any longer.

The racial dimension of the rising wave of crime and violence in 1993–4 was an important one, not just in terms of 'black on white', but of 'white on black' as well, as gangs of white racists, organized by extreme right-wing groups, attacked and often killed individual blacks and Asians, and firebombed their homes and shops. But the racial dimension was by no means the only one. Equally in evidence, in cities such as Liverpool and Glasgow, were violent clashes along religious, or perhaps tribal, lines. These had been mainly precipitated by the recent distressing sequence of events in Northern Ireland.

The previous year, partly in furtherance of its policy of cutting public spending, but mainly in order to protect the American bases in Britain from the assaults of an increasingly anti-American public, the government had withdrawn half of the 12,000 troops stationed, at great expense, in Northern Ireland. The weakened force left behind found it increasingly difficult to keep the situation in the Province under control, and casualties among the remaining troops had mounted alarmingly. Growing demands in Britain that the rest of the troops be withdrawn and Ulster left alone to sort out its own problems had coincided with the deteriorating law and order situation in Britain itself. Accordingly – even though the new American

172

President had now withdrawn all US troops from Britain and the bases no longer needed protection – in the late autumn of 1993 the remaining troops were brought back in order to strengthen the Cabinet's hand in the event – however unlikely it might seem – of the escalating violence in the streets coming to constitute a threat to the continued existence of the democratically elected government. In Northern Ireland, the consequences of British withdrawal had been horrendous. Freed of all external restraints, except for the improbable prospect of intervention by an Irish government that was itself paralysed by political divisions, the killers on both sides – the IRA and the Protestant extremist organizations – got to work on each other with a vengeance. Killings and revenge killings mounted and multiplied; and it was the reverberations of this which echoed in outbreaks of communal violence in the Protestant and Catholic areas of Liverpool and Glasgow.

A third dimension of the crime and violence that swept Britain in 1993–4 – and perhaps the most significant one of all – was neither racial nor religious. It was simply an uprising of the impoverished and dispossessed, a cry of frustration and fury by those who had lost out in a nation that had once been great, that even now ought to be one of the richest and most contented countries in the world, but which somewhere, somehow, had taken a wrong turning.

By the beginning of 1994, the situation was largely beyond the control of the government. Whether the inflation rate had fallen to zero, as the Prime Minister had predicted, nobody could be sure, because figures of retail prices were no longer being properly collected or processed, and in any case many goods had disappeared from the shelves as people who could afford to hoarded food and other essentials. The idea that the government could now relax its fiscal and monetary policies, and inaugurate an era of non-inflationary growth, was simply laughable. The banks were refusing to lend money except against the most cast-iron collateral, and the mechanisms for increasing effective demand by undertaking urgent public sector investment projects or even reducing taxation were hopelessly clogged up by activities and responses ranging from simple non co-operation to outright sabotage. The people had totally lost confidence in the government, but showed not the slightest disposition to repose it in the opposition parties. The processes of British parliamentary democracy had lost all credibility.

And yet, in Britain, democracy was a hardy plant: its seeds had been sown a long time ago, and its roots went deep. It seems clear, in the light of hindsight, that one thing saved Britain, in 1993–4, from sliding so far downhill into chaos and anarchy that either a left-wing revolution or – more probably – a right-wing military-backed dictatorship soon resulted. This was the widespread belief that although both the present government and the previous one had palpably failed to combine a tolerable level of unemployment and a tolerable rate of inflation, there must nevertheless be *some* way in which this could be done which was still consistent with democracy. And, so it seemed, there was.

From late 1992 onwards, as discontent and disillusionment with the existing party political system in Britain deepened, Le Rith and the fourteen EFM members who had won seats in the Westminster Parliament earlier in the year made sure that the British people were told again and again what that way was. Only the Europe First Movement, with its Europe-wide vision and its Europe-wide approach to the continent's economic problems, could provide the answer. As Britain plunged into the disruptions and dangers of the winter of 1993–4, an increasing number of its citizens were coming to believe that there was one last chance of restoring economic normality while maintaining democratic institutions; and they fixed their gaze, as if on the coming of the millennium, on the Euro-elections due to be held in June 1994.

And so, by the beginning of 1994, for a variety of different reasons and with a wealth of different expectations, very large numbers of people in Germany, in France and in Britain had their sights firmly set on the coming elections for the European Parliament. The same was true in Italy, where chaos and anarchy had gone even further than in Britain, with people refusing to pay their taxes, civil servants and other public sector workers no longer receiving their wages and salaries, and communists and neo-fascists fighting in the streets. And much the same applied in many of the other member countries of the European Community.

Only a decade before, no one had heard of Le Rith, and the

Europe First Movement had not been born. Now, in consequence of the total and continuing failure of the European nation-states to combine low unemployment and low inflation, the man's shadow fell across the entire continent, and even most sceptical observers sensed that things would never be the same again.

And so, indeed, it was to prove. The results of the elections held for the European Parliament in June 1994 were remarkable. In both France and Germany the Europe First Movement obtained over 50 per cent of the total number of votes cast. In Britain, although it obtained slightly under half the total vote, the first-past-the-post electoral system meant that it won sixty-eight of the country's eighty-one seats in the European Parliament. The overall result was that the EFM won 51 per cent of all the votes cast throughout the twelve nations of the European Community, and 54 per cent of the seats in the European Parliament.

It took some time for the rest of the world – and indeed a great many people in Europe itself – to comprehend what had happened. In a free, democratic election, the largest electorate on earth had voted by a clear majority for a new political movement and a new political leader.

What did this mean? Did it – in view of the apparent impotence of the European Parliament – mean anything at all? How would national governments react? The questions came thick and fast. And before long, the answers were coming thick and fast, too.

CHAPTER VII

The United States:
Decline and Fall

More than one foreign observer who visited the United States in April and May of 1994 reported a palpable tension in the air, and predicted that the approaching summer might prove long and hot in more than a literal sense.

The rich – those in the top 5 or 10 per cent of the income distribution – were happy enough. They had done exceedingly well during the 1980s, some of them because they were directly engaged in the nation's most lucrative activity – buying and selling pieces of paper on Wall Street; most of the others because they owned assets which were trebled or quadrupled in value by the great stock market and real estate boom which got under way in 1982; and all of them because of the huge tax cuts they had enjoyed during the Reagan years – tax cuts which the 1989–93 Democratic Administration had hardly reversed at all. Their man was in the White House and their party controlled both houses of Congress – and there was no reason to suppose that it would not continue to do so after the mid-term elections in six months' time. America's military defences were being built up, wasteful welfare expenditures were being cut back or eliminated, and inflation was falling rapidly towards zero.

Yet not all was entirely well with the world, even as viewed from penthouses in Manhattan or villas in Beverly Hills: the rich had their worries, too. There was still a budget deficit, although it was smaller than it had been, and was more than fully accounted for by interest payments on the national debt – more than two-thirds of which had been accumulated since President

176

Reagan took office in 1981. The federal government's continuing need to borrow, combined with the very tight monetary policy being pursued by the Federal Reserve Board in order to eliminate inflation, had resulted in a very high level of interest rates, despite the developing recession. So far the financial markets had weathered these high interest rates reasonably well, the bearish effect of falling output and employment being neutralized by the favourable influence of the rapid and continuing decline in the inflation rate. But rumours were beginning to spread of severe difficulties in a number of companies and banks, particularly those which had financed acquisitions and leveraged buyouts in the 1980s by issuing high-yielding, variable-interest 'junk bonds': these institutions were now having to face the fact that a very high ratio of debt to equity capital, at a time of falling sales and high interest rates, was a recipe for disaster. The possibility, although it might not seem a strong one, of a stock market crash and an associated collapse of property values conduced to a jittery feeling on the part of many of those in the highest income groups at this time. But underlying this nervousness were the stirrings of a deeper and darker fear: one from which the rich are never entirely free, though it lies dormant for long periods of time. It is the fear the haves feel of the have-nots; the fear that one day the dispossessed will rise up and take what they want by force; the fear of the revolution and the tumbrel.

The fear of the mob which lurks in the hearts of the rich is not unknown to the 60 or 70 per cent of the population which is neither rich nor poor: they have less to protect than the rich, but also fewer resources to protect it with. By and large, they will support any measures which seem necessary to preserve law and order, and the existing distribution of property. But it was not these considerations which were uppermost in the minds of these middle-income groups in America in the spring of 1994; it was the threat posed to their standard of living by the faltering performance of the economy. They welcomed the fall in inflation; but many of them were seeing their small businesses going bankrupt, and many more were losing their jobs. For an ever-growing number, high interest rates not merely put out of reach the possibility of moving into a better house or buying a new car; they led to evictions and repossessions, as

177

mortgage and instalment credit payments could no longer be kept up.

Thus the rich were edgy, and the middle classes worried. Among many of those in the poorest quarter of the population, however, stronger emotions were brewing: resentment and anger. This was particularly true of the younger blacks and Hispanics living in the big cities. Minimally educated, unemployed, appallingly housed, virtually cut off from public assistance programmes, inhabiting a squalid and dangerous present and facing a future that promised nothing better, they glowered and simmered in the ghettos as the summer heat intensified. In June, as temperatures soared into the upper 90s, frustration and resentment boiled over.

Almost any incident might have served to spark the explosions which occurred simultaneously in New York and Los Angeles, and were rapidly followed by others in nearly every part of the continent in between, from Chicago and Detroit in the north to Houston and Miami in the south. The actual final, unendurable provocation, it is clear, was a co-ordinated series of raids in the inner cities, conducted by local police departments and agents and officials of the Drug Enforcement Administration and the Immigration and Naturalization Service in furtherance of the President's recently declared war on illegal immigration and drug-trafficking. These raids were large-scale and ruthlessly conducted, and resulted not only in a great deal of damage to property as tenement blocks were ransacked in the search for drugs, unauthorized weapons and illegal immigrants, but also in considerable loss of life, much of it in the form of shooting deaths of people 'resisting arrest'. In spite of the explosion of anger occasioned by the first of this series of raids, and the widespread street fighting, arson and looting which followed, the raids themselves continued over a period of several weeks, until the President called a halt, claiming that 'we have broken the back of the problem of drugs and illegal immigration'.

This claim was, in fact, far from accurate. It is true that very large quantities of drugs were seized, and tens of thousands of illegal immigrants – a large proportion of them allegedly involved in the drug trade – were detained. But the main effect of the drug seizures was thoroughly perverse. As the supply was cut, prices went sharply up, and the crimes committed by addicts desperate for a fix increased in boldness and in number. Moreover, with heroin and cocaine suddenly in short supply, the big drug rings started hi-jacking each other's shipments, and for a short time there was an eruption of inter-gang warfare on a scale that not even the most sanctimonious citizen could remain indifferent to. On top of this, the automatic weapons to which these gangs appeared to have unlimited access were often turned on the police and federal agents when the hunt for drugs and drug-traffickers grew too hot, and this resulted in a very high rate of police casualties and, in two notorious cases, in uncontrolled police reprisals which caused scores of deaths among innocent people.

Many of the bigger fish netted in these operations were neither poor nor black: the extensive Mafia and Italian-American involvement in the drug business saw to that. But the great majority of those arrested were poor, and either black or Hispanic. At the beginning, most of those arrested were charged with drug offences or with being in the country illegally. But inevitably, as the level of violence escalated, an increasing proportion of those arrested were charged with more serious crimes, ranging from arson to murder. It was widely believed in the black community – and later investigations frequently vindicated this belief – that in many cases a combination of fear and anger was leading inexperienced police and federal law enforcement officials to arrest young blacks on a more or less arbitrary basis and accuse them of committing serious crimes. This was bad enough; what was even worse was that the courts very quickly became overwhelmed by the huge number of cases they were now being called upon to hear, and delays of many months before a case could come to trial became commonplace. Since state and federal prosecutors naturally, and nearly always successfully, opposed the granting of bail in serious – and indeed in many less serious – cases, a very large number of people, many of them guilty of nothing more than having been in the wrong place at the wrong time, found themselves remanded in custody for a period that would probably last for several months, and sometimes looked as though it might stretch into years. Moreover the prisons, long since overcrowded, now started to overflow, and many of those remanded in custody were detained in designated 'holding areas' – camps rapidly constructed in order to accommodate the swelling numbers of remand prisoners, ringed by barbed wire perimeter fences patrolled by dogs, and in which living conditions were frequently even worse than in the prisons themselves.

This state of affairs not only provoked the most profound resentment in the black ghettos; it stimulated acute criticism from liberals of whatever colour. Quite apart from the specific issue of the arbitrary arrest and lengthy detention without trial of many people who were probably innocent, a large number of liberal lawyers were convinced that the entire search and arrest operation was being conducted in a manner for which there was no proper authority in either state or federal law, and which indeed probably violated the fourth amendment to the Constitution. Accordingly, and with the backing of a number of civil rights organizations, attempts were made in a carefully-selected series of test cases to challenge in the courts, and particularly the federal courts, the validity of the arrest of the accused, the charges levelled against him, or the nature of the evidence submitted by the prosecution. And it was at this point that something which had long been a matter of small talk in the legal profession suddenly came to be appreciated by a much wider public: something once rather ghoulishly expressed in terms of 'Reagan controlling the country from beyond the grave'.

In the last forty years, Reagan had served as President for longer than anyone else except Eisenhower, and in one crucial respect – though by no means this one alone – had been a luckier President than Eisenhower: during his term of office a very large number of federal judges, at both district and appeal court levels, had died, retired or resigned. The consequence was that by the late 1980s more than half the members of the federal judiciary had been appointed by Reagan, and the position had altered little since then. The overwhelming majority of these Reagan appointees were ideologically conservative, some of them extremely so; and this had been demonstrated in a long series of rulings and sentences down the years. It therefore came, or should have come, as no great surprise, in the late summer and early fall of 1994, that the federal district courts should in the main have ruled in favour of the prosecution in cases of disputes over the legality of search and arrest procedures or the admissibility of evidence; or that these rulings should usually have been upheld by the federal appeal courts; or that very severe sentences should have been passed not only on those found guilty of major crimes, but also on those convicted of lesser offences which happened to come under federal jurisdiction.

In the fall of 1994, however, and to the undisguised relief of liberals, the best traditions of American justice temporarily reasserted themselves. The Supreme Court, like the lower judiciary, was now dominated by conservatives: the retirement of Chief Justice Burger in 1986 had marked the beginning of a marked tilt to the right on the Court, and of the nine justices at least six, and perhaps seven, could now be described as conservative or very conservative. Unlike the majority of lower court judges, however, several of these men and women were of outstanding intellectual ability, and one or two of the most persuasive of them had, or liked to think that they had, something of the extra-judicial feel for what was required of the acceptable interpretation of the law in a changing and evolving society that had characterized the incumbency of the great Chief Justice Marshall in the early 19th century. Whatever the precise reasons, the fact was that in one test case which it consented to hear the Supreme Court now ruled, five to four, that the police had exceeded their powers under the existing law; and that in another it ruled, six to three, that a lower court had unreasonably refused to grant bail to a defendant whose case could not be expected to come to trial for more than six months. The liberals were jubilant. Their jubiliation, however, was to prove short-lived.

White, middle-class America was thoroughly disconcerted by the Supreme Court's decisions – or at any rate by the way they were represented in the popular media. Rioters, looters, arsonists, even murderers, it now appeared, might be immune from arrest on technicalities; or, if arrested, might be released on bail, no doubt to disappear back into the ghettos to commit more crimes at a later date. Irrational though these apprehensions might be, they augmented a climate of fear provoked by the urban disturbances themselves, and by another factor which was causing increasing concern to even the most sober opinion. This was that, precisely because the lower courts had been so

181

prone to give the prosecution the benefit of all possible doubt about the validity of charges and the admissibility of evidence, and so ready to impose maximum jail sentences in cases where the accused was convicted, juries had reacted perversely, and had been increasingly inclined to acquit defendants, however strong the evidence against them. Few objective observers doubted that, in consequence, many dangerous criminals who should be behind bars were freely walking the streets.

Middle-class America could do nothing about Supreme Court verdicts or the irresponsible behaviour of particular juries; but it could still express its opinion at the ballot box. In the November mid-term elections hardline, law and order conservative candidates received overwhelming support, both in Congressional and gubernatorial contests. Most of the remaining liberal Representatives disappeared from the House; in the Senate, virtually the only liberals to survive were those fortunate enough not to be running for re-election this year. And the fruits of this landslide soon became evident. Convening early in 1995, the new Congress rapidly passed legislation that gave both federal and state governments extensive powers to search premises reasonably suspected of harbouring illegal immigrants or housing drugs, explosives or unregistered firearms; to arrest people reasonably suspected of involvement in drugs, explosives or firearms offences; and to detain such suspects without trial for a period of up to six months where such detention was deemed by local police departments or federal security agencies to be in the public interest.

This legislation – signed into law by the President in a ceremony televised from coast to coast – provoked uproar in liberal circles in the United States, and was widely condemned by democratic countries around the world. Academic experts asserted that the legislation was demonstrably unconstitutional, several political correspondents compared it with legislation in force in South Africa in the final years of apartheid, and a German television company (conveniently ignoring equally sinister developments closer to home – *see* Chapter VIII) made a programme full of heavy Teutonic symbolism, showing the Statue of Liberty – expensively refurbished less than a decade before – being eaten away by the effects of atmospheric pollution. The Supreme Court, however, as was only proper, remained magnificently impervious to academic experts, political correspondents and German television programmes. By a decisive seven to two vote it ruled that the new law was designed, in the difficult circumstances of the late 20th century, to maintain the integrity of the Union, preserve the security of the nation and guarantee the safety and freedom of its citizens, and was accordingly fully consistent with the Constitution. To a large majority of Americans, the day this verdict was handed down by the Supreme Court was probably a day like any other. To a small minority of concerned citizens it was the day on which a great historical experiment, begun in 1776 and officially blessed in 1787, finally came to an end.

On the economic front, the situation was going from bad to worse. American exports were spiralling downwards as the world recession deepened, as Europe started closing its markets to imports of food and manufactured goods, and as developing countries found it impossible to pay for imports. More recently, another factor had been at work, similar to the one which had caused America's trade balance to plunge so heavily into the red in the early 1980s: the high interest rates implicit in the Fed's tight monetary policies, and investors' confidence in the present Administration's ability to bring the inflation rate down towards zero, had induced a big inflow of capital into the US, and this had substantially raised the value of the dollar, further inhibiting exports and stimulating imports – which were already on a rising trend as other hard-hit countries endeavoured to create jobs by encouraging business to export to the still huge American market. The net result of all this was to aggravate the contractionary effects on output and employment in the US that were already in operation in consequence of high interest rates and tight credit. By the spring of 1995 the national unemployment rate was approaching 15 per cent, and rising with alarming speed.

The rational policy response in this situation – as had been recognized by a series of American administrations on a number of occasions between the beginning of the 1960s and the early 1980s – would have consisted, at least in part, of the adoption of an expansionary fiscal policy. Government expenditure would have been increased, or taxes reduced – or perhaps both – in order to stimulate effective demand to the extent necessary to halt and then reverse the fall in output and the rise in unemployment. However, the President and most of his advisers were firmly wedded to the ideology of the free market and the conviction that the government must at all costs keep its hands off the economy. Provided that the government balanced its own budget, and the Fed kept the growth of the money supply under control, all would be well. (The President's personal antipathy to Keynes and all that he stood for was remarked on in Chapter V.)

By an unfortunate irony, hostility at this time to the idea of unbalanced budgets was by no means confined to ideologues like the President or the neo-monetarist economists who advised him. The persistent attacks made on the large budget deficits of the mid- and later 1980s by economists of all persuasions, including leading Keynesians – attacks wholly justified in the economic circumstances of the time – had eventually so impressed themselves on the public consciousness that now it was almost universally believed that budget deficits were a bad thing at all times and in all economic circumstances – a repudiation of Keynes's analysis that put the clock back sixty years. Thus, despite economic recession and rising unemployment, the present Administration sought to eliminate the budget deficit in the same way that governments around the world had done in the early 1930s. And the consequences of these endeavours were equally perverse. As the recession deepened, tax revenues fell and – to the extent that they still existed in the United States of 1995 – various welfare payments and subsidies automatically rose. Thus the budget deficit rose, too, and further efforts were made to cut government expenditure and raise certain taxes; and this in turn further reduced demand in the economy, and drove it further into recession.

Although falling output and rising unemployment had no impact on the President's view of how the economic system worked, or his belief that the very notion of a discretionary fiscal or monetary policy was something close to heresy, it did affect his attitude towards protectionism. Although he had been a critic of the protectionist measures introduced by his predecessor in 1989, he now seemed to have very little difficulty in accepting the time-honoured and self-serving argument that the reason for America's surging imports and widening trade gap

184

was nothing to do with the level of exchange rates or the inefficiency of America's manufacturing industry, but was the consequence of other countries' 'unfair trade practices'. There was, of course, some truth in this accusation – though not nearly as much as there would be in a year's time, when Europe's massive new import restrictions would be biting very hard. Accordingly, and under the stirring slogan 'America must be strong and self-reliant', a series of steps were taken to reinforce such protectionist measures as were still in place as a result of the 1989 measures, and to impose a number of further restrictions which appeared to be urgently needed.

Over the next year or so these import restrictions unquestionably created some jobs and saved many others; but the impact they had on the overall unemployment situation was relatively slight. If anything, their main effect was to emphasize how much further, even during just the last six years, America's ability to produce the goods that people wanted to buy had deteriorated. The factors that had so worried the previous President had continued to operate, and the termites had continued to eat away at the basic foundations of American prosperity. There had been too much consumption and too little saving and investment. Research and development had gone on being devoted, to a wholly disproportionate degree, to the arms industry and the space race. The low level of real wages and the seemingly inexhaustible supply of cheap immigrant labour from Mexico, Central and South America had inhibited innovation and capital formation. All these things – even the inflow of mainly illegal immigrants, despite the Administration's efforts to stop it – were still going on, and were taking an even heavier toll.

Of course, there were areas of manufacturing where the United States still led, or almost led, the field. These included advanced weaponry and military aircraft – though in an increasingly impoverished world these were a much less lucrative export than they had been ten or twenty years ago; many types of civil aircraft; communication equipment; and some types of computers. But in many other areas, particularly the fastest-growing ones, the United States had fallen behind, and in some cases far behind, Japan, two or three European countries, and even some of the newly-industrializing countries of South-east Asia. These areas included much of advanced electronics, computer-controlled machine tools, new materials, fibre optics and biotechnology.

In the field of high-tech services, including financial, legal, medical and miscellaneous professional services, America had been more successful in maintaining its pre-eminence. But for various reasons this was not as reassuring as it seemed. Despite the emergence in the 1980s of the global financial marketplace, barriers of one kind or another still existed in this business, and a number of other countries had managed to limit the expansion of American firms, or at any rate the employment of American nationals and the remittance of profits to the US. Moreover, whatever the national income statistics might show, the real value of much of this high-tech service activity could reasonably be questioned. The fact that most legal offices were now computerized and connected with vast data-banks, for example, seemed more conducive to increasing the cost and complexity of litigation than to improving the administration of justice.

But the real problem was more basic than this. Even at the more glamorous end of the service sector – financial and legal services, television, and the other media – the productivity of the great bulk of the employees, measured in any plausible way, was low, as were their real wages. This was even more true of the far greater number of people employed in the remainder of the service sector, such as wholesale and retail distribution, enter-tainment and leisure activities, the hotel, catering and fast food business, and so on. Of course the value of a person's output in these service sectors is, in accounting terms, what someone else is willing to pay for it; but the argument soon becomes circular, and there is an element in the situation of everyone taking in each other's washing. In some sense which might elude the official statistics, but which was very apparent to visitors from Japan and the more prosperous Western European countries like Germany and Switzerland, the America of 1995 had become, in the main, a low-wage, low-productivity economy.

This phenomenon was not confined to the decaying areas of the great cities; nowhere was it more starkly apparent than in the sunbelt states of the south and the west which, only a decade or two ago, had been so enviably prosperous. In huge areas, conditions now resembled those in the Third World rather than the First. Tens of millions of recent immigrants, and – for this was a population with a very high rate of natural increase – the American-born children of recent immigrants, occupied great stretches of land. They worked, if employed, in low-paid agricultural and service jobs. They lived in shanty towns that resembled the surroundings of Mexico City or São Paulo. They spoke little or no English. They absorbed such educational and medical services as were available, but were too poor to contribute much by way of taxation or user fees to the cost of providing these and other services.

From a general humanitarian point of view there was much to be said for permitting these mainly illegal immigrants to stay, and even for turning a blind eye to their continuing arrival from south of the border. Abysmally low though their living standards in the US might be, they were higher than where they had come from. And the problems of unemployment and poverty in their home countries would be even worse than they were if these migrants could not enter the United States, attempt to find jobs, and remit some of their earnings back to their relatives. But from the point of view of the United States – whatever the benefits to employers looking for cheap labour – the phenomenon had some markedly adverse effects. Not only did it increase unemployment among native-born Americans, and depress their real wages, thus contributing powerfully to racial and ethnic tensions; it had probably also played a major part in the long stagnation of American productivity, and the nation's growing inability to provide its citizens with the standard of living they demanded.

The stock market had weathered the disturbances of the summer of 1994 remarkably well: there had been a couple of very sharp falls, but these had soon been followed by substantial recoveries. During the later part of 1994 and the early part of 1995 there had been a modest advance in share prices, in spite of the deteriorating economic climate, the bankruptcy of a number of well-known companies, and the failure of several medium-sized banks and many smaller ones. Clearly, the virtual eradication of inflation, the election in November 1994 of a Congress determined to maintain law and order at all costs, the embodiment of this attitude in new legislation and the validation of this legislation by the Supreme Court, had together been seen as thoroughly reassuring factors, guaranteeing that any recurrence of the rioting and violence of the previous summer would bring swift and merciless retribution.

But quite suddenly, in April 1995, the stock market collapsed. As in the case of the crash of the London stock market two years earlier, there seemed no particular reason why it should have collapsed then, rather than earlier or later. Possibly it was only then that some of the deeper implications of the events of the previous summer sank in, and a few key people started to hear the beat of a more distant drummer. Whatever the reason, many investors, as in any stock market crash, were caught napping. They watched in dismay as large paper profits started to evaporate. Some sold in order to realize some profit while it was still there. Others stayed in the market, hoping for a recovery, and saw, with incredulity, their paper profits turning into losses; and then they sold to cut their losses. The more people sold, the more prices fell; and the more prices fell, the more people sold. In seven trading days, the Dow Jones industrial average fell by more than 15 per cent, and then, after a two-day rally, plunged again. Expert commentators explained that because of tight margin requirements, the weight of institutional investors, the existence of options and futures markets, and much else besides, there was no question of anything like a recurrence of the 1929 crash, which by the middle of 1932 had resulted in a fall of nearly 90 per cent in the Dow Jones industrial average. But the market failed to listen. After a month the Dow Jones had fallen by nearly 30 per cent, and after six weeks by more than 40 per cent. Nervousness turned into demoralization, and in many cases demoralization degenerated into panic. Few members of the financial community jumped out of windows, as they had in 1929, because nowadays the windows did not open. But lethal doses of sleeping pills and the carbon monoxide emitted by car exhausts proved an adequate substitute; and before long, on most days, the *New York Times* was devoting an entire page, or even more, to its obituaries.

The news of collapsing share prices on Wall Street caused little concern in the black ghettos and the Hispanic shanty towns; it had no obvious relevance to most of their inhabitants – though many of them felt some jubilation at the troubles being experienced by the rich. Nevertheless, it is clear in retrospect that the stock market crash acted as a catalyst of the events of the next eighteen months. The stock market represented, after all, the most visible and obtrusive embodiment of an economic system in which the allocation of resources was determined largely by short-term considerations of profit and loss, in which the rich often got richer and the poor poorer, and the workings of the democratic process were too hamstrung by an antiquated system of checks and balances, too enervated by the inertia of a vast bureaucracy, and too trammelled by the pressures from powerful vested interests, to prevent inequalities from widening to a point at which they became socially explosive. The stock market crash seemed to betoken a sudden loss of confidence in the system on the part of those who operated it and most benefited from it; and this loss of confidence emboldened the more aggressive and disgruntled of those who most suffered from the system to start taking a few good kicks at it while it was down. And this set in motion a process of disintegration which was to prove irreversible.

The early summer of 1995 witnessed the beginning of a series of major outbreaks of urban rioting, arson and looting. City police forces did their best to cope with the situation, but found it increasingly difficult and beyond their capacity to do so. Years of cuts in federal funding of the big cities, together with the erosion of the local tax base caused by businesses and better-off families moving out to the suburbs, had left police forces under-manned and under-equipped. The same was true of firefighting and hospital services, with the result that whole areas of large cities were sometimes destroyed before fires caused by a single incident of arson could be brought under control, and many people injured in the spreading urban violence suffered long delays, and sometimes died, before receiving medical treatment. In some places life came to a virtual standstill as the most basic amenities of an organized society, such as water, electricity, sewerage and garbage disposal services ceased to be provided, as accident or sabotage destroyed facilities which it then became too dangerous for municipal crews to attempt to repair or replace. Similar disturbances occurred on a number of occasions in the predominantly Hispanic shanty towns of the south and west, as boredom and despair bred of unemployment and atrocious housing and sanitary conditions, and harassment by local police and government officials, provoked explosions of violence. Sometimes this took the form of large-scale fighting between different national or ethnic groups within and around the shanty towns; but sometimes it was directed at the prosperous inhabitants of nearby small towns and suburbs.

This was a new and alarming phenomenon. Even in parts of the country close to the great cities, the residents of small-town and suburban America had always been insulated from the intermittent violence of the inner cities: they might read about it in their newspapers and see it on television, but it seemed to have nothing to do with them. Now this started to change. Isolated instances of violence and armed confrontation in these hitherto safe areas became more common, and were played up in a sensational way by the media. Perhaps encouraged by the publicity they were receiving, such incidents multiplied. Generally committed by people who drove into the area from outside, usually from deprived urban neighbourhoods, some of these crimes took the traditional form of armed holdups of banks and supermarkets; but frequently they took the more horrific form of mindless destruction, with car-bombs exploding without warning in crowded places, and vehicles crammed with youths speeding down main streets hurling petrol bombs at stores and restaurants and spraying pedestrians with automatic fire. It sometimes seemed that poor America had declared war on rich America, and what this largely meant in practice was that black America – mainly young black America – had declared war on white America. In many parts of the country, particularly the small towns and rural areas, retaliation was swift, as armed white vigilante groups seized individual blacks, and sometimes members of other ethnic minorities, most of them completely innocent, and made short work of lynching them. Groups of blacks sometimes took reprisals in their turn, and the cycle of violence intensified. A corrosive fear gripped the nation. No one, anywhere, seemed safe any longer.

The fact that local police forces frequently became overstretched, particularly in the big cities, meant that on a number of occasions the National Guard had to be called out. This was the last resort available to the state – and the second to last resort available to the federal government – for restoring law and order. But as often as not this step exacerbated the situation instead of bringing it under control. Efforts had been made after the 1967 civil disorders to effect various improvements in the National Guard, but with the long period of calm that succeeded those disturbances, and the numerous other pressures on state budgets, these initial efforts had soon slackened, and once again the National Guard appeared to be insufficiently trained and inappropriately equipped for modern riot control operations. It was also, overwhelmingly, white. Its arrival in black urban ghettos was usually seen as highly provocative, and led to frenzied assaults, which in turn sometimes caused panicky young National Guardsmen to over-react and shoot indiscriminately at anything that moved. Casualties on both sides were high; and the mounting toll of deaths among the National Guard further hardened the mood of white America. In several cases federal troops had to be called in to supplement or replace the National Guard. The federal units employed in these operations were properly trained and equipped, and often used techniques developed in Japan, where the need to counter armed groups of left-wing militants was becoming an increasingly acute problem. But the deployment of federal troops was not without disadvantages. By contrast with the National Guard, where they were heavily under-represented, blacks formed a relatively large proportion of the army, and riot control operations in black areas sometimes led to friction between army and National Guard units, and within the army itself. More generally, the spectacle of US armed servicemen going into action in US cities, and sometimes killing or being killed, aggravated the deep unease within America itself, and contributed to a growing sense of anxiety in other democratic countries around the world.

Bad though all this was, there was worse to come. Until now it had been widely supposed that the urban violence, and even the armed attacks on the suburbs and small towns, were the product of a spontaneous outburst of anger which would soon subside provided it were controlled by the use of whatever force was necessary, and in addition, perhaps, bought off by the promise of increased funding for the inner cities. But now it was beginning to be clear that not all of the rioting and violence was adventitious and spontaneous; much of it was systematic and organized.

The long history of racial discrimination in the United States had only ended, in a formal sense, in the 1960s, and in practice still persisted in a variety of ways. It was true that individual blacks, if sufficiently talented, motivated and lucky, could now get to somewhere near the top, and thousands had done so. It was true that hundreds of thousands of others – the majority of them women – had found employment in white-collar jobs in the burgeoning service sector of the economy. But all this was little more than cosmetic. Bold 'affirmative action' programmes, designed to reverse the effects of centuries of discrimination, had frequently been stymied by the executive decisions of Republican Administrations, and sometimes sabotaged by the decisions of an increasingly conservative judiciary. In most places, and particularly in the inner cities, blacks were still massively disadvantaged in their access to jobs, housing, education and health care. Over the last couple of decades all this had created a growing sense of alienation within the black community, which had intensified during the later Reagan years. The flame of hope ignited by the election of a liberal Democratic President in 1988 had flared only briefly, flickering in the face of that President's inability to make any substantial inroads into the problems of unemployment and poverty, and being brusquely extinguished by the contractionary economic policies, welfare cuts and tough law and order measures of his successor. Among many blacks, alienation was now being transformed into an irreversible radicalization. This process had been accelerated and intensified by the detention of thousands of blacks for long periods in the so-called 'holding areas', and their exposure there to the influence and teachings of a sizeable number of black intellectuals and activists.

At first, the basic theme of most of this teaching fell on stony ground, for it was alien to American – even black American – political tradition. But gradually it took root and spread. The basic theme was that blacks and other exploited minorities in the United States would remain in a position of permanent economic and social subjugation to the white, middle-class majority as long as change depended on the workings of the traditional democratic process. That process, for all its windy rhetoric and

192

superficial achievements, had never served to lift from the backs of minorities, and particularly the black minority, the yoke of poverty and oppression, and it never would. There was only one way to make the middle-class white majority concede blacks their place in the sun; and that was 'the armed struggle'. There was, of course, no way in which blacks, who accounted for only 15 per cent of the population of the country – even if backed by a sizeable proportion of other exploited minorities – could hope to win any armed confrontation with the forces of the federal government. But that was not the object of the exercise. The object was to make life for the average American white so uncomfortable and so unsafe that in the end the white majority would have to come to terms with the black minority. That would not happen quickly: for a long time the white majority would react with coercion and brutal suppression. But that would only serve to increase radicalization and militancy among the blacks and other minorities, and make more certain the day of ultimate victory.

The growing realization among the white establishment that the violence and destruction it was witnessing were not simply a temporary eruption of frustrated and probably drug-crazed individuals, but to an increasing extent represented the staging of a drama that had been meticulously plotted and scripted, led to some predictable responses. The first response was to brand the black and other activists involved as 'communists under orders from Moscow'. This charge was entirely false. There was, to be sure, a communist element among the radicals, in the sense that some of them had read the works of Marx, Lenin, and Mao, and derived from them valuable insights into the workings of economic and political processes. But no one involved would have dreamt of taking orders from Moscow, Beijing or anywhere else; though the experiences of Cuba, Nicaragua and other Latin American countries where left-wing guerillas had succeeded in overthrowing corrupt right-wing dictatorships were closely studied. Another charge was that some black leaders were taking their instructions from other old enemies of the United States, particularly Libya and Iran. There was slightly more substance in this allegation, since in recent years the Black Muslim movement in America had gained many new recruits, and – particularly since the spectacular rocket attack on the

Waldorf-Astoria in May 1991 – Shiite ideas had spread widely among American Muslims. But once again, there was no question of the American black radical movement taking orders from foreign governments. The movement certainly absorbed relevant ideas from whatever quarter they might come; but it was a home-grown movement, stemming from the civil rights campaigns of the 1960s and the traditional concerns of the liberal wing of the Democratic Party. What had happened was not that some of the heirs to these noble traditions had started taking orders from abroad. It was simply that they had finally been driven to the conclusion that the intolerable degree of inequality and injustice from which the black minority in America suffered would only be eradicated by recourse to the use of armed force.

However, while the radicals were in no sense agents of some worldwide communist or Islamic conspiracy, it was certainly true that they accepted help from anyone willing to provide it. One kind of help they accepted took the form of advice on the strategy of guerilla warfare, and training in its actual tactics. This came from the considerable number of people now in the United States – many of whom had gone underground – who had experience of guerilla fighting in Central and South America. Many of these men and women had fought unsuccessful campaigns against military dictatorships, and had been among the fortunate minority that had escaped and, despite the acute disfavour with which the American authorities had been viewing political refugees since the early 1980s, had managed to find their way into the US.

Even the most liberal white Americans were naturally outraged by the revelation that foreigners who had found sanctuary in the United States should now be assisting in plots to murder American citizens; and this was one of several factors which further deepened divisions between the black radicals and some of those who had earlier championed the cause of blacks and other racial minorities. But the refugees from Latin America retorted to this charge that the right-wing regimes in their own countries, which mercilessly tortured and murdered those who expressed any kind of opposition, only retained power because they were supported by American money and American armed might. They themselves, therefore, just as

194

much as oppressed minorities in the US, had a stake in forcing white America to do what was needed to remove an intolerable degree of inequality and injustice in their societies.

A second kind of help accepted by the radicals took the form of weapons and explosives. Ironically, some of these came from caches accumulated by groups of right-wing exiles from Cuba and the two other Latin American countries which at this time had revolutionary left-wing governments. The Central Intelligence Agency, which seemed to have learnt nothing since the Bay of Pigs fiasco in 1961, but forgotten such useful lessons as it must have learnt from that episode, had continued to arm these groups against the day when they would, supposedly, stage a triumphant invasion of their home countries, to the accompaniment of cheers and hosannas from a grateful populace. Although the previous President had put a stop to this nonsense as soon as he assumed office in 1989, the policy had been secretly reinstituted under the present Administration – which, in its turn, seemed to have forgotten the lessons of the 1986–7 Reagan Administration scandal, when it was revealed that arms had surreptitiously been sold to Iran in the hope of securing the release of American hostages in Lebanon, and some of the proceeds of these sales even more surreptitiously channelled to the 'Contra' rebels trying to unseat the government of Nicaragua. Because of the covert nature of the policy, a raid by radical groups on a right-wing arms hoard in Miami in July 1995 was dismissed by the local police as a trivial incident in a dispute between rival gangs of drug dealers. In fact there is every reason to suppose that the radicals acquired a very large haul of arms and explosives.

This was, however, by no means the only source of weapons and other military *matériel* available to black radical groups. As they tightened their grip on the inner cities, they acquired increasing control over the profits made by the still-flourishing drug business, and this enabled them to finance large-scale arms purchases from abroad. Many of these shipments were seized as they were being smuggled in, and others fell victim to routine police and army searches and the activities of informers; but enough got through to the hands of guerilla fighters to constitute a formidable armoury.

Many of these weapons were of Russian origin, but there was

no evidence for the inference unanimously drawn by conservatives in the United States that they were being knowingly supplied by the Soviet Union. At this time the Soviet government was almost wholly absorbed in its own internal problems. Attempts to move towards a more efficient, market-oriented economic system had foundered on the rock of Communist Party conservatism and entrenched bureaucratic officialdom; and the increasing resistance in the Soviet Asian republics to the domination of the Russians, who now constituted less than a third of the country's population, was facing the Kremlin with the prospect of either widescale secession or something close to civil war. In so far as it could spare time and energy to devote to foreign affairs, the Politburo seems to have been deeply perturbed by the developments now taking place in the United States, and fearful that the President, untrammelled by the constraints of the kind of collective leadership that operated in Moscow, might be tempted to adopt the time-honoured remedy of national leaders facing unrest at home, and decide to engage in foreign military adventures which, in a nuclear age, could bring destruction to everybody. It seems far more likely that these weapons were being supplied by some of the radical Middle Eastern regimes which had no love for the United States. There is some evidence, too, that the new black government of South Africa, under domestic pressure to assist the black struggle in the United States, and remembering the shameful support that the US, like Britain, had continued to provide for far too long to the country's former white apartheid regime, was involved in some of these arms supplies as well.

Although the most widespread reaction to the growing realization that the rioting, violence and killing were systematically organized may have been that it was all a communist plot orchestrated by Moscow, the fact remained that calling it names was not going to stop it. Something had to be done to restore law and order to the streets, and make sure that people were once again safe in their homes and local communities. Essentially, there were two views about how this should be done.

The first view, widely held among intellectuals, academics, liberal Democrats and others, was that, totally unacceptable though the violence it had provoked might be, the deeply felt sense of grievance of blacks had a legitimate basis, and that far more must be done to remove it. The kind of policies the former Democratic President had tried to implement in 1989–90 must now be put in hand as a matter of urgency, they argued, but on a much bigger scale than envisaged then; and must be persisted with year after year, regardless of which party occupied the White House and controlled the Congress, until the problem was solved.

Perhaps inevitably, given the increasingly conservative mood of the country since 1992, and the near-hysteria induced by the shootings and bombings which had been occurring on a rising scale since the early summer of 1995, this reasoned appeal for a programme of massive and continuing assistance from the federal government to the deprived section of the population – 'a kind of domestic Marshall Plan', as one proponent put it – got nowhere. It was the second view which prevailed. This view was that the violence had to be stamped out by force, whatever it took. Bleeding-heart liberals, soft on communism, it was argued by the President and many Congressional leaders, were nearly as much the enemy as the black radicals who were trying to take over the country by violent revolution. The first duty of government, after preserving the state from external aggression – and there was a large element of that here as well, they claimed – was to maintain law and order at home, regardless of cost. People must be free to go about their business, and lead normal lives, without the constant fear of attack. The free market system must be protected. Democracy must be preserved. If it took half the army to put down this insurrectionary violence, so be it. If it meant that half the black population ended up in jails and detention centres, or on Death Row itself, so be it.

This uncompromising stance received the unequivocal backing of the overwhelming majority of white Americans of every class and ethnic origin, of Asians and other small racial groups, and indeed of many blacks. Nevertheless, it made little sense. Black radicals were in a minority even among blacks, and a small minority of the population as a whole. All the same, they were numbered not in thousands but in millions; they were well-armed; and they enjoyed the active or passive support of hundreds of thousands of people of other races who found themselves at the bottom end of the very unequal income distribution, with no hope, unless major changes in social

197

arrangements were made, of ever being anywhere else. Moreover, the blacks were becoming increasingly radicalized and militant – the result, as their leaders had anticipated, of the ferocious assaults on black ghettos now being mounted by federal troops in the interests of 'stamping out the violence by force'. And another factor was at work. Among black muslims, the Shiite interpretation of Islam had been growing in influence by leaps and bounds, with the consequence that more and more young blacks believed that to die in battle was to win an immediate passage to heaven. Thus the kind of fanaticism that had inspired the Japanese kamikaze pilots who had wreaked such havoc among the American fleet in World War Two, and had turned the Gulf War between Iran and Iraq in the 1980s into a bloodbath comparable to the fighting in France and Flanders in World War One, was now unleashed upon carefully chosen targets within the United States itself. And so, as one head was cut off by the forces of law and order, two even fiercer ones seemed to grow in its place.

Another factor soon began to operate as well, which served to frustrate the ability of even the most massive show of federal force to put down the black insurrection. Radical leaders started to place less emphasis on direct armed confrontations which resulted in many of their members being killed or captured, and more emphasis on subtler forms of economic and political sabotage, and operations in which relatively small numbers of guerilas were put at risk. Political and business leaders particularly associated with the hardline policies of the present Administration became prime targets for kidnapping and assassination attempts; and despite security precautions so stringent that most of these people were hampered in discharging their professional duties, as well as unable to lead normal domestic lives, many of these attempts were successful. Internal airline flights, notwithstanding regulations that required passengers to arrive at the airport four hours before departure, were regularly hi-jacked, and passengers ransomed against the release of black militants from federal prisons, where in many cases they awaited execution. At first the Administration refused to negotiate in these cases, but within a month more than thirty passengers had been murdered by hi-jackers, and the nation's airlines came to a standstill. The Administration had to change its tune. The result was like equipping the prisons to which radical leaders were sent with revolving doors, and lowered national morale even further. Meanwhile, other kinds of sabotage calculated to make life difficult for the white majority – though not only for them – were continuously undertaken: electricity and water supplies to middle-class white neighbourhoods were frequently cut off, for example, and in one horrendous case a reservoir was actually poisoned, causing hundreds of deaths before the problem was identified.

In short, the President, his Administration, and white America generally had miscalculated. Black guerilla warfare could not be eliminated, or even reduced to a bearable level, by the use of force. But if the whites had miscalculated, so had the blacks. The black leaders had supposed that their widespread and unremitting use of violence would eventually compel the white establishment to grant the blacks what they demanded. These demands were not, after all, something which no sovereign nation could readily contemplate, like the demand for a separate state which had been heard for many years from the Basques in Spain, the Sikhs in India, and the Tamils in Sri Lanka; or the demand for unification with another country heard from the Catholic Republicans in Northern Ireland. All that the blacks were demanding was full economic and social equality within the United States: the same access to jobs, housing, education and health as the whites – an end to the unemployment, poverty, hunger and homelessness that afflicted the poorest 15 or 20 per cent of the population. It did not seem too much to ask.

The blacks had miscalculated not because the white establishment made a conscious decision to put up with a state of violent guerilla warfare indefinitely rather than concede black demands; some hardliners adopted this position, but they were in a minority. The blacks had miscalulated because, as it turned out, the very nature of the American economy and the American political system made it impossible for their demands to be conceded. Under the free enterprise, free market American system, those who were successful grew rich, and those who were unsuccessful stayed poor. The system could only function by creating these great inequalities. But inequalities were not created from scratch in each generation: however powerful the rags-to-riches myth in America, and however easy to illustrate by pointing at this millionaire or at that, the fact was that great and persistent inequalities were deeply entrenched at the very heart of the American way of life. Wealth begat more wealth, and poverty spawned more poverty. The political system proved incapable of changing this situation, because it was itself a reflection of the existing economic and social order: the large campaign contributions to conservative candidates from corporations and wealthy individuals, and the very low election turnout of the most disadvantaged groups in society, were only two of the more visible manifestations of this. Whoever first observed that money buys power and power generates money might have had his eye on America.

The consequence of this double miscalculation, by the white leadership and the black, was a stalemate. Insurrectionary activity was unremitting, a continuous level of minor violence being punctuated from time to time by spectacular acts of assassination and physical destruction. The responses of federal and state authorities followed a similar pattern: a continuous process of search, arrest and detention without trial was interrupted by occasional massive reprisals against neighbourhoods believed to be sheltering guerillas or storing weapons. America did not come to a standstill: people still went about their daily business, and lived their lives as best they could. Nevertheless, the mainspring was broken. America was no longer a happy, hopeful, easy-going, friendly country. It was a place under siege.

In the November 1996 election, the incumbent President, though having no salvation to offer his fellow-countrymen – at least in this world – was re-elected by a large majority. It required no hardened cynic to connect this event with a bill the President had signed into law a few months earlier. This made it possible – on the grounds that many respectable citizens were understandably afraid to venture out into the streets to get to polling stations – for people to vote by telephone from the relative safety of their own homes. The arrangements for counting and checking these telephone votes left, to put it mildly, much to be desired; and liberal intellectuals talked – though circumspectly – of the similarities between this 'electronic election' and elections in the Third World which also, mysteriously, always seemed to confirm the tenure of those already in power. Perhaps the world's oldest democracy was also in the process of becoming a one-party state.

The reinauguration of the President in January 1997 was held in the Pentagon, the only place regarded as offering adequate security. No members of the general public were admitted, though there were plenty of microphones and television cameras. Among the assembled dignitaries upon whom the cameras focused for a moment was the former Democratic President, attending this ceremony only because of an iron sense of the constitutional proprieties, and looking twenty years older than when he had assumed office only eight years ago. It did not require a great deal of imagination on the part of the television viewer to guess what he was thinking. During his four years in office he had tried to promote the low level of unemployment, the high rate of economic growth, and the fairer distribution of the national income that would enable America to travel onwards into a happy and prosperous future. But he had been defeated – defeated by the greed of the rich and the would-be rich, by the self-serving demands of a multiplicity of special interests, and by the obstructions placed in the way of progress by the workings of the political system and by conservative interpretations of the Constitution. The failure had not been his alone; it had been the failure of all privileged Americans. The nation, in its obsession with material consumption, with short-term profits, with getting-rich-quick and devil-take-the-hindmost, had sown the wind. Now it was reaping the whirlwind.

CHAPTER VIII

Western Europe and Japan: The Reckoning

It was not only in the United States that the mid-1990s witnessed a political and economic débâcle on a scale that would have been difficult to credit only a decade earlier. The same thing happened in Western Europe and Japan and, in consequence, in much of the rest of the world as well. The actual course of events varied in different countries and regions, but the fundamental cause was the same: the failure of the existing political system to provide people with the minimum amount of economic security – in terms of adequate employment and reasonably stable prices – to which they believed they were entitled.

The downfall of Japan was one of the most remarkable developments of the 1990s. In the 1970s and 1980s, Japan had looked increasingly like the economic superpower of the 21st century, with its long time-horizons, its close and constructive links between government and industry, its skilled and disciplined workforce, its huge expenditures on innovation, research and development, and investment, its relentless introduction of new products and new processes, and its ever-rising share of the world market for sophisticated consumer and capital goods. But the whole operation had come unstuck: Japan had become the victim of its own success.

The heart of the problem had lain in Japan's chronic trade surplus. Year after year, throughout the 1980s, Japan had notched up trade and current account surpluses of many tens of billions of dollars. One reason for this had been that Japanese goods were of high quality and reliability, and in demand all over the world; and although the appreciation of the yen against many other currencies in the later 1980s had increased the price of Japanese exports, this effect had been smaller than appeared, because the Japanese inflation rate had been very low, and thus the appreciation of the *real* exchange rate had not been nearly as great as many people thought. Another reason for the chronic balance of payments surplus lay in Japan's low propensity to import. This was not simply – as Americans and some Europeans believed – a matter of hidden trade barriers, but rather of the deeply held, and to some extent justified, belief of Japanese consumers that Japanese goods were superior to foreign goods. But the fundamental reason for these chronic balance of payments surpluses, some shrewd observers believed, was simply that the Japanese *liked* to have such surpluses. The Japanese, they suggested, had an 18th-century mercantilist attitude to foreign trade. The bigger the excess of exports over imports, the argument went, the better, because such a surplus helped to provide employment at home, while at the same time piling up wealth, in the form of gold or foreign exchange reserves, or assets overseas, that provided the nation with security against the rainy days that the future might bring.

The trouble about this, of course, was that the countries whose balance of payments deficits were the counterpart of the Japanese surpluses suffered corresponding disadvantages: they lost jobs to competition from Japan, and saw their external assets dwindling, or their external liabilities piling up. Ever since the 1970s, Japan had been under mounting pressure from many of these countries to restrain its exports to them on a voluntary basis, and had increasingly done so: voluntary restraint agreements on Japanese car exports, for example – quite inconsistent, incidentally, with the spirit of the General Agreement on Tariffs and Trade (GATT) – had been in operation in North America and Western Europe for many years. Increasingly, the Japanese had side-stepped these pressures by locating manufacturing plants in the United States and Western Europe, and sourcing the output of these plants from local suppliers. But none of this had been enough. These other countries had continued to lose jobs because of imports from Japan, and had continued to see their external financial position getting weaker. Anger had mounted, and eventually exploded, first in the form of the import controls imposed by the US in the later 1980s, and particularly in 1989, and then in the controls introduced by a number of European countries a few years later.

By 1994, this surging tide of protectionism had hit Japan very hard, bankrupting many smaller firms and causing unemployment to rise to the highest levels in living memory. Up to a point, the Japanese administration tried to counter these contractionary influences by encouraging higher domestic consumption and increasing its own expenditures on the country's often inadequate and antiquated physical infrastructure. But the Japanese propensity to save stayed stubbornly very high, and for reasons in which party political calculations seemed to be mixed with a quasi-theological attachment to fiscal austerity, the government refused to budget for deficits large enough to absorb these private savings, and thus maintain a high level of effective demand. And so output stagnated, businesses collapsed, and unemployment rose.

Under a superficial appearance of consensus and agreement, Japan was deeply divided over how to react to this mounting crisis. On one side were the internationalists, or 'externalists', who were convinced that a densely populated country like Japan, with virtually no natural resources of its own, must at all costs be deeply and acceptably integrated into the world economy as a whole. For far too long, they argued, Japan had recklessly run huge balance of payments surpluses, without heeding the adverse effects of these surpluses on other countries; and for far too long it had refused to play the positive and constructive role in managing the world's trading and financial system which its huge economic strength should have obliged it to do. It was essential for its own economic survival that Japan eliminate its chronic current account surplus by genuinely opening up the whole of its internal market to imports, and by massively increasing its aid to the developing countries. Only a responsible, generous, outward-looking approach, they concluded, would enable Japan to continue to prosper; and, by the beginning of 1994, the time left for adopting such an approach was looking exceedingly short.

On the other side of the argument were the nationalists, or 'internalists'. Many different points of view were represented under this heading, by no means all of them consistent with each other. Some internalists rejected the whole of the Western, materialistic, consumer-oriented ethos, and sought society's return to an ascetic, spiritual, contemplative life-style, consistent with what they saw as Japan's cultural heritage. Others were less ambitious, seeking only to de-link the Japanese economy as far as possible from an international trading and financial system which they saw as fundamentally hostile to Japan's true interests, and to rely on individually negotiated barter arrangements to secure from such countries as China and Australia the food and raw materials it needed.

On methods, as well as on objectives, internalists differed among themselves. Some believed that it was vital to pursue the argument within the context of the democratic constitution set up by the Americans after the war. Others regarded Western-style democracy as a creed alien to the Japanese tradition, and felt under no obligation to conform to democratic procedures in the pursuit of objectives they considered to be of overriding importance. What all internalists had in common, however, was a pronounced antipathy to the externalists' attempts to integrate Japan more fully into the world economic system, and a determination to block such attempts by one means or another.

For several years there had been a stalemate between internalists and externalists, with the result that there had been no decisive policy thrust in one direction or the other. After 1994 it became apparent that this paralysis had lasted too long, and that Japan's ability to choose had been overtaken by events. Well before the end of the century the internalists, helped by dramatic developments in Europe, and using tactics that were frequently illegal and undemocratic, had gained the upper hand, and Japan had turned in upon itself in an orgy of mutual recrimination and expressions of individual guilt and failure.

Back in 1989, Olaf D. Le Rith had watched with disdain, though without surprise, the leisurely pace at which the new President of the United States had gone about trying to put his country to rights. Here, Le Rith told his lieutenants, is a man who has been elected with an overwhelming majority, but who – with the sole exception of the imposition of import controls – is failing to use the authority his election victory has given him to get things done quickly, before the inevitable opposition begins to consolidate. A leader with a mandate, he said, must strike while the iron is hot, if he is to change the course of history. But not on every front, he added. A leader needs not only the speed of the blacksmith, but also the patience of the farmer, waiting until the moment is ripe to gather in the harvest. And above all, perhaps, the wisdom to judge when it is the approach of the blacksmith that is called for, and when the approach of the farmer.

No doubt some of these lieutenants remembered these ruminations, as they observed Le Rith's tactics, and obeyed his instructions, in the weeks and months that followed the European Parliament elections of June 1994. On some fronts, he moved swiftly and decisively. On others, he played a waiting game. Overall, in hindsight, it has to be said that his sense of timing was masterly.

Le Rith's first act, after it had become clear that the Europe First Movement now controlled the European Parliament, was to organize a victory celebration. This was described by apprehensive enemies as 'a pure public relations stunt', and that is exactly what it was. It was also one of the most spectacular public relations stunts in history. Le Rith had at first toyed with the idea of staging this event in Rome, the Roman Empire being one of the major paradigms of his own political vision. But the chaos that reigned throughout much of Italy was nowhere more pronounced than in Rome, and anyway the summer heat was unbearable. And so the choice fell on Venice, itself once the centre of a great empire, and still the world's most breathtakingly beautiful city.

With maximum publicity, all the victorious EFM Euro-MPs were summoned to a Europe First Victory Convention at the Excelsior Hotel on the Lido at Venice. The occasion was to be preceded by a non-denominational service in St Mark's Square, at which the Pope in person had agreed to preach. Later, there would be a keynote speech by Le Rith. Finally, there would be a spectacular 'Europe First Victory Convoy' down the Grand Canal, culminating in the most dramatic fireworks display that even the Italians – the world's greatest pyrotechnicians – had ever devised. 'This one has everything,' said the head of the largest of the American TV networks, explaining to his executives why they were going to give it maximum coverage. 'The Pope and fireworks? – the sacred and profane. Venice and Le Rith? – beauty and the beast. We can't miss.' The rest of the world's media seemed to agree. No Soviet-American summit, no royal wedding, no Olympic Games, no Papal visit had ever attracted more camera teams, more specialist correspondents, more technical miracles of communication or indeed more furious battles between rival papers and broadcasting channels than descended on the quiet Venetian lagoon in July 1994.

Le Rith had thought twice about asking the Pope to preach, and the Pope had thought twice about accepting. Le Rith had calculated, coolly, that the presence of the Pope at the Victory Convention would do the Europe First Movement more good in the eyes of Catholic Europe than damage in the eyes of Protestant Europe. And the Pope had calculated, equally coolly, that if, as seemed possible, the EFM were going to be the new masters of Europe, then the Vatican had better get on the right side of them at the start.

In his sermon the Pope took as his text Christ's treatment of the money-changers in the temple; and, in the spirit of non-denominationalism, not to say pantheism, he referred also to the labours of Hercules in the Augean stables. While there was not a syllable that was directly political in his words, there must have been many who watched the service, in person or on television, who were reminded by the story of the money-changers of the old, corrupt politicians in the national capitals of Europe, and the need to cast them out. For those whose education had veered towards the classical rather than the Christian, the sixth labour of Hercules offered an even more persuasive parable for the contemporary state of affairs in Europe; for had not filth accumulated in the vast Augean stables for thirty years, and had not Hercules, by diverting two rivers, cleansed them in a single day?

Inevitably, however, it was Le Rith's speech, rather than the Pope's sermon, which was the high point of the Victory Convention. Beamed directly into nearly every home in Europe, and hundreds of millions of others around the rest of the globe, it commanded attention from the first sentence. 'We have no victory to celebrate,' said Le Rith, '. . . yet. We have gained an admission ticket to the real contest. That is all. Now we must resolve and dedicate ourselves to victory in that contest, the real victory, the only victory for the future of Europe and all its people.' The speech lasted barely half an hour

– and to many of its viewers it seemed much less – but by the time he had finished the leader of the Europe First Movement had made millions of new converts.

It is impossible to convey in print the effect that Le Rith's oratory had on his listeners. This is so despite the fact that his sentences, when transcribed, turned out to be entirely grammatical and literate – a quality rarely encountered in demagogues of genius. An extract from his Venice speech may, however, give some impression of the nature of his message and the reasons for the powerful, visceral response it elicited.

'Thirty million Europeans,' he thundered, 'have no work. The old, out of date politicians in the old, out of date national capitals have nothing for them to do. They have nothing to say to them except "We are sorry. We are doing our best. Trust us. We hope that things will get better one day." Thirty million sons and daughters of true-born European stock, waiting and wanting to serve, to serve themselves, to serve their families, and to serve Europe; and all that these inert, corrupt, discredited parish-pump politicians can say is "Please be patient. We have nothing for you just now. Come back tomorrow."

'Well, they will not be patient any longer. The blood is running in their veins today. Their sinews and muscles are flexing today. They will not come back to the old leaders at all, ever. They are here, now, in this great place. They are on the march. They have their feet on the threshold of every capital in Europe. Their hands are on the bars of the prisons which the old, discredited politicians have fashioned for them. The bars, like the politicians, are old and rotten; and their shoulders are young and strong. They know the truth. They know how to shrug off the insidious net of American seduction and subjugation. They know how to trample under their feet the leeches and parasites from alien races who suck away at their strength and drain their vitality. They know that to do this, two things are needed: work, and discipline. Work, for every man and woman who can and will. Discipline, which turns a rabble into an army, and without which civilization degenerates into a jungle. The Spartans and the Athenians did not turn back the million-strong army of the Persian king except with discipline. The Roman Republic did not build the greatest empire of ancient times, except with discipline; and they did not watch it decline and fall for any other reason than the loss of discipline. It is the American empire that, alone, has been built on self-indulgence, on the easy affluence of empty fertile lands, on the ignoble foundations of commercial purchase and of shameless appeal to depraved appetites, not on the honest foundations of legitimate arms or on the strong base of high principles and self-discipline. And therefore the American empire is rotten, it is resented throughout the world, and it is crumbling away before our eyes . . .

'We, in the Europe First Movement, speak for Europe. We control the Parliament of Europe. The people of Europe have given us their trust. They have given us their mandate, their authority to carry out our programme. We will not betray that trust. We will not flinch from carrying out our programme. No commission, no council of corrupt, out of date politicians, no procrastination from the old national capitals, no piece of paper waved by the very men who have brought Europe to its knees shall stand in our way. We have a job to do. We must have the tools. We will take them and we will fashion them and we will shoulder them and we will use them. A great task lies ahead of us. We are ready to begin.'

Some of the political correspondents who covered the Europe First Victory Convention dismissed this speech as nothing but windy rhetoric. One of them was incautious enough to quote *Macbeth*: it was a tale told by an idiot, he said, full of sound and fury, signifying nothing. But the most experienced of them took a very different view. They knew that the speech was not aimed at political sophisticates, but at the masses, and its impact on them had probably been immense – a supposition soon confirmed by reports from correspondents in every corner of Europe, and indeed around the world. They knew, too, that Le Rith was a man of action as well as of words, and that when he said the Europe First Movement was ready to begin, he meant it. As the great firework display which marked the end of the Convention came to its climax, late on a warm, clear evening, and twenty huge star-bursts exploded simultaneously over the Venetian lagoon, they knew that what was about to begin might mark a momentous turning point in European history.

The governments of the twelve member countries of the European Community had been surprised, even startled, by the results of the Euro-elections, but they had not been particularly perturbed. The powers of the European Parliament, under the various Treaties and the interpretations of them by the European Court of Justice, were quite limited. The place, in the view of most governments, was little more than a talking-shop where, with a little luck, obstreperous national politicians could be diverted by generous salaries and allowances, and thus given less opportunity to cause trouble at home. The impotence and inefficiency of the institution were epitomized by the fact that it sat in Strasbourg, while its secretariat was housed more than a hundred miles away in Luxembourg.

The real decision-making power in the European Community lay partly with the EEC Commission in Brussels, but mainly with the Council of Ministers – which meant national governments. And although in recent years the Council of Ministers had moved towards a system of majority voting on some issues, in practice no country – and certainly no big country – could be overruled on an issue of importance to it by other Community members. In short, within the EEC, national sovereignty remained largely intact, and there was no way in which this state of affairs could be changed by the activities of the European Parliament. So, at any rate, national governments reassured themselves, and each other, after Le Rith's Venice speech.

But they were deluding themselves. They had overlooked the crucial fact that a directly elected parliament, whatever paper limitations there may be on its jurisdiction and powers, has a political potency and legitimacy which cannot be gainsaid once the leadership and the opportunity arise to use it. And, in the case of the European Parliament, this had now happened. This Parliament was no longer composed of people who owed allegiance to, and were often leading members of, the main political parties in the individual member states. It was now controlled by people who had explicitly repudiated the 'old' politics and the 'old' governments based in the 'old' national capitals, and who owed allegiance to a leader who had been insisting for nearly a decade that the individual governments of Europe had no answer to their countries' problems, and that only action on a Europe-wide scale could provide a solution.

This was a new and unprecedented situation. Europe was entering territory never explored before. It was a journey without maps or guidebooks. But one thing seemed absolutely clear. Even those national governments most firmly in the saddle, like the German Social Democrats – let alone governments barely in control of events at all, such as those in Italy and Britain – would now find it very difficult to pursue policies in conflict with the will of the EFM majority in the European Parliament, or even to appear to obstruct the policies the EFM seemed determined to pursue. The people of Europe, in a free and fair election, had said that they wanted Le Rith and the Europe First Movement to solve their economic problems. Unfamiliar though this situation might be, it was a political fact of the first magnitude, and sooner or later every government in Europe would have to come to terms with it.

The first thing Le Rith did after the Venice Victory Convention was to send his 270 Euro-MPs off on three weeks' holiday. 'Make the most of it,' he told them grimly. 'It may be your last holiday for a long time.' The second thing he did – using his power to command a majority in the EP – was to insist that the Parliament be reconvened in three weeks' time, early in August. He was unconcerned by the howls of protest from non-EFM Euro-MPs all over Europe. If they turned up in Strasbourg, he could outvote any proposal to go back into recess until October. If they preferred to stay sunning themselves on Mediterranean beaches, so be it: his own MEPs constituted a quorum many times over. Once reassembled, the European Parliament debated in detail, and then voted on, Le Rith's programme. By the time that members of individual European governments got back from their holidays at the beginning of September, Le Rith was ready to present them with a list of the demands of the European Parliament.

The list was staggering.

The first, and most modest, demand was that the eighteen members of the European Commission, hitherto appointed by national governments, should now be appointed, from among its own members, by the European Parliament.

The second demand was that all European governments should explicitly acknowledge that the European Parliament must now be recognized as the sovereign parliament of Europe. The parliaments of individual countries would remain responsible for exercising those functions which it was more appropriate to discharge at a national rather than Europe-wide level, such as the provision of health care and the organization of primary education. (To soften the blow a little, Le Rith used as an analogy to the proposed new arrangements the relationship that existed between the German Bundestag and the relatively powerful German state governments, rather than the relationship which existed between the Westminster parliament in Britain and the relatively impotent local authorities.) All the powers needed to cope with the great and desperate problems of unemployment, inflation and economic growth, however, must be ceded to the European Parliament, since those problems could only be dealt with by action on a fully European basis.

These powers were then listed. The two most important ones were as follows.

First, the EP would have the sole power to levy income tax, corporation tax, value added tax (VAT), and customs and excise duties. Although the mechanical task of assessing and collecting these taxes would continue to be performed by individual countries, the rates of tax would be determined by the European Parliament, and the revenues collected would accrue to it and it alone. Individual countries would continue to determine the rates of minor taxes, such as wealth, inheritance and capital gains tax, and to retain the revenues accruing from these taxes.

Secondly, the EP would have the sole power to determine how its revenues from taxes and duties should be spent. Much of this revenue would be allocated to individual governments, earmarked for expenditure on such items as social security, primary education and health care. Much of it would be allocated by the European Parliament to developments vital to the economic regeneration of Europe, such as increased expenditure on physical and social infrastructure, on industrial investment, and on secondary and higher education, and training and re-training of every kind. And much of the remainder of its revenue would be spent by the European Parliament on the establishment and equipping of the new European Security Forces. These centrally controlled forces, which would have a large conventional element, but which would also incorporate and update the British and French nuclear deterrents, were essential to the protection of Western

212

Europe against aggression – from any quarter – now that all American forces had been withdrawn from Europe and NATO had effectively collapsed.

The individual European governments, once they had recovered from their astonishment, rejected these demands out of hand, and put on a great show of conducting business as usual. It reminded one French journalist of the way that Louis XVI had continued to sign royal decrees after the fall of the Bastille.

Le Rith was unworried. The vast extravaganza at Venice, and in particular his own speech, had had the kind of impact throughout Europe that was normally associated with major catastrophes, such as the assassination of President Kennedy in 1963 or the American space shuttle disaster in 1986: everyone knew about it, and everyone remembered what they were doing when they heard about it. At the beginning of October, as the unemployment queues lengthened throughout Europe, as tens of millions of people faced the onset of another winter without adequate food or shelter, Le Rith, with every eye in Europe upon him, made his next move. He unleashed a devastating propaganda barrage, with one simple message: we have been elected to put Europe back to work and back on the path to greatness, but the 'old' national governments are refusing to give us the tools to do the job. Within a few weeks, no one in Europe who had seen a billboard, opened a newspaper, or turned on a radio or television set, could have failed to receive this message loud and clear.

Meanwhile, day by day, the work that Le Rith had promised to provide in his Venice speech was proving in ever shorter supply, as was the discipline. Employers laid workers off as they found they could not market their output because nobody could afford to buy it, or because they could not produce it in the first place, as a result of strikes by key personnel, power cuts, and the shortages of materials and components created by the constant disruption of road and rail communications. As workers were laid off, purchasing power declined further, and more people were thrown out of work. By the end of October more than 6 million people in Britain, for example, were unemployed – a quarter of the labour force – and in most of the rest of Europe the position was little better.

Meanwhile, throughout the continent, order and discipline

213

were fast disappearing from large areas of national life. Strikes and demonstrations – some of them organized by Le Rith supporters, but many of them spontaneous – erupted in major cities in nearly every European country. Strikers attacked people seeking to go to work, and sometimes set their own factories and offices on fire. Demonstrators ignored police instructions about designated routes, and bloody battles ensued. Wild outbreaks of arson and looting in city centres and suburban shopping malls often proved uncontrollable, subsiding only when destruction was total. Gangs of youths, some white, some black, some North African or Turkish or Asian, roamed the streets, assaulting or killing anyone they disliked the look of. Day by day, week by week, life in the European cities became increasingly intolerable, and the war of nerves between Le Rith and the national governments rose in screaming crescendo. It could not last. Something had to give.

It was the national governments who blinked first. Following three days of frantic consultations between national capitals, the governments of the twelve members of the European Community agreed to Le Rith's demand that the eighteen members of the Commission should henceforth be appointed by the European Parliament, from among its own members, instead of by national governments. After all – these governments seem to have assured each other – the EEC Commissioners in Brussels are essentially faceless bureaucrats, and it does not matter a great deal who appoints them. The real power will continue to lie, as it always has done, with the Council of Ministers, and thus with national governments. Armed with this comforting rationalization, the European member governments made Le Rith a formal offer of this change in arrangements, on condition that he immediately use all his influence over his EFM supporters throughout Europe to bring an end to the strikes and demonstrations that were threatening to bring the continent to its knees.

To this offer Le Rith gave only the briefest of replies. The demands made by the sovereign, democratically elected European Parliament must be met in full, he said. Nothing else would do.

Throughout Europe, the chaos intensified, and the public clamour for governments to 'give Le Rith the tools he needs to do the job' became deafening. Behind the scenes, Le Rith gave a sharp further twist to the screw. He privately informed a number of governments that in their countries' next national elections – which the gathering crisis seemed likely to force on them sooner rather than later – he would field an EFM candidate in every single constituency; he would also put up the leader of the French national section of the EFM to contest the forthcoming Presidential election in France. In view of the strength of the Movement's current popularity – opinion polls taken at this time showed that the EFM would now get 65 per cent of the vote in a Euro-election, compared with the 51 per cent it had actually received in June – this would almost certainly mean the return of EFM governments with large majorities in the national parliaments. These EFM governments would immediately concede the demands of the European Parliament. And the members of the existing national governments, instead of being able to carry on as ministers, exercising the limited but still substantial powers that the European Parliament would devolve to them, would instead be finished, as politicians, for good.

Whether – as cynics would aver – it was this last threat which was decisive is unclear. But it is certainly true that within a few weeks of Le Rith's ultimatum the landscape had changed completely.

Italy was the first country to cave in, though here the chief motivating factor was brutally unsubtle. During the last week of October and the first week of November, in three separate incidents in Rome, the four politicians who were the most vocal opponents of Le Rith and his demands were assassinated. The killings bore the hallmark of the Mafia rather than of an extreme terrorist group like the now largely defunct Red Brigades; but evidence later emerged – consistent with a long tradition in Italian politics – that there were links between the killers and extreme right-wingers who were members of the Italian section of the EFM. Within a day of the last of these assassinations, the Italian Parliament had voted by a large majority to concede the demands of the European Parliament, piously noting that this decision had been taken 'in order to strengthen and advance the cause of democracy in Europe'.

France was the next country to give way. Although there was

a clear majority in the country for conceding Le Rith's demands, the situation was more complex than in most other European countries. Many of the industrial workers engaged in strikes and demonstrations owed allegiance to the Communist Party, and had no desire to cede power to a European Parliament which they saw as under the control of fascists; what they were seeking to do was overthrow the French government, which had presided over an intolerable attack on workers' living standards and job security, and replace it with a left-wing coalition which included the communists. Correspondingly, within the government itself, there was an extreme Gaullist element which would under no circumstances agree to the ceding of French sovereignty to a European body. This complicated deadlock was resolved by a bizarre development. Only a development of this kind, perhaps, could have united France; and only in France could such a development have had such an impact.

Late one afternoon in the middle of November, several hundred EFM militants, many of them armed with all-plastic guns and plastic explosives which escaped the scrutiny of the metal detectors at the entrance, and posing as ordinary visitors, gained admission to the Musée d'Orsay, the huge gallery of late 19th- and early 20th-century French art and sculpture opened by former President Mitterrand in 1986. While a small group gained access to the museum's computers, seized the technicians working there, and closed all the great steel gates and doors, sealing the entire building off from the outside world, others rounded up the security guards and visitors, and assembled them all in the museum's vast, vaguely Egyptian, central nave. Breaking into the main Paris radio frequency, the group demanded an announcement by the government, backed by a two-thirds majority in the National Assembly, that France would immediately concede to the European Parliament all the powers stipulated by Le Rith. The government had until three o'clock the following afternoon to meet this demand. After that, every fifteen minutes until the demand was met, a work of art would be destroyed – starting with the most valuable, and working downwards.

Within minutes, television shots of the huge museum, and the tiny figures who could be dimly seen moving about inside, were being beamed around the world. In America particularly, where the deepening economic crisis and the right-wing landslide in the mid-term elections ten days earlier were already threatening to plunge the country into an internal conflict as violent as anything yet seen in Europe, the incident brought a touch of light relief. The men who had hi-jacked the museum were not threatening the *hostages*, only works of *art*? 'Gee, man,' said one New Yorker, interviewed on the street, 'those French are real weird, y'know.' His view would have been amply confirmed had he managed to be a fly on the wall at that evening's more sophisticated Paris dinner parties. Optimists wondered whether it might not be possible to persuade the terrorists to eliminate hostages at fifteen-minute intervals, rather than paintings. Pessimists dismissed this possibility and broke into furious arguments about the order in which the exhibits would be destroyed. Which would be first? Manet's *Dejeuner sur l'herbe*? Courbet's *Atelier*? Cézanne's *Card Players*? Rodin's *Gates of Hell*? A Van Gogh? A Gauguin? On only one point was there general agreement. If the 5,000 exhibits were to be destroyed in descending order of value, then Couture's vast canvas of *Romans of the Decadence*, which dominated much of the museum, would be approximately the five thousandth to go – and not just because it so aptly illustrated one of Le Rith's pet themes.

To the beleaguered French government, the occupation of the Musée d'Orsay came as manna from heaven. The Minister of Culture pointed out to his colleagues that, short of storming the building on a scale that might lead, directly or indirectly, to the destruction of the museum and all its contents (and, of course, the 500 or so people inside), there was no way in which the government could stop the terrorists from carrying out their threat. The contents of the museum were, he said, invaluable, beyond price (though, he added, the Getty Museum, which had recently acquired a large new site next to its existing premises in Malibu, California, had recently had the effrontery to make an offer for the entire building and contents of $6.8 billion). In these circumstances, he went on, the government had no option but to concede the terrorists' demands – which were in line with what a majority of the French population wanted anyway. Governments and constitutions, he concluded, at any rate in France, were ephemeral – here today and gone tomorrow. French art and sculpture, on the other hand, were eternal.

217

The Cabinet found this argument persuasive and, before the deadline expired, had secured the necessary two-thirds vote in the National Assembly for the ceding to the European Parliament of the powers it had asked for. It was to be clearly understood, the Prime Minister said, that the government was acting in the best interests of France, and that the decision would be reversed unless it was ratified by a majority of the French people in a referendum to be held at some unspecified time in the future.

If the French government's reactions to EFM attempts to force its hand were characteristically Gallic, the British government's reactions to similar efforts were just as characteristically Anglo-Saxon. In the small hours of the morning of Saturday, 5 November a small group of hardline Le Rith supporters assembled at the top of Parliament Hill in London, and launched a Russian surface to surface missile at a target that lay five miles to the south-east. Neatly bisecting the space between the Post Office (or British Telecom) Tower and Euston Tower, this missile landed with total accuracy on the chamber of the House of Commons. In contrast to Guy Fawkes' failure exactly 389 years earlier, this attack destroyed the chamber just as comprehensively as Hitler's bombers had done in 1941. Assembling after the weekend in the chamber of the House of Lords – just as their bombed-out predecessors had done – MPs voted overwhelmingly to defy Le Rith – though less overwhelmingly than their predecessors had voted to defy Hitler.

But in 1994, unlike 1941, it was all play-acting. The situation was out of control, and the government was near the end of its tether. A state of near-anarchy existed throughout much of the country. In many of the big cities there was open racial warfare. In some areas entire housing estates had been gutted by fire. In one north London borough the frustrations engendered by a decade and a half of rising unemployment and deepening poverty and deprivation had exploded into a horrendous, mindless orgy of killing and destruction. Troops brought in to try to restore order had been decimated by petrol bombs and sniper fire, and one of the helicopter gunships flown in with reinforcements had been destroyed by a heat-seeking missile from a home-made but effective rocket-launcher. The nation's toughest paratroops, brought in as a last resort by the government,

218

overreacted, and when relative calm descended on the area two days later the dead were numbered in hundreds, and the wounded in thousands. And yet so great was the chaos and violence elsewhere that the rest of the country hardly noticed.

It could not go on. Late in November the government recommended to the House of Commons that, 'in view of the grave emergency with which the nation is now faced, and the widespread belief of the British people that in the increasingly difficult world economic situation with which we are confronted, it is essential that the European Community – of which we have been a leading member for more than twenty years – should now adopt a united stand in order to cope with the acute economic difficulties which are afflicting the entire continent, we accordingly recommend to the House that for a period not exceeding six months in the first instance – such period to be extended only by positive affirmation of this House – the powers requested by the Parliament of the European Community should be vested in that body, and that for the aforesaid period that body should supersede, in the exercise of sovereignty, this House.'

'What on earth,' Le Rith was asked by a bemused aide, when the news came through, 'does all that mean?'

'It means,' said Le Rith, 'that the British are in the bag. Now the only people who matter are the Germans.'

The Germans looked like proving a tougher nut to crack. The SPD government had been badly shaken by the Euro-election results, in which it had got barely 30 per cent of the vote compared with over 50 per cent for the Europe First Movement. Nevertheless, it still had a solid majority in the Bundestag, and it was determined to resist any ceding of power to a European Parliament now controlled by a movement and a man which it regarded as right-wing, and indeed fundamentally undemocratic. Moreover, with another three years to run before the next federal elections, the German government was less susceptible than most to Le Rith's threat to run EFM candidates for every seat in the next national elections.

These factors proved insufficient, however, to stem Le Rith's momentum. In Germany – more than in any other country where similar circumstances prevailed – a great deal was made of the argument that an absolute majority of the electorate had voted for the EFM in the Euro-elections, and that now that the

EFM had a majority in the European Parliament, it was an unacceptable flouting of democracy for the German federal government to refuse to cede to the European Parliament the powers for which it was asking. Some might condemn this argument as sophistry, but it cut very deep in a country where the collapse of democracy after the First World War had led to consequences so horrendous that no one would ever forget them. The idea – actively promoted by former CDU and CSU officials and members who had transferred their allegiance to the Europe First Movement – that the 'democratic' thing to do was to cede the European Parliament the powers for which it was asking quickly gained very wide currency. Huge demonstrations, orderly but menacing, were held throughout the country, at which the slogan 'We want democracy' was paraded on thousands of placards, and chanted by tens of thousands of voices. The largest of these demonstrations, held in Bonn early in December, coincided with the news of a further sharp rise in unemployment, to the highest figure for sixty years. Nearly half a million people surrounded the Parliamentary building and refused to budge until the European Parliament's demands were met. In a secret briefing, the Cabinet was informed that there was widespread sympathy with the demonstrators' demands among both the police and the army, and that their loyalty could not be counted on if ordered to remove the demonstrators by force.

Things might have turned out differently if the rest of Europe had stood firm. But by this time Britain, France, Italy, and two of the smaller countries had all agreed to Le Rith's demands. The German government decided that further resistance would be futile, and on 14 December it conceded defeat. At least, unlike Britain and France, it made no attempt to save face with meaningless stipulations about 'a limited period' or 'a subsequent referendum'. Perhaps this was because the government was fully conscious of the agonizing paradox inherent in the situation. In the interests of 'respecting democracy', it was being forced to cede vast power to a body that had been democratically elected, but was controlled by a man who, many were convinced, was not a democrat. Nobody made the point explicitly, but there were few members of the Cabinet who had forgotten that in 1933 Hitler had come to power in Germany as the result of a democratic election.

Once Germany had thrown in the towel, the other half dozen members of the European Community soon fell into line. The country to hold out longest was Denmark, which had always viewed Le Rith and the Europe First Movement with the deepest misgiving. But the Danes enjoyed the highest per capita income in Europe entirely as a consequence of the way they benefited from the EEC's Common Agricultural Policy, and to refuse to concede the powers demanded by the European Parliament was to invite almost certain expulsion from the European Community. No government could hope to survive the devastating effects of that on the Danish economy. Reassembling early in January 1995, after the Christmas recess, the Danish Parliament voted by a small but sufficient majority to follow the example of the other eleven governments of the European Community.

Less than ten years after he had published *Europe First*, Olaf D. Le Rith was in charge.

Le Rith's first step was administrative. The eighteen members of the European Commission in Brussels were relieved of their posts – the blow being softened by exceedingly generous redundancy payments – and replaced by twenty Commissioners selected by Le Rith from among the 270 EFM members of the European Parliament, he himself assuming the role of President of the Commission. The Commission was now, in effect, the government of Europe, answerable only to the European Parliament, which now exercised all the important sovereign powers previously exercised by the parliaments of the individual European countries. As long as the Commission could command a majority in the European Parliament – and discipline among the EFM Euro-MPs was such that there was little doubt about that – and as long as Le Rith was in control of the Commission – every member of which was personally loyal to him – Le Rith's position was impregnable. He now wielded more power in Europe than anybody since Hitler – with the difference that Le Rith's power was democratically legitimate whereas, outside Germany itself, Hitler's had not been.

The day that the new Commission was confirmed in office by the European Parliament, Le Rith moved into action. Some things he accomplished within days; others took two years or more. But once again his sense of timing proved almost faultless. Things were done in orderly and logical sequence; but the timetable also took account of the need to maintain the popular support which had swept the Europe First Movement into power, until other mechanisms for consolidating that power were in place.

The financial markets were Le Rith's first priority. European stock markets were, in general, at a low ebb, but this did not cause him undue concern: he was confident that as his policies started to revive the economy of Europe, and restore order to the streets, stock markets would pick up strongly. The foreign exchange markets were a different matter. Putting Europe first meant, crucially, providing work for all able-bodied Europeans. This could not be done as long as Europeans were free to spend their money on foreign goods instead of European ones, or to invest their money in factories or offices or shops that created jobs overseas instead of at home. An essential step towards achieving this objective was to impose restrictions on the purchase of foreign exchange by European residents, whether companies or individuals. Thus while individual European currencies would continue to be freely convertible into each other (pending the creation of a single European currency unit, to be called the Europa), the purchase of gold and other currencies such as dollars and yen was to be severely curtailed.

Le Rith closed all European foreign exchange markets for a week, and when they reopened the landscape had been transformed. There was now a new European Central Bank, whose headquarters were located in the premises of the Bank of England, and which had a Governor – a German – who was a former head of the Bundesbank, and one of Le Rith's earliest and strongest supporters. The central banks of the individual European countries had been downgraded to being national branches of the European Central Bank.

The ECB, which was directly answerable to the European Commission, and had the power to lend directly to the European government, assumed control over the gold and foreign exchange reserves of all the former European central banks. Henceforth, all earnings of foreign exchange accruing from European exports and other receipts from abroad would have to be deposited with the ECB, which would in turn allocate this foreign exchange only in accordance with the principles laid down by the Commission. It would be made readily available, for example, to finance imports of commodities with which Europe could not supply itself, such as oil, coal, raw materials and tropical foodstuffs; but it would not be made available, except during a transitional period, for imports of goods which Europe could make for itself. Nor would it be made available for European investment overseas. The foreign exchange earnings of existing European overseas investments – mines, plantations, factories, office blocks, shopping complexes – had to be remitted to the European Central Bank, except in so far as it could be demonstrated that they were needed for the profitable expansion of existing facilities.

The network of foreign exchange restrictions was completed by one further measure. A travel allowance was introduced for those wishing to take holidays outside Europe. For the great majority of European citizens, who never travelled outside Europe anyway, this presented no problems, but for those accustomed to taking holidays or visiting friends or relatives in the United States or other parts of the world it proved irksome, because the allowance was set so low: it permitted little more than one week's comfortable (or two weeks' uncomfortable) foreign travel per person per year.

The effects of this restriction did not become widely appreciated until six months later, during the 1995 summer holiday season, and by then things in Europe had changed quite a bit. They had changed even more by January 1996, when Le Rith announced that it had become clear that the previous summer there had been widespread evasion of the foreign travel restrictions, that the consequence was a haemorrhage of foreign exchange which Europe could not afford if the process of economic recovery was to continue and work was to be provided for everyone, and that, accordingly, exit visas would now be required by all European citizens wishing to travel outside Europe, in order to ensure that the rules governing the travel allowance were properly adhered to.

That still lay in the future, however, in January 1995, a month in which Le Rith set in motion a number of other policies, apart from those relating to foreign exchange transactions. One of these was a comprehensive programme of import restrictions, reinforcing the effect of foreign exchange controls, and aimed in particular at raising the level of employment in Europe. Some of these restrictions took the form of tariffs, ranging up to 200 per cent, on imports of capital and consumer goods; others took the form of quotas, imposed initially at 80 per cent of the level of imports in 1994, but to be reduced rapidly to zero over the next three years, as Europe moved towards complete self-sufficiency in the provision of manufactured goods.

Another policy which Le Rith started to put into effect as soon as he assumed the Presidency of the Commission was the creation of the European Security Forces. Here, however, he encountered difficulties. Although the European Parliament's power to create these forces had been explicitly conceded by individual governments during the crisis a month or two earlier, when the time came to put the policy into effect several of them began to prevaricate. Clarification, they said, was needed. Further discussions would be valuable. Experts should prepare a report. And so on. This, Le Rith knew, was the crunch: this was the battle he had to win.

The struggle went on for two months. Although Le Rith made judicious use of his public relations skills, this was not an issue on which the views of the general public had much bearing; it was an issue that was going to be decided behind closed doors. In urgent discussions with national political leaders, Le Rith and his principal lieutenants made much of the fact that now that all American troops had been withdrawn from Europe, and NATO had collapsed, the separate national armies of Western Europe were in too much disarray, and too inadequately equipped, to defend their countries against attack from the east. The economic confusion in the Soviet Union, he insisted, and the general turbulence created by the drive for greater autonomy by minority ethnic and religious groups and the Soviet Asian republics, could not be counted on for ever to absorb Russian attention, to the exclusion of its long-standing aim of world domination; indeed history suggested that these were precisely the circumstances in which a country might be tempted to strike at a neighbour in the interests of preserving national unity.

And it was not only from the Soviet Union that a military threat might come, Le Rith would claim, in those circles in which the argument might fall on a receptive ear: one could not rule out the possibility of aggression from across the Atlantic. America might be looking increasingly isolationist, but there were powerful groups in that country that were bitterly opposed to Europe's democratic decision to break out of the American commercial and cultural stranglehold, and reassert its own historic identity. Unless Europe rapidly equipped itself with powerful, centrally commanded security forces, these groups might attempt to prevent Europe following its chosen course, either by explicit aggression from outside, or by a process of internal subversion.

Some of the politicians and their civilian advisers in the national capitals found Le Rith's arguments persuasive; some were suspicious and unco-operative; some fought tooth and nail the idea that ultimate authority over their country's armed forces should pass to the European Parliament, which really meant the Europe First Movement, which really meant Le Rith. But – what Le Rith had heavily banked on, though he had never been completely sure – it was the military men – the generals and the colonels – who were decisive in the end.

By and large, these men were fed up with Europe's military backwardness, compared with the United States and the Soviet Union. They were fed up with the defence cuts which nearly every European government had been making for nearly a decade, in order to appease the civilian electorate with tax cuts, and the work-shy with social security benefits. Above all, they were fed up with the weak and cowardly national politicians, who had not only sabotaged their countries' external defences, but in most cases refused to call in troops in support of the civil power, despite the state of anarchy to which strikers and demonstrators had been allowed to reduce most of Western Europe over the past couple of years. To these men, Le Rith had come in recent months to look like a saviour: a strong leader, on a European scale, who would spend what was needed to bring the European armed forces up to both nuclear and conventional parity with the two superpowers, and who would at the same time deal ruthlessly with the left-wing intellectuals, the students, and the troublemakers in the trade unions, who together bore such a heavy responsibility for Europe's military and economic weakness.

By the end of March 1995 the argument was over. All army,

navy, air force and marine units of the twelve members of the European Community were placed under the command of the new Commander-in-Chief of the European Security Forces, a French general whose personal friendship with Le Rith had dated from their student days in Paris, and who now reported directly to Le Rith in his capacity of President of the European Commission. Although it was to be nearly a year before the military reorganization was complete, and the armies of individual countries fully integrated into – and made to feel a loyalty to – a genuinely European force, the decisive step had been taken.

After the creation of what came to be known as the European Security Forces (External), or ESF(E), the creation of the European Security Forces (Internal), or ESF(I), presented Le Rith with few problems. Based on a nucleus of national police forces, including riot and paramilitary police forces such as the French CRS and the Italian Carabinieri, the Internal Security Forces were made directly responsible to the European Commissioner for Internal Security. Like the External Security Forces, units of the Internal Forces were composed of a mixture of nationals from most member countries, though generally under the command of a national of the country in which they were stationed. They, like the ESF(E), were soon trained, equipped – and paid – to a very high standard.

By the middle of 1995, therefore, the structure of the procedures for the enforcement of law and order in Europe was clear. First, there were the ordinary police forces, responsible in each country, in accordance with tradition, to local authorities, state governments, or the central government. With authority to override these national police forces were the European Security Forces (Internal), answerable to the European Internal Security Commissioner. And, as a last resort, there were the European Security Forces (External), primarily responsible for defending Europe against external aggression, but available to assist the ESF(I) if needed, and directly responsible to Le Rith.

Meanwhile, Le Rith began to implement his plans to reduce unemployment. It was an intolerably high level of unemployment that had brought him to power; he was pledged to do something about it; and that was what he was going to do. Europe could not be great again until every able-bodied man and woman was at work.

He adopted a three-pronged approach. First, with a few exceptions – such as the physically or mentally handicapped, and females with young children – all those in the 16–25 year old age group who were out of work – and there were more than 15 million of them – were enrolled in a European Pioneer Corps. This corps, composed of tens of thousands of units of mixed nationality, whose members were constantly exhorted to be 'loyal to Europe' and 'think as Europeans', was put to work 'building the new Europe'. Units were housed in accommodation which ranged from empty palaces and country mansions to deserted tenement blocks and tented camps: it was largely a matter of luck. Members of the Pioneer Corps were put to work on projects as various as digging irrigation ditches in rural areas, and chauffeuring the rulers of the new Europe, and their sometimes glamorous spouses, around the continent's great cities: that, too, was largely a matter of luck. It might not be the pattern of resource allocation posited by neo-classical economics, and it might not be to the taste of all those involved, but it brought the European unemployment figures down with a bang loud enough to be heard around the world.

The second prong of Le Rith's employment strategy was directed at unemployed workers between the age of twenty-six and the new compulsory retirement age of sixty. Many skilled workers in this age-group were quickly drawn back into employment as the European economy started to grow again, under the influence of Le Rith's expansionary fiscal policies – increases in civil and military expenditures, unaccompanied by any tax increases – and the stimulative monetary policies pursued by the European Central Bank, which relaxed credit and lowered interest rates. Other unemployed workers were offered re-training in new skills, entirely at the expense of the European Community, where they seemed likely to benefit from it; or jobs on various kinds of public works project, similar to those being undertaken by the European Pioneer Corps, where they did not. Only workers unable or unwilling to be re-trained or employed in any of these ways were accommodated in 'residential rehabilitation centres' where, it was understood, they would be encouraged to modify their attitudes.

The third prong in Le Rith's programme for eliminating

unemployment lay not in measures to increase the demand for labour, but in a measure designed to reduce its supply. Apart from helping to bring down unemployment, this measure was entirely consistent with Le Rith's long-held view that one of the major things that had gone wrong with Europe over the past forty years was the torrent of immigration from alien cultures and inferior genetic stock. 'Immigrants' were now offered free passage back to the countries from which they had come, together with a modest resettlement allowance. Immigrants were defined as those (other than people of clearly European stock) who were born outside the European Community, or whose parents had been born outside it, or who, in the opinion of local tribunals established to apply certain criteria laid down by the Commission, were clearly *de facto* immigrants even though not falling into the standard categories. Only in rare cases, where immigrants could demonstrate that they were 'socially useful' to the European Community, would the rules be waived. Immigrants who, within six months, had failed to take advantage of this offer, would be forcibly repatriated; and any immigrants whose 'home countries' refused to admit them would be interned in 'transit centres' pending a satisfactory resolution of the problem of their disposal.

The other main policy put into operation by Le Rith when he took power at the beginning of 1995 was directed at the control of inflation. Although the widespread disruption of the last two years had led to shortages of individual items, and the emergence of a kind of black market for certain goods, in which prices were very high, the heavy and rising level of unemployment had seen to it that there was none of the widespread and accelerating inflation which had characterized the beginning of the 1990s. But now that policies designed to bring unemployment down to a low level were being put into effect, there was obviously a danger that inflation would pick up speed again – just as it had done during every period of falling unemployment in Europe over the last thirty years.

Le Rith's policy was drastically simple. First, a 'family price index' was constructed, which covered all the main essential items of a family's expenditure – basic foodstuffs, low-income housing, energy, public transport and a few others. The detailed composition of the index varied somewhat in different parts of

228

Europe, according to national tastes: bread was one of the fifteen basic foods in the British version of the index, for example, whereas in the Italian version its place was taken by pasta; but the overall pattern was the same. Then, by a combination of controls and subsidies, the prices of the items in the family price index were frozen, so that 'the cost of living' was stabilized.

Secondly, wages were frozen. With the cost of living stabilized, Le Rith pointed out, there was no need for wage increases – not, at any rate, until the European economy had recovered, and the process of switching resources to such essential expenditures as investment, training, and the European Security Forces had been completed. And with wages frozen, the main cause of the great inflations of the past thirty years would be eliminated.

In short, Le Rith proclaimed, his policies were going to provide everyone with work, and everyone with a guaranteed standard of living. This was enormous progress, by comparison with the state of affairs he had inherited. Soon, it would be time for living standards to start rising again, as the new Europe emerged from the chaos of the recent past. But in the meantime, what was required was work, and discipline; discipline, and work.

It was over a year before discontent with the new Europe that Le Rith was constructing began to surface in any systematic way, and even then it was confined to a small minority. The old, on the whole, were well satisfied with Le Rith's policies. They could no longer afford luxuries, of course, but then who could? The great blessing, to them, was that the cost of living had been stabilized: no longer need they fear that rising rents or prices would suddenly lead to eviction, or put basic foodstuffs out of reach, or make it impossible to keep warm in winter.

Many of the young, too, were quite content. Le Rith had provided them with jobs or training, and in many cases with the excitement of new challenges, new experiences, new places and new friendships. Some of the most obdurate and unhappy had been allowed to drop quietly out of the Pioneer Corps, and sink unobtrusively into a squalid underground sub-culture of drugs and alcohol – as long as they remained invisible to the rest of the community, and stayed relatively few in number. At the other end of the spectrum, the most intelligent and enterprising, who had emerged as natural leaders of the individual Pioneer Corps units, were being creamed off and recruited into the first stages of glittering careers in the service – civilian or military – of the new Europe. And most of the rest of the young workers recruited into the Pioneer Corps, like the great majority of older workers, were glad enough to have a job and a living wage – a marked improvement on the state of affairs when Le Rith had taken over.

Nevertheless, by the spring of 1996 the darker side of Le Rith's economic programme was becoming increasingly apparent. For millions of people, the policy of providing all the unemployed with jobs 'in the construction of the new Europe' meant direction of labour: they could not change the jobs assigned to them by the authorities nor, accordingly, their place of residence. This effect, however, was felt only by a minority; another effect of the policy to eliminate unemployment was felt by everybody (except for leading members of the Europe First Movement, and senior and middle-ranking civilian and military officials, for whom special shops selling imported goods started to be discreetly provided). This was the consequence of the import and foreign exchange controls which Le Rith had imposed at the beginning of 1995, in order to keep out the foreign manufactured goods which Europe ought, in his view, to be making for itself.

Over the next few years imports of manufactured goods did, indeed, fall rapidly away, under the influence of very high tariffs, tightening quotas, and the allocation to importers of an ever-diminishing supply of foreign exchange. But the closing of Europe's markets to foreign manufacturers, while stimulating output and employment in a number of European industries, had a highly adverse effect on European living standards. Most of the substitute European goods – from cars and computers at one end of the spectrum to clothes and shoes at the other – were high in price and low in quality and reliability. As time went on, the problem got worse, as the wage controls designed to prevent a recurrence of inflation, even though somewhat relaxed from their original stringency, inhibited flexibility in the labour market, led to bottlenecks and inefficiency, and smothered the incentive for improvements in productivity. Within a few years, the rise in European living standards which for decades those in work, at least, had taken for granted, was a thing of the past; living standards were now set on a declining trend.

One of the greatest ironies about all this – though no one seems to have dared to point it out to Le Rith – was that the jobs created in Europe by his import and foreign exchange restrictions were fewer in number than the jobs lost in Europe as a result of the falling incomes abroad, and the import controls imposed by foreign countries, which were a direct consequence of the European measures. To keep unemployment at a low level, therefore, even more jobs had to be provided in the public programmes responsible for 'constructing the new Europe', where productivity was usually very low, and the usefulness of what was achieved often exceedingly difficult to discern.

The eruption of opposition to Le Rith's programme for Europe, in the spring of 1996, did not get very far, or last very long. By this time the European Parliament had passed all the necessary legislation. Strikes, unless specifically sanctioned by the Commissioner for Employment, were illegal. 'Subversive elements' – people, possibly in the pay of the United States or the Soviet Union, who were suspected of intending to sabotage the construction of the new Europe – could be detained without being charged, and without trial, for an initial period of six months, which was extendible indefinitely. The Commissioner for Communications had been given the power to censor all television and radio broadcasts, and all newspapers and periodicals, in the interests 'of shielding the European people from the insidious propaganda of Europe's sworn enemies'; and the possession of antennae and satellite dishes capable of receiving direct television transmissions from the outside world had been made an offence punishable by long terms of imprisonment. By this time, too, the European Security Forces, both Internal and External, were fully operational. The ESF(I), in particular, was ready and eager to deal vigorously with anyone who seemed guilty of defying European law, or questioning the authority of the European Commission and its President.

Accordingly, students who organized demonstrations were detained, as were trade union leaders who urged their members to strike, and intellectuals who sought to promulgate

231

'anti-European' views in speech or in writing. The treatment of these and similar 'undesirables' varied at different times, and in different parts of Europe. In certain cases of 'particularly anti-European behaviour', Le Rith himself was sometimes consulted, and enjoyed the opportunity of using his knowledge of the different national traditions within Europe to devise appropriate forms of punishment. When 700 German Greens (some of whom had once believed that the Europe First Movement would impose tough anti-pollution policies on Europe) demonstrated outside one of the nuclear power stations in Germany kept operational in pursuance of Le Rith's policy of making Europe independent of coal and oil imports for electricity generation, Le Rith had them transported to Greece, to start digging the foundations of a new nuclear breeder reactor. When several hundred French train drivers went on strike for higher pay, their families were arrested on charges of 'incitement to industrial sabotage', and only released from particularly unpleasant conditions of imprisonment when the men went back to work. In Spain, a harsher tradition was invoked: when several thousand coal miners went on strike, the seventeen men identified as ringleaders were summarily shot. In Britain, on the other hand, it amused Le Rith to apply a different kind of punishment: a motley group of some fifty journalists, university teachers and white-collar trade unionists suspected of meeting secretly to co-ordinate a leaflet campaign against the policies of the European Parliament were incarcer-ated in the monolith of London University's Senate House for 're-education', which consisted of memorizing the whole of Le Rith's book *Europe First*. No one, Le Rith stipulated, was to be released until he demonstrated that he knew the book by heart.

By the end of 1996, many people were trying to escape from the new Europe, even though by now life in most of the rest of the world was looking little more attractive. With few excep-tions, however – mainly the very rich, who had something to bargain with – they were refused exit visas. Many others sought escape of a different kind, in recourse to the drugs and alcohol that seemed among the few products in plentiful supply. If drug addiction in the later 1980s had – as the popular press of the time maintained – reached epidemic proportions, by the later 1990s it was more like a pandemic. But this was no more than an accurate reflection of the deterioration in the conditions of life in Europe over the same period.

In January 1997 the President of Europe (as he was now styled) flew to Washington to be present at the reinauguration in the Pentagon of the President of the United States. Some observers – though no longer encouraged to air their reflections in public – were puzzled as to why the great anti-American Euro-chauvinist should lend his presence to this occasion. But the answer was simple. Le Rith could not resist pointing out to the American President, in person, the fact that the United States was wracked by an interminable and apparently insoluble guerilla war. Le Rith's Europe, on the other hand, was firmly under control.

EPILOGUE

By the beginning of the year 2000, three years after the reinauguration of the American President, the state of the world had grown even worse.

In the United States, new investment was at a standstill. Officially, unemployment was less than 20 per cent, but in reality it was much higher. Productivity and real wages continued to decline. Poverty and despair was engulfing an ever-growing proportion of the population. Violence had become endemic. From time to time, in and around the major cities, large-scale battles were fought between heavily armed guerillas and state or federal security forces. Some of the people who had the necessary money and influence had managed to gain admission to the few countries around the world that still seemed a desirable place to be; others lived in a state of siege in compounds armoured and patrolled like fortresses. And the great mass of the population existed as best it could amid the encompassing destruction and pervasive fear. Life in much of America in 2000 was like it had been in the Lebanon in the mid-1980s, or in South Africa towards the end of that decade.

In Europe, the two great scourges of an earlier era (privately referred to by the population as BLR, or 'before Le Rith') had been eliminated. There was, according to the official figures, no unemployment, and no inflation. But if there was no unemployment, the underemployment of those in jobs was massive, because of the appalling inefficiency with which the over-centralized and over-regulated economy was now operating. And if there was no inflation, it was because the items measured by the official price index were heavily subsidized, and often in short supply or even unobtainable: the suppressed inflationary forces at work in the economy were immense. The economic state of affairs was well summarized in one of the 'Polish jokes' that were now told about Western Europe more often than about its counterpart east of the Elbe: 'Why have the dole queues disappeared?' 'Because everyone's in the bread queue instead.'

On the political front, both individual national elections, and the Euro-elections due in 1999, had been postponed until further notice, on the grounds that such elections would be divisive at a time when Europe's enemies abroad – both to the east and to the west – were awaiting the chance to destroy the burgeoning new Europe before its power could be consolidated. Meanwhile, an attempt had been made by three of the smaller member countries – Denmark, Portugal and Ireland – to secede from this new Europe. Contingents of the European Security Forces (Internal) rapidly crushed the Portuguese rebellion; in Denmark they needed some assistance from the External Security Forces. Ireland's announcement that it was leaving the European Community, on the other hand, was immediately accepted by Le Rith, who remarked to an aide that it had taken the English 600 years to rid themselves of the Irish problem; he had done it in less than six. But if the Irish escaped, nobody else did. By the beginning of the year 2000, there was no one in Europe who did not fear the knock on the door in the middle of the night.

In Japan, despite the fact that the markets of Europe and the US were now closed to Japanese goods, the living standards of those in employment were still very high, in the narrow sense that they could afford to buy all the consumer goods that human ingenuity had ever invented and produced; and the world-wide depression meant that by bartering manufactured goods Japan could obtain all the food and raw materials it needed from developing countries on favourable terms. In a wider sense, nevertheless, the quality of life had deteriorated. Pollution and congestion were worse than ever, and there had been little improvement over the past decade in the state of the housing stock. On top of this, the country had failed to come to grips with the problem of its rapidly ageing population, and millions of old people lived in poverty, and without access to proper health care. Among younger people, unemployment, both open and hidden, was higher than anyone could remember. Frequently, frustrations and tensions built up until they exploded publicly in great pitched battles between communist and nationalist youth armies, or between these armies and the heavily equipped riot police. Even more frequently, a sense of frustration and failure culminated in private, behind closed doors, as an ever-increasing number of people, sometimes after killing their families, resorted to the ultimate solution of suicide. The nation had sunk into a seemingly irreversible psychological depression.

Some historians are determinists, believing that what happened in history, had to happen. Others incline to the 'great man' theory, arguing that historical developments are heavily influenced by the accident of birth, and the appearance on the scene of an Alexander, a Caesar, a Christ or a Napoleon. The present historian is more sanguine. The destiny of nations, he believes, is under the control of the men and women who live in them. The distressing catalogue of events which unfolded between 1989 and 2000 could, and should, have been avoided.

The simplest case, perhaps, is that of Japan. Once it had recovered from the physical and psychological trauma of the war, Japan had astonished the world, from the early 1950s on, by the speed and range of its export-led economic growth. Thirty years later it was an economic superpower. But it refused to accept the responsibilities attaching to such a major world player; and therein lay its downfall. One country after another closed its markets to Japan, and the mainspring of its economic growth was broken.

Why did successive Japanese governments refuse to countenance the public expenditure and the budget deficits needed to accommodate the very high Japanese personal savings ratio? Why did Japan persist in policies that led to huge chronic trade and current account surpluses? Why did it not use a large part of these surpluses to provide untied aid to developing countries? Why, for example, did it not provide the Philippines with enough economic assistance in 1986–7 to save the beleaguered democratic government of Mrs Aquino? Only the Japanese can know the ultimate answers to these questions; though unfortunately it is not only the Japanese who have cause to rue the fact that they need to be asked.

In the United States, the problems were more complex and the remedies more difficult to apply. But that hardly excuses

236

the combination of complacency, indifference, cowardice and greed which led the country to disaster.

What went wrong? What caused the high hopes entertained in the early and mid-1980s, and again at the time of the inauguration of the new Democratic Administration in 1989, to be so comprehensively quenched?

The kernel of the answer to this question, in the opinion of the present historian, is this. After about 1970, the American economy gradually ceased to function properly, and this created economic and social problems that the political system proved incapable of putting right.

For a couple of decades, by the time the crunch came in the early 1990s, America had been consuming too much. Individual households, the federal government, and the nation as a whole all went increasingly into debt – particularly after the beginning of the 1980s. The high level of consumption in the US, and the corresponding low level of saving, were in no way surprising. The driving force of the American free enterprise system had always been the urge to identify – or to create – consumer wants, and then make money by satisfying them.

This emphasis on consumption was partly an effect, and partly a cause, of a level of personal taxation which was low compared with most other advanced industrial democracies: because taxes were low, people consumed a lot; and because people consumed a lot, there was relentless pressure to keep taxes low. This was all very well as long as the federal government did not need to spend a great deal. But in the later part of the 20th century the federal government needed – or thought that it needed – to spend quite a lot.

One reason for this was that from the late 1940s on, successive US administrations were preoccupied, with varying degrees of intensity, with the threat of world-wide Soviet expansionism. To many people in Western Europe, and indeed in the United States itself, the degree of this preoccupation sometimes appeared to border on the obsessive; the notion, in particular, that groups of rebels who sought to overthrow brutal and corrupt dictatorships in Africa and Latin America were necessarily agents of the Kremlin often seemed to verge on paranoia. However that may be, the consequence of this preoccupation with the Soviet Union was a high level of military expenditure by the United States, particularly at the time of the Korean and Vietnam wars, and again after 1980.

A second reason for high federal spending was that after the New Deal of the 1930s, and the Great Society reforms of the 1960s, the nation was committed to providing a reasonable standard of living for many of those unable to work, and especially for retired people. As the proportion of these 'senior citizens' in the population grew, and as they lived longer and demanded ever more sophisticated and expensive health care, the cost of maintaining them snowballed.

Thirdly, an increasingly complex and technologically advanced society cannot function efficiently unless government spends large sums on a whole range of infrastructural, environmental and social programmes, extending from highways and air traffic control systems, through water projects and toxic waste disposal, to a variety of education and training programmes. Although in the United States many of these kinds of expenditure have traditionally been undertaken by state or local governments rather than the central government, in many cases federal funds are essential if money is to be available on the necessary scale.

Thus, for a series of compelling reasons, federal government expenditure during the last few decades of the 20th century was relatively high – not by European standards, but by comparison with earlier decades in the US. The problem, particularly during the fatal dozen years between the early 1980s and the mid-1990s, was that the population, pursuing the Holy Grail of high levels of private consumption, was unwilling to pay for all the public expenditure it demanded as well. Or, to be more precise, the political system, with its separation of powers, its lack of party cohesion, its subservience to special interests and its short time-horizons, failed to agree on whether or how to increase taxes sufficiently to pay for it. And so too much of this expenditure, for too long, was not paid for.

This had two consequences. First, the federal government borrowed the difference between its income and its expenditure, and did so not only at times of recession, when mainstream economic theory sanctions such borrowing as legitimate, but at all other times as well, when it certainly does not. The upshot was that between 1980 and 1990 the National Debt trebled, and by the latter year more than 20 per cent of federal revenue was required simply to pay interest on this debt. Even more serious was the fact that America's high propensity to consume and low propensity to save meant that much of the federal government's borrowing had to come from abroad. By the mid-1980s the United States had become the world's biggest debtor, and by the mid-1990s more than 2 per cent of the GNP was being swallowed up each year solely in making interest payments on this external debt.

The second consequence of the country's prolonged unwillingness or inability to raise taxes was that throughout much of the period after 1980 successive attempts to reduce the budget deficit, unable to make much headway in cutting the military expenditure and middle-class entitlements that were so jealously protected by powerful special interests, concentrated on slashing the types of expenditure that had no strongly organized political constituency. One of these was federal funding of reasearch and development, and scientific and technical education and training; and cuts in these programmes had an increasingly serious effect in depressing innovation and the growth of productivity, and in weakening the country's longer-term competitive position. Another target was welfare payments of every kind; and cuts in these had the effect of reducing the living standards of the poorest 20 per cent of the population to an extent that eventually became insupportable.

In a full-employment economy, in which productivity and real wages were growing at a respectable rate – the type of economy the US was for twenty-five years after the end of World War Two – this would not have mattered so much: the private sector, confident of future expansion and profits, would have played a bigger role in funding research and development, and essential training programmes; and even the least skilled and most disadvantaged members of the community would have had a chance of finding a job and enjoying a rising standard of living. But after 1970, and certainly after 1980, the US was not a full-employment economy, or one in which productivity and real wages were growing at an acceptable rate. It was an economy in which unemployment was high, living standards stagnating, inequality widening and poverty deepening. In the light of hindsight, at least, it was an economy, and a society, riding for a fall.

The reasons for this shift in the character of the economy between the quarter century or so after 1945 and the quarter century or so that ended in the year 2000 are complex, and indeed not fully understood. But to the eye accustomed to survey the broad terrain of history, two features stand out sharply.

First, around 1970 there was a sea-change in the main preoccupation of economic policy. For the first time in nearly forty years, the major emphasis ceased to be on full employment and growth, and started to be on the control of inflation. There were good practical and political reasons for this. The combination of the Vietnam War and the Great Society programmes – the attempt to have both guns and butter – had created an excessive level of demand in the US economy, and by the late 1960s the inflation rate had begun to rise alarmingly. It was no coincidence that it was also at about this time that the doctrine of monetarism, which had been making converts for nearly a decade, suddenly came into its own. Monetarism condemned Keynesian attempts to maintain full employment and promote economic growth by managing the level of effective demand, claiming that it was exactly this kind of interventionist meddling in the workings of the free market which brought unemployment down below its 'natural rate', and made inflation inevitable. To eliminate inflation, the monetarists said, the government and the central bank should simply balance the budget and control the growth of the money supply. This would enable the economy to grow at the rate permitted by the underlying growth of productivity and the labour force, with a level of unemployment as low as was compatible with such structural factors as the flexibility of the economy and the mobility of labour, and at a low or zero inflation rate. This seductive doctrine did not sweep the board all at once, or for good: in 1971, President Nixon is reported to have said that 'I am now a Keynesian'; President Carter had no great patience with the creed; under President Reagan the balanced-budget part of the prescription was largely stood on its head; and the 1989–93 Democratic President thought it was misconceived. Nevertheless, the thirty years since 1970 were as thoroughly imbued with the spirit of monetarism as the previous thirty years had been with the spirit of Keynesianism.

Unfortunately, monetarism was fatally flawed. It may be true that a sufficient squeeze on the money supply can reduce the inflation rate: the experience of the United States in the early 1980s is often cited as evidence of that. But it can be powerfully argued that the fall in the US inflation rate between 1980 and 1985 was the consequence not of the squeeze on the money supply as such, but of the huge rise in the value of the dollar resulting from the high interest rates associated with the tight monetary policy, of the collapse of world commodity prices caused by the global recession of the early 1980s, and of the dampening effect on wage claims of the high rate of unemployment. In short, a government can bring down the inflation rate by following restrictive monetary policies, provided it is willing to push those policies far enough to create high unemployment and low, or even negative, economic growth. And the evidence is that these adverse effects are not temporary phases in a fairly rapid adjustment process, as monetarists claim, but must continue or even intensify if inflation is not to start rising again. Certainly this was the American experience: despite short-term ups and downs, the thirty years after 1970 saw an underlying rise in the unemployment rate and a virtual absence of growth in productivity – but no lasting solution to the problem of inflation.

The fact that, after 1970 or thereabouts, the United States tolerated a high and for the most part rising rate of unemployment, and a rate of growth of productivity that was little better than zero, is a vivid pointer to the second feature that stands out in the economic and social landscape of the second half of the 20th century. These evils were tolerated because they seemed inevitable by-products of policies designed to control inflation; and to the rich and even moderately affluent people who play such a disproportionate role in the American political process, inflation is a much greater threat than unemployment or a stagnating growth rate. The beginning of a feeling of indifference to unemployment and stagnant or even declining living standards for much of the population can also be placed in or around 1970. Perhaps this watershed marked the end of the idealism and sense of comradeship that had characterized the New Deal, the fight against fascism in World War Two, and the attempt to create a Great Society in the mid-1960s. It probably had something to do with the loss of innocence and the growth of internal tensions associated with the war in Vietnam. For whatever reasons, around 1970 the nation seems to have begun to move back towards an older and harsher tradition: the tradition of unfettered 19th-century capitalism, of the ruthless, rugged frontier, of greedily grabbing what one could for oneself, and the devil take the hindmost.

With a brief pause during the Carter years, this new, harder, more mercilessly self-seeking philosophy gathered pace, reaching its first peak under the Reagan Administration in the mid-1980s, with the frenzied activity in the stock market and the explosive spate of mergers and acquisitions which had no purpose but to enhance the wealth of those directly involved, often by criminal means. Unfortunately, while the financial sector of the economy prospered mightily, the far more important 'real' economy of industry and agriculture rotted. There was too little investment and innovation and – the result also of large-scale illegal immigration – productivity and real wages stagnated, and unemployment and poverty worsened. When, in 1989, a Democratic President assumed office and tried to turn all this around, he found himself fatally frustrated. A political system designed to prevent the executive from wielding too much power was now blocking the adoption of the activist, interventionist policies that the gathering crisis so clearly called for. Opposition to needed change on the part of those who benefited from the status quo was too strong to be overcome.

In short, after about 1970 the American economic system, for whatever complex of reasons, progressively failed to perform: growth stagnated, unemployment rose, inequality increased and poverty worsened. And the political system failed to put things right. The consequence of this double failure – the economic and the political – was to deny the poorest 20 per cent of the population even the minimal living standards they would have found acceptable. In the end, they revolted. Supplied with money from the drug trade and other sources, armed with weapons provided by America's enemies abroad, and implacable in their demand for the justice and equality that the American system had denied them for far too long, these people, mainly young and mainly black, embarked on a path of armed struggle against the American establishment. They have conclusively demonstrated that a relatively small minority of the population, if alienated from the predominant philosophy, if sufficiently determined and adequately armed, can make life in a complex modern society virtually intolerable for everyone else.

What, then, should have been done, back in the 1980s, before the situation started to move out of control? Of the various morals that may be suggested by the preceding analysis, two in particular seem of overwhelming importance.

First of all, far more vigorous action should have been taken to adjust the huge imbalances in the American economy represented by the budget and balance of payments deficits. Unlike Japan, where the very high private propensity to save made budget deficits structurally necessary if the country was not to run huge and disruptive balance of payments surpluses on current account, in the US the private savings ratio was too low even to finance a satisfactory level of new investment, let alone a $200 billion budget deficit, equivalent to about 4 per cent of GNP. This combination of a low propensity to save and a large budget deficit had many damaging consequences. One was high American interest rates, which inhibited investment and the longer-term growth of productivity. Another – until 1985–6 – was a sky-high dollar, which did untold damage to American manufacturing industry, and contributed to a current account deficit that within a few years transformed the US from the world's largest creditor to the world's largest debtor. These effects, in turn, precipitated the American plunge into protectionism, which played a major role in the breakdown of the whole post-war international trading and monetary system.

What was needed in this situation was a major stimulus to saving (of the kind long built into the Japanese tax structure); and a tax increase, to eliminate most of the budget deficit. An opportunity was missed in 1986. The Packwood-Rostenkowski tax reform bill of that year was a remarkable tribute to the ability of the US Congress, on occasion, to do the right thing and ride roughshod over the many powerful interest groups opposed to any change. But the bill, although in some ways it simplified and improved the tax system, did not increase overall tax revenue. Moreover, it repealed the main investment tax credit, reduced tax incentives to saving, and shifted a considerable part of the tax burden from individuals to corporations. Thus the net effect of the bill – despite some steps to restrict tax relief on consumer borrowing – was to increase the nation's propensity to consume and reduce its propensity to save and invest. At the very least, drastic further steps should have been taken to increase tax revenue and private saving in 1987 and 1988.

The second main moral of the history of the last decade of the 20th century, and the analysis given above of what went wrong, is that vigorous action should have been taken in the US in the 1980s to reduce the gross inequalities in the distribution of income, and the disparities in access to such fundamental necessities as jobs, housing, education and health care. The American free enterprise system inevitably throws up huge inequalities. In the 19th century these may have been tolerated; in the last quarter of the 20th century they were tolerated less and less. It was the task of the political process to reduce these inequalities, and to alleviate in some measure the hardships suffered by the poorest fifth of the population. Taxes on the rich should have been increased, to help pay for better services for the poor. This was not done. Indeed, throughout much of the 1980s the trend was in the opposite direction: taxes on the rich were significantly reduced by the Reagan Administration, and federal expenditures on programmes that assisted the poor were repeatedly cut back. There were those who warned at the time of the explosive forces that might be unleashed in reaction against the greed and indifference which lay behind these policies. It is tragic that their voices were not heeded.

In Europe, some of the same mistakes were made as in the United States. As in America, after about 1970 there was a shift away from the idea that full employment and a respectable rate of growth should be the main objectives of economic policy, to the notion that governments could have little effect on these things, and that their main responsibility was to minimize or eliminate inflation by balancing the budget and controlling the money supply. But monetarism not only proved as false a god in Europe as in America; its worship proved much more damaging.

One reason for this was that in Europe tight fiscal policies were pursued, as well as tight monetary policies: there was little of the fiscal laxity introduced by President Reagan in 1981. The consequence was that unemployment went higher in Europe than in the US at the beginning of the 1980s, and stayed there long after American unemployment had come down again. Another reason was the relative inflexibility of the European economy and European labour markets, which was partly the legacy of history, and partly a consequence of the fact that in most European countries there was little parallel to the huge flood of illegal immigration from south of the Rio Grande.

There were, of course, enormous variations between different European countries. At one end of the spectrum was West Germany, a country which, throughout much of the 1980s, enjoyed an enviable combination of steady if unspectacular growth, a low inflation rate, a rock-hard currency and an unemployment rate that, though high, was below the European average. But even West Germany had an Achilles heel: its complacent absorption in its own material success alienated its unemployed youth, and many others besides, and led eventually to irreconcilable political divisions. In Britain, at the other end of the spectrum, things were far worse. After 1979, in a vain attempt to turn the British economy into a miniature imitation of the American economy, Mrs Thatcher doggedly pursued policies which led to the destruction of much of the country's manufacturing industry, the emergence of a huge structural deficit in the balance of payments, and the creation of a pool of over 3 million unemployed, whose social security receipts largely swallowed up the unconvenated benefit the country had received from North Sea oil.

Taking the European Community as a whole, however, many things should have been done differently. Europe should have embarked on bolder and more sustained policies to meet the challenge of the new technological age that was emerging in Japan and parts of the United States. It should long since have swept aside the artificial barriers to genuine free trade within Europe, which still existed in the late 1980s, thirty years after the signing of the Treaty of Rome, in order to strengthen competition and enable European firms to reap the economies of scale enjoyed in America and Japan. It should have phased out much sooner the subsidies to older industries – including agriculture – which could no longer compete on world markets, and should have encouraged resources to flow faster into the new information-based technologies of the 1980s and 1990s. It should have promoted more research and development, and encouraged more training and re-training in the skills demanded by the micro-electronic age. It should have exercised far more ingenuity in devising ways of minimizing the inflationary impact of reductions in unemployment, through incomes policies or profit-sharing schemes. Indeed, it can be argued that nothing short of a radical transformation in the organization of society, and particularly in the relationship between work and pay, could have done the trick.

In the last resort, however, Europe's real failure lay not in the fact that it did not adopt better economic policies or techniques of economic and social organization. It was a moral failure. Year after year, from 1980 onwards, European unemployment rose. By the end of 1986 it numbered more than 16 million, or 11 per cent of the labour force. Among the young, and deprived minorities of various kinds, the figures were far higher. Much lip service was paid to the need to do something about the economic waste and human desolation represented by this heavy and persistent unemployment, but nothing effective was done. Governments, and those who elected them, simply did not care enough about this deprived minority to insist that unemployment be reduced to a tolerable level.

In 1987, or even 1988, this could still have been done. After that, it was too late. The eleventh hour for Europe had come and gone, and the midnight bell had started to toll.

INDEX